Discourses in Mormon Theology

Philosophical and Theological Possibilities

Discourses in Mormon Theology

Philosophical and Theological Possibilities

Edited by James M. McLachlan and Loyd Ericson

Greg Kofford Books
Salt Lake City, 2007

Published in the USA

Library of Congress Cataloging-in-Publication Data

Discourses in Mormon theology : philosophical and theological possibilities / edited by James M. McLachlan and Loyd Ericson.

p. cm.
Includes index.
ISBN 978-1-58958-104-3
1. Church of Jesus Christ of Latter-day Saints--Doctrines. 2. Philosophical theology. I. McLachlan, James M., 1955- II. Ericson, Loyd.
BX8635.3.D57 2007
230'.9332--dc22

2007029585

Contents

Theological and Philosophical Possibilities of the Mormon Religion

James M. McLachlan
Western Carolina University

Fawn Brodie didn't think much of the possibilities of Mormon philosophical theology. In the last paragraphs of her epilogue to *No Man Knows My History* she uses a metaphor of the church's monument at Joseph Smith's birth place in Sharon, Vermont. A sign on the road, she writes, says "Visit the Joseph Smith Monument, World's Largest Polished Shaft." She finds this message a fitting sign for Joseph Smith, "for it only symbolizes the barrenness of his spiritual legacy." Brodie could see nothing in Joseph Smith beyond a "genius for improvisation" who created a theology which was only "a patchwork of ideas and rituals drawn from every quarter." Then her tone changes, "Yet Joseph's theology . . . became in his hands a thing of color, warmth, and originality."[1] Though Brodie's contention in *No Man Knows My History* is that Joseph Smith was no more than a lovable, humane, and creative charlatan, she hits on something incredibly important. Joseph Smith found truth everywhere. He loved the good in this world so much that he saw it becoming a celestial kingdom, where the same sociality that exists among us here would exist in an ever better and glorified state (D&C 130). It is the love of friends and family here that will be fulfilled in the eternal realms. Joseph Smith loved the joys of this world and saw them as moments of the experience of the eternal. In this sense, he did not just look toward an ideal unlike the world

1. Fawn McKay Brodie, *No Man Knows My History* (New York: A. Knopf, 1945) p. 404.

in which we live. Instead he saw that in this life we experience something of the bliss of the eternal realms. Because they differ in such important ways from the main strands of traditional Christian theology Smith's revelations demand philosophical and theological reflection on their radical originality.

In the early years, Mormonism spawned an incredible amount of original and mightily creative theological reflections on Joseph Smith's revelations. These were made within the church by leaders such as Brigham Young, Orson and Parley Pratt, John Taylor, and eventually B.H. Roberts, James Talmage, and John A. Widtsoe. While these were read widely within the LDS community, Mormon theology was almost completely ignored or misunderstood by the non-Mormon world. For most non-Mormon theologians, Brodie's assessment of Mormon doctrine and theology seemed true. It was an interesting and highly eccentric sect which was "spiritually barren" and theologically naive.

Serious philosophical and theological debate among academics over the nature and meaning of the Latter-day Saint revelation through the last hundred and fifty years has been fairly scant. Even the exceptions like William H. Chamberlin, E. E. Erickson, Sterling McMurrin, and O. C. Tanner seem to prove the rule. They published little specifically on Mormonism, and what they did publish was usually only for the Mormon community, quickly going out of print. Mormon studies in general, however, has changed greatly over the last forty years. Since the emergence of the "New Mormon History" and the Mormon History Association in the 1960s and '70s, there has been considerable historical interest in Mormonism with an exceedingly long list of scholarly publications and debates. Since Thomas O'Dea's *The Mormons*, there has also been a significant number of works on Mormonism in the social sciences. In 1984, Rodney Stark even claimed that Mormonism may be the emergence of a new religious tradition. With Jan Shipps's *Mormonism: A New Religious Tradition*, and much more recently Douglas Davies's *An Introduction to Mormonism*, as well as Terryl

Givens's *The Viper on the Hearth* and *By the Hand of Mormon*, there is more interest in Mormonism in religious studies. An LDS group now meets at meetings of the Society of Biblical Literature and a Mormon Studies group is just beginning its work at the American Academy of Religion.

However, with the exception of a smattering of articles in *Dialogue: A Journal of Mormon Thought*, *BYU Studies*, *Sunstone*, *The FARMS Review*, and a short selection of books over the last forty years, there has been little specifically philosophical and theological work done on Mormonism since Sterling McMurrin's little classic, *The Theological Foundations of the Mormon Religion* in 1965. It is not that interesting and provocative work in Mormon philosophical thought wasn't being done by people like David Paulsen, Truman Madsen, and Jim Faulconer at BYU, or independent scholars like Blake Ostler, Janice Allred, and Margaret Toscano, but like William Chamberlin's writing, such work had no home, reached a fairly small audience, and has had no community of readers to debate it. Also like Chamberlin's work, they have not been significantly read beyond the Latter-day Saint community.

This has begun to change on two fronts. Interest in Mormon philosophical and theological reflection has increased both within and without the Mormon community. In 2001, Greg Kofford Books published Blake Ostler's *Exploring Mormon Thought: The Attributes of God* which has gone through several printings and has been followed with a second volume in 2006. Since 2000, Oxford University Press has published Terryl Givens's *The Viper on the Hearth* and *By the Hand of Mormon*, as well as Douglas Davies's *An Introduction to Mormonism*. Furthermore, the 2005 celebration of Joseph Smith's bi-centenary at the Library of Congress included papers examining Smith's impact on religious thought.

The papers in this volume were drawn from the first meeting of the Society for Mormon Philosophy and Theology (SMPT) that took place at Utah Valley State College in March 2004. The Society was formed a year earlier in March 2003, during "God, Humanity, and Revelation: Perspectives from Mormon Philosophy and History," a conference organized by Kenneth West and held at Yale University. However, the emergence of the Society can be traced to two previous events: Dennis Potter's formation of LDS-Phil, an email discussion list on Mormon theology and philosophy in 1995, and the March 2002 Mormon Philosophy Conference at Utah Valley State College, organized by Brian Birch, director of the Religious Studies Program at UVSC. This trajectory indicates the growing interest in Mormon philosophical and theological thought over the last few years by scholars both within and without the LDS Church.

The Society for Mormon Philosophy and Theology brings together scholars and others both within and without the Mormon tradition who share an interest in studying the teachings and texts of the Church of Jesus Christ of Latter-day Saints. It facilitates the sharing and discussion of work by sponsoring an annual conference and publishing *Element: A Journal of Mormon Philosophy and Theology*. Its statement of purpose reads as follows:

> The purpose of SMPT is to promote disciplined reflection on Latter-day Saint beliefs. Its aims include constructive engagement with the broader tradition of philosophy and theology. All its publications, conferences, and other forums for discussion will take seriously both the commitments of faith and the standards of scholarship. . . .
>
> As the Church of Jesus Christ of Latter-day Saints becomes an increasingly global church, SMPT calls attention to the Latter-day Saints' distinctive theology, and its philosophical context and implications. Moreover, it provides a forum for Latter-day Saints and other interested scholars to explore in a disciplined way the message of LDS scriptures and prophets.

The papers collected in this volume indicate an effort to live out the ideals of the society's statement of purpose. It seeks to call attention to Mormonism's distinctive theology and its philosophical implications. The Society attempts to do this by bridging two worlds: the inner faith tradition of Mormonism and the outer theological, philosophical, and scholarly tradition. Thus, it attempts a kind of translation between two languages, faith and scholarship, in order to speak to both Mormons and others beyond Mormonism in the wider philosophical and theological community. Of course this itself is an important philosophical question that concerns some of the papers presented here: whether and to what extent such a translation is possible. Thus, the papers in this volume represent a wide diversity of viewpoints.

Although all the writers follow the commitment of the society to "take seriously both the commitments of faith and the standards of scholarship," the papers in this volume reflect a wide variety of positions in regard to the LDS faith. They exhibit the religiously, theologically, and philosophically diverse points of view in the book and in the Society. This should be apparent from a mere perusal of the titles of the papers in the table of contents. For although the writers agree that one should take the commitments of faith seriously, what that means and how one does it are areas for theological and philosophical discussion. If anything, this variety of positions, like the burgeoning growth of the Mormon tradition, points to Brodie's error. Joseph Smith's spiritual legacy is anything but barren.

As editors we have chosen to divide the papers into four sections: "Thinking about Mormon History and the History of Mormon Thought," "Theological Questions," "Themes of Liberation," and "Scripture and Doctrine."

Thinking about Mormon History and the History of Mormon Thought

The first section contains two papers: Grant Underwood's "A 'Communities of Discourse' Approach to Early LDS Thought" and James McLachlan's "The Modernism Controversy: William Henry Chamberlin, His Teachers Howison and Royce, and the Conception of God Debate."

In his fascinating piece, Grant Underwood recommends a "communities of discourse" approach to discuss the changing usage of terms in LDS thought. Underwood finds that by examining the historical context of the religious discourse of the time we can understand the development of LDS doctrine. He uses examples of the understanding of divine embodiment, and terms like *apostle* and *confirmation*.

The discourse about the body in anti-trinitarian discussions, though they were quite concrete in referring to hands, feet, etc., referred to a spiritual and not physical body. He cites works by Parley Pratt and Lorenzo Snow to illustrate that this was how they also understood this. Underwood contends that the Saints did not take the position that God was materially embodied until the Nauvoo period of the 1840s. Before then they fit into a community of discourse that saw God as spiritually embodied, perhaps even material. Rather than a body of flesh, God's spiritual embodiment was as a higher type of matter, a celestial substance.

Underwood also gives the example of two other terms that fit into the community of discourse approach: *apostle* and *confirmation*. An apostle among the members of the early church referred to a function more than to a position. Early usage understood the term as the descriptive "one who is sent." Consider Doctrine and Covenants 20:38 where missionaries were considered apostles. In 1835, a dozen men were selected based on D&C 18:26–40 and received the special designation of "twelve apostles." Gradually afterwards the term became limited to that body. The use of "*confirming* the church(es)" appears in several places in Joseph Smith's early revelations (D&C 20:43; 24:9; 26:1). Here "church" meant not "the Church" but individual congregations, and mirrors the use of the term in Acts 15:41 where Paul and Silas "confirm the churches." Similarly, "confirm" means to strengthen, establish, or consolidate.

Underwood maintains that what the community of discourse approach reveals is how "the beautiful monarch butterfly of the restored gospel gradually emerged from the cocoon of contemporary Christianity." Just as humans did not spring full-grown from the hand of God, neither did the gospel. He believes that this connects our own LDS community of discourse to the "line-upon-line" principle of the unfolding of doctrine.

James McLachlan's "The Modernism Controversy: William Henry Chamberlin, His Teachers Howison and Royce, and the Conception of God Debate" attempts to situate the modernism controversy that rocked BYU at the turn of the century within the philosophical debates of the period on higher criticism of the scripture and evolution. William H. Chamberlin was the first professionally trained LDS philosopher, and in his time became an influential figure in shaping the thought of a generation of Mormon intellectuals. Chamberlin studied with some of the great figures of the golden age of American philosophy, including John Dewey at the University of Chicago, William James, George Palmer, Josiah Royce at Harvard, and George Holmes Howison at Berkeley. He had a close relation with Royce during his first year at Harvard, and Howison with whom he wrote his master's thesis at Berkeley. Chamberlin is interesting because despite Mormon "materialism," he selected two personalist and idealist philosophers (Howison and Royce) as his mentors, and produced a Mormon idealism which he called "Spiritual Realism." Just ten years before Chamberlin sought out Howison at Berkeley, Howison and Royce had clashed in what the *New York Times* called the great philosophical debate of the century on "The Conception of God." Howison proposed a pluralist, personalist notion of the eternal persons existing with God in the "City of God." Later in his efforts to respond to some of Howison's criticisms from the debate, Royce would offer his personalist "philosophy of loyalty" in 1907 and 1908, the years that Chamberlin studied with him at Harvard. Chamberlin's LDS personalistic philosophy grew out of these sources as an effort to respond to difficulties posed by evolution and higher criticism to LDS faith. This response had tragic results for Chamberlin.

Theological Questions

This section deals with theology proper, moving from questions of method with Benjamin Huff and Brian Birch to theological issues of prayer and the divine attributes with Richard Sherlock, and the relation of God and moral obligation with Blake Ostler.

Benjamin Huff's "Theology in the One-Room Schoolhouse" tackles an essential problem of theology of whether or not we should attempt to think about our religious beliefs systematically. Some critics suggest that a systematic theology can not be open to continuing revelation. Huff thinks that this problem is not necessary to the systematic approach, though at times it has accompanied systematic thought on religion. He gives examples of the necessity of the systematic approach to the understanding of particular doctrines and images in the scriptures. Huff responds to objections that the systematic approach leads to the rigidity and rejection of continuing revelation, because rejection of continuing revelation is the result of ignorance, pride, or both, and not a result of systematic theology. In relation to the polyphony of scripture, he argues that a pluralism of theological approaches would also be helpful.

Huff uses the analogy of a one-room school house where six year olds and eleven year olds share the same classroom, requiring a creative approach to teaching. He compares this to LDS sacrament meeting and Gospel Doctrine classes where a range of stages of spiritual and intellectual development is present. We are united by certain core doctrines. We also have the scriptures which we may picture as a planar space over which we rove as we learn. We could see them as simply an expansion of core doctrines without them meaning just one thing. Rather, they possess layers of meaning.

Like Huff's paper, Brian Birch's "Theological Method and the Question of Truth: A Postliberal Approach to Mormon Doctrine and Practice" starts out with the empirical fact that Mormonism has had an uncomfortable relation with theology. Mormons don't rely on a theological tradition to shape our discourse but instead look to continuing revelation. Mormons don't have an academically trained clergy and frequently claim that mainstream Christianity has enslaved itself to intellectual methods that don't allow it to see the simple truths of the gospel. Some LDS scholars have used insights from postliberal theology to bolster this position. However, postliberal critiques of liberalism and conservative attempts to link religious truths to a propositional-realist method of inquiry imply "the idea that religious beliefs and doctrines have the epistemological status of hypotheses." Birch thinks that it is a mistake. The propositional approach to authoritative teaching is too rigid and makes it difficult to understand how new doctrines can develop, how old doctrines fade, or how they are transformed to fit new circumstances. It can't answer the question of what changes and what remains the same or how they become reconciled with doctrines that at one time at least seemed to contradict them. Postliberal theology has made itself irrefutable and thus set itself apart in a "conceptual ghetto" free from criticism. Thus it makes itself irrelevant. Mormon scholars who adopt this position would thus end up talking to each other and to no one else. It is thus a mistake to tie Mormonism to the arguments of a theological tradition under the guise that it preserves Mormon tradition, the understanding of which (as Huff and Underwood pointed to), are living and evolving. Rather, meaning is located in the symbolic relations of the community and not severed from it. The point of postliberal theology is to offer an account of how the language functions in the community, how this community understands reality, and how this develops as cultures come into contact, intermingling in both time and space.

Birch argues that we don't have to appeal to a common rationality or universally shared experience. There is an aesthetic quality to our experience. Some things come to the forefront and organize experience in various ways. Here interreligious dialogue is the sharing of patterns. Birch claims the rejection of metaphysical realism and epistemological foundationalism does not entail that religious believers cannot make absolute claims. It is the pattern of religious belief that we make absolute claims. Some Mormon apologists have made the claim that reason must serve revelation, but this is saying that reason can only serve apologetic ends—thus making it impossible for any scholarship to offer a valid critique of authority. Once one has appealed to external standards of reason to reflect on Mormon history or ritual, one must allow the theory or argument to be applied to all relevant data. Birch makes this resounding point about the problem of Mormon apologetics; when one employs reason against the detractors of a religious position, one must also expect the possibility that such reasoning can be equally applied in return. This type of criticism is commonly employed in LDS scholarly circles as a way to preserve the religious integrity of a Latter-day Saint understanding of history and scripture against causal explanations for events that depend upon naturalistic methods of inquiry. However, this same "environmental argument" has been repeatedly employed in LDS scholarship to argue that Christian doctrine was co-opted by Greek philosophy such that it became theoretically misguided. The implication seems clear. Critical methods cannot only apply in one direction and maintain any *scholarly* respectability. One must employ a kind of theoretical "golden rule" in these cases: Apply only those critical methods to others you are willing to be subjected to yourself.

In his paper "Prayer and Divine Attributes," Richard Sherlock argues that the fundamental problem of all theology is its ground or foundation. Though frequently ignored, this is the first question of any theology. There are four fundamental possibilities for the grounding of theology: (1) philosophical reason, (2) scripture, (3) prophetic teaching, or (4) the beliefs and practices of the faith community. Sherlock opts for grounding in the beliefs and practices of the faith community. He claims that the generally accepted classics of Mormon theology (by the Pratts, Roberts, Widtsoe, and McMurrin) amount to little more than stipulative theologies that ignore the ground and simply declare something to be "Mormon

Theology." He cites examples of LDS arguments for the eternality of individual spirits or intelligences following Roberts and Widtsoe, and compares that to Bruce R. McConkie's claim that spirits were created by God from primal intelligence. Both claim to be the "normative" Mormon view. Against this, Sherlock claims that "the community creates theology not the other way around." Since there is almost no way that a correspondence theory of truth can provide any meaning to the common Mormon statement, "I know the gospel is true," Sherlock rejects "without apology" the liberal claim that theology must make the gospel plausible to modern man (or enlightenment reason). Sherlock illustrates his point by considering two fundamental practices of the community: private prayer and temple commitment. From these, he seeks to derive the Mormon beliefs about the attributes of God. These are the beliefs that the community is least likely to give up. Sherlock's point is that prayer and temple commitment indicate a much more traditionally theistic notion of God and the relation of God and humanity, than has been found in much of the more "stipulative" Mormon theology.

Blake Ostler's essay, "The Relation of Moral Obligation and God in LDS Thought," accomplishes two tasks. He answers some of the critics of Mormon theism as a foundation for ethics (particularly LDS critic Francis Beckwith), and sets out to outline an LDS theory of ethics based on an LDS conception of God. Critics of Mormon theism have argued that traditional Christian theism can better explain the ground of ethics because they associate God with *Being* where as Mormon theism associates God with *Becoming*. The idea here is that a God who is becoming is finite, and though not responsible for the evils of the world, cannot provide the unchanging basis that is required for ethics. Ostler thinks that such views are short sighted with respect to the Mormon view of the relation between ethics and God. "The revelations of the restoration point to a profound and thoroughly Christian view of ethical obligation that is not available to creedal Christians." Francis Beckwith rejects divine command theory and sees the moral law as within God's nature. Ostler argues that his position leads to the view that God must obey the moral law that is ulterior to God in order for God to achieve divine status. God is not the source of the moral law but subject to it. Whereas, in traditional theism, all God's commands are good because they are issued by a perfect being who is the source of all goodness, Ostler asserts that if God's nature is logically prior to God's will, then God is stuck with whatever his nature happens to dictate, and in this sense moral values are arbitrary. In Beckwith's position the moral law cannot be the result of a personal mind given his assumptions about God's nature, because the moral law is prior to any thought or rational input on God's part. Ostler argues that if God is a perfectly good being by nature rather than by choice, then God is an amoral being. For God is not morally good in the sense that He is subject to any moral obligation. If so, then God is not morally praiseworthy because God does not have the ability not to do good. God cannot be tempted. This point was made by Ivan Karamazov in Dostoevsky's parable of the Grand Inquisitor. If Jesus, a God, was not tempted by the three temptations, not only must we ask how could we praise him for something that he did not have to overcome, but we must also ask how He could, in turn, expect human beings to resist any such temptation. Ostler doesn't deny the logical possibility that God could do evil, but denies "that the logical possibility of God's doing something evil is a reason for failing to trust or have faith in God." In addition he claims that without the ability to do wrong we cannot genuinely trust God as we trust our most intimate beloved or friend. Were we to think that they merely were faithful because they logically, necessarily could not be otherwise, it seems their actions would be more automatic than personal. If our friend were an immaterial spirit who could not be unfaithful, then our faith in them would be based on logical meanings and usage of terms not on trust. We only trust persons. Semantic guarantees are not trust.

Ostler then moves to outline an LDS theory of ethics, which begins with Joseph Smith's teaching that our relationship with God gives us the opportunity to advance in knowledge, and that God has instituted laws that the weakest of us might be exalted with God. Ostler states that the "most natural view" grounds moral obligation in the eternal nature of uncreated realities. Moral laws are thus communal and define the conditions necessary for individual growth and the growth of the community. Good is whatever leads us to greater love and unity in interpersonal relationships. Personal growth is the increased capacity to love and be loved. Evil is what destroys a relationship—it is alienation.

Themes of Liberation

The next section deals with themes of liberation in Mormon thought. Two essays by Dennis Potter and Margaret Toscano deal with liberation of the oppressed.

In "Liberation Theology in the Book of Mormon," Dennis Potter claims that the 1978 revelation that extended the blessing of the priesthood to all worthy males was the act where "the LDS Church began the process of coming out of its moral childhood." In its adulthood it must let its moral conscience guide its increasing activity in the socio-political realm. The Book of Mormon could guide this development. It could take the United States from a "biggest-kid-on-the-block" foreign policy to an adult morality akin to King Benjamin's teachings. The message of the Book of Mormon is a theology of liberation. However, the ideal of liberation is not realized. Rather it is a story of damnation, narrating the consequences of what happens when riches and power lead to pride and self-insulation from others, instead of identification with the poor and oppressed. It is sometimes claimed that the Book of Mormon advocates only the "spiritual" but not the "material" liberation of the oppressed, but this is to miss that LDS doctrine has virtually annulled this distinction. LDS theology undercuts the distinction between this world and the next.

Potter believes there is a unique quality to the liberation theology in the Book of Mormon. For most Christians in North

America liberation theology does not speak to them, they are not poor. However, the Book of Mormon's theology of liberation speaks to the powerful, the rich, the privileged, and the prideful. It warns of their damnation. In the Book of Mormon the righteous become wealthy and prideful, creating socio-economic divisions which are sinful. He cites the ideal in 4 Nephi 1:2–3 and notes there is no discussion of personal morality here—only a communal morality. It is not an individual matter. It is not the case that all problems in society can be traced back to personal sins. Sin should be considered as the absence of fellowship and the loss of relationships. For King Benjamin the fundamental sin is economic. It is the failure to take care of the poor. His is a theology of salvation that undercuts the meritocratic theologies that support economic inequality. From King Benjamin's point of view you can't make the argument that someone earned her money and deserves it. Benjamin sees that circumstances have much to do with where we end up in life, and links salvation to our ability to obey the command to help the poor. In Mosiah 3:19, Benjamin claims that the natural man is an enemy to God and denies the ability to be good or evil in isolation from the community. Before the fall, Adam and Eve are in communion with God. They lose this in the fall. Without a community, they have to struggle for themselves, becoming like animals. This is their natural state. True community eliminates the need for struggle. In this reading we are no longer talking about natural as a metaphysical state of the individual, instead it is a social character.

In the next essay, Margaret Toscano asks the difficult question about the position of women evident through the enterprise of this book. She begins her essay, "Is There a Place for Heavenly Mother in Mormon Theology? An Investigation into Discourses of Power," with the questions: "Why are most Mormon theologians white males? And what does this question have to do with the nature of Mormon theology and how it is done?" Toscano points out that we seldom consider how power structures influence the nature of knowledge and our perceptions the world. Often we cannot even see structures of oppression because they uphold the very way we see. She analyzes a recent *Ensign* article by LDS President Gordon B. Hinckley on the four cornerstones of the faith. Each cornerstone centers on male figures and thus have implications for how women are positioned in the organization. This is reinforced by the visual imagery that illustrates each principle with a male figure. She writes: "The absence of female figures underscores the way women are excluded from participating with God in the most essential work of salvation, thus raising the question of how these basic principles even apply to them." Authority structures predetermine who and what gets included in Mormon theological discourse.

Toscano uses the concept of a Heavenly Mother as an example of what gets marginalized in LDS theological discussions. She discusses the intricacies of authorization and authority in LDS discourse and uses the Mother in Heaven doctrine to illustrate her point. For although President Hinckley has reiterated her existence, and *The Encyclopedia of Mormonism* asserts "that the belief in a living Mother in Heaven is implicit in Latter-day Saint thought," the doctrine of a Mother in Heaven does not appear on the Church's website, informal surveys among the Saints indicate unease about discussing the doctrine openly, and the doctrine seldom turns up in discourses by General Authorities in the last thirty years. Such sparse referencing of the Mother in Heaven implies that she should not be a topic of major concern for members of the church. Toscano argues that the prohibition against praying to Mother in Heaven makes her secondary in some way to Heavenly Father. While some regard silence about the mother as reverence, Toscano is concerned that it erases her. Latter-day Saints may not talk about what goes on in the temple for example, but they constantly talk about the temple. However, interest in the doctrine still abounds in the Church as might be indicated by the phenomenal popularity of *The Da Vinci Code* among Latter-day Saints.

The irony of Mormon belief in divine embodiment makes for strange discussion of God's gender in Mormon philosophical writing for which the "God of Mormon philosophical writing is usually male but sexless and thus, in a curious way, is both instantiated in and at the same time beyond gender." She cites passages in LDS scripture about salvation and exaltation that are male centered and priesthood conditioned. It can be said that the texts apply to both men and women but they do not in fact include women in any literal sense. Toscano argues the very structure of the discourse makes it that even when a Mother in Heaven is recognized, the subordination of the Mother to the Father is guaranteed. Male authority is at every level of the text and subtext.

Toscano does not believe that feminism is at odds with LDS doctrine, for one thing Mormonism's open canon and doctrine of continuing revelation makes possible a fuller revelation of the doctrine of the Heavenly Mother. Mormonism goes so far to say even the scripture may contain mistakes (Ether 12 and Mormon 8). Continuing revelation is not only the addition of new doctrine; it is the correction, clarification, and recontextualization of doctrine. There are texts which support equality (Galatians 3:28; 2 Nephi 26:33) and the breaking down of hierarchies of oppression (D&C 1:19, 20, 35). Also, current prophets have reasserted women's dignity and worth with men. The Proclamation on the Family states that they are "equal partners." This is also a goal of feminist theology. The problem, according to Toscano, is that currently this equality is at best a notion of "separate but equal." Like the Mother in Heaven, the mother of a family is supposed to be silent and at home.

Toscano ends her essay where she began by asking the question, "Is there a place for Mother in Heaven in Mormon Theology?" While she is discouraged with the lack of progress Toscano feels that "core LDS texts and doctrines give greater justification for women's equality than perhaps any other Christian tradition."

Scripture and Doctrine

The final section discusses the LDS canon, the meaning of LDS scripture, and what counts as LDS doctrine. In "Messianic

History: Walter Benjamin and the Book of Mormon," Adam Miller gives us an ingenious and playful response to Fawn Brodie and a long line of critics who claim the Book of Mormon is full of historical anachronisms. At the same time he gives a new way to look at revelation as an anachronistic eruption into linear history. Miller elaborates a thesis in connection with the work of Walter Benjamin that messianic time is necessarily anachronic. He then reformulates this thesis eleven times showing how Benjamin's notion of the messianic as anachronic finds expression in the Book of Mormon. The messianic, as messianic, involves the rediscovery of that which was lost. It occurs within history without belonging to history. The messianic, as messianic, interrupts the tyranny of homogeneous time. It breaks through the causal sense of time. It interrupts the homogenous chain of cause and effect. In fact, this is the point of repentance: it is a break of the chain of repetition, to change direction, and to start anew. Miller calls repentance a one word summary of what is meant by heterogeneous time. When Benjamin wishes to describe the kind of history proper to the heteronymous messianic time, he uses the term *constellation*. A historian who takes messianic time "as his point of departure stops telling the sequence of events like the beads of a rosary. Instead, he grasps the constellation which his own era has formed with a definite earlier one." Time moves by means of novel repetition. To look at history this way is to see constellations form on the basis of affinities and resemblances. Not only does Mormon watch the destruction of his people, but as an "angel of history" he sees that he is incapable of making things whole again. "The messianic, as messianic, speaks from the dust." It is less a matter of facts anchored firmly in memory as it is a convergence in memory of unconscious data. These constitute what Benjamin calls an "aura." The Book of Mormon is both familiar and other. It speaks from the dust. It shows us a world from the dust-filled perspective of the forgotten and oppressed. The Book of Mormon is a monad, a microcosm. It reveals a world from beginning to end. In Reformulation 10, Miller writes that "The messianic, as messianic, persists out of its time, irremediably." The past subsists but it is beyond our intellectual reach. It not as something available to our intellect, rather it is the book itself as a material object. Terryl Givens noted that this was also what was most interested to early Mormons—not just the contents of the book, but that it existed as an angelic interruption of the status quo. Finally, the messianic, as messianic, is anachronistic. A messianic constellation is formed when present events align with, repeat the lost, and reveal revolutionary possibilities. It provides "a revolutionary chance to fight for an oppressed past." Only if the past is reconfigured anachronistically, can repentance be possible. Miller writes that the wager of his paper is that its anachrony is the very condition for the Book of Mormon to operate in messianic fashion.

In his paper, "On Scripture, or Idolatry versus True Religion," James Faulconer writes that there are three factors distinguishing Zion from idolatry. The first he calls *Theos versus Person*. This pits the metaphysical first cause against a person. The philosophical/theological tradition saw God as the first cause of the universe. In this sense God is a part of a system of thought. We use God to structure the world for us. Faulconer argues that in contrast to this impersonal system we should think of God as a person rather than a metaphysical origin. In this sense, the scriptures are "*a-theistic*," they deny the unmoved, first cause, God of a metaphysical system, whether it is called theos, law, or reason. God is a person with passions. LDS theology sees God as not only personal but as embodied, not a metaphysical foundation. The Jewish thinker Emmanuel Levinas argues that both the self and ability to repent have their origins in the Other. But the Other is no foundation in the usual sense of that term. The Other is not a founder like the metaphysical God. Rather the founding of the person occurs in the face-to-face relation. An example might be Joseph Smith before God. Joseph becomes who he is in relation to this other person. Of course Joseph was already in relation with other mortal persons, and his response to these relation created who he was. Persons are fundamental—one is who he or she is in relation to these others and the ultimate person, God. "True religion posits no ultimate thing; instead it responds to an Ultimate Person."

Second, pure religion is not founded by a first cause, it has no *theos*, it recognizes no raw power before which it must bow. It bows but its humility is free. It is because of an ethical, not ontological, obligation—not because of superior and threatening power. It refuses to bow before power, but only because of an ethical demand toward a God that it loves and respects.

So third, Zion is based on the notion that obedience is a matter of service rather than appeasement to a powerful tyrant. True religion is a response to an obligation to the Other rather than to a reasoned and coherent understanding of the Other (where I list all his/her metaphysical, social, or individual aspects and this list of concepts replaces the person). Thematizing the Other, placing her in a system of thought, and reducing her to a list of conceptual properties, is one of the few areas in which human beings can dominate. In this way I can fantasize that I have the whole universe and every creature categorized in my head. Pure religion is beyond thematizing, beyond the mere law, it deals with obligations. It encounters real others. Faulconer says that this will seem nihilistic to those who insist there must be a *Theos*, a founding concept that governs all the rest of the understanding. Thematizing of the ethical demand necessarily occurs as we represent the obligation to ourselves in consciousness, but the temptation is then to fall down and worship my thematized image. This is the source of idolatry—where I mistake the image for the person.

This is where humility should enter the philosophical and theological enterprise. We often read scripture as a naive philosophy and ontology that awaits philosophical or theological exposition to point out the conceptual foundations of the religion. However, this is merely the point of convergence that the theologian and philosopher are translating into conceptual language—a concrete meeting with another. If I mistake the concept for the Other, I have transformed the person into an idol. Zion makes a demand for our ethical response in the world. Philosophical conception may be a part of this response but it is not primary. Faulconer makes the claim that "God's oneness is the unity of Zion, a unity of multiple individuals who remain individual in their unity. God's unity is not the unity of an overarching, metaphysical *theos*, for, as Latter-day Saints have pointed out for years, God is spoken of in the multiple, not the singular."

Faulconer exegetes two scriptural stories to illustrate his point. In the story of Adam and Eve, the woman is now the other who stands against Adam—not merely an extension of man, but "the mother of all living." Their relation cannot be reduced to some third term that encapsulates them both. This exegesis of the creation of man and woman illustrates the ethical point of view that Faulconer wants us to see. He writes "The story of Adam and Eve is the story of the necessity of the Other—a sexed Other—with whom one can stand before God, as a god, in ethical labor and ethical knowledge. It is a story that undoes philosophical knowledge in favor of personal and even sexual knowledge."

In Abraham's binding of Isaac the key question is not "what are you?" but "where are you?" Not what is your location in being, but where are you standing face to face with God. In this story, unlike Adam hiding himself, Abraham responds to God's call both in his act of binding Isaac and also in his not performing the sacrifice when he hears the call of the divine messenger. Both stories are stories of unity that warn us about looking for unity in a conceptual totality. Both concern welcoming the Other. The scriptures invite us to be reborn in Zion.

The final essay in this volume is Robert Millet's "What Do We Really Believe? Identifying Doctrinal Parameters within Mormonism." Millet claims that Mormons, like other Christians, hold to the central and saving doctrine "that Jesus is the Christ, the Son of God, the Savior and Redeemer of humankind; that he lived, taught, healed, suffered and died for our sins; and that he rose from the dead the third day with an immortal, resurrected body (1 Cor. 15:1–3; D&C 76:40–42)." However, since Mormons have had no councils or creeds, people have difficulty figuring out what LDS doctrine might be. Millet suggests the following "rules of thumb" for thinking about the official doctrine of the LDS church.

> 1. The teachings of the Church today have a rather narrow focus . . . ; the central and saving doctrine is what we are called upon to teach and emphasize.
> 2. Very often what is drawn from Church leaders of the past is either misrepresented, improperly weighted, or taken out of context. Further, not everything that was ever spoken or written by a Church leader in the past is a part of what we teach today.
> 3. In determining whether something is a part of the doctrine of the Church, we might ask: Is it found within the four standard works? Within official declarations or proclamations? Is it taught or discussed in general conference or other official gatherings by general Church leaders today? Is it found in the general handbooks or approved curriculum of the Church today? If it meets at least one of these criteria, we can feel secure and appropriate about teaching it. We might also add that included within the category of "all that God does reveal" would be certain matters about which we maintain "sacred silence." For example, the content of the temple endowment today would certainly be considered a part of the doctrine of the Church.

Following his "rules of thumb," he gives a list of interesting but also problematic doctrinal points from years past, pointing out that a plethora of anti-Mormon attacks deal with these peripheral doctrinal points. Almost no one criticizes Mormons for belief in Christ or his resurrection. Instead, the following items show up continually in anti-Mormon literature.

- God's life before he was God.
- How Jesus was conceived.
- The specific fate of sons of perdition.
- Teachings about Adam as God.
- Details concerning what it means to become like God hereafter.
- That plural marriage is essential to one's exaltation.
- Why blacks were denied the priesthood prior to 1978, etc.

Millet points out that since Mormons don't endorse the infallibility of the scripture it should not be surprising that their attitude to apostles and prophets would be the same. Not everything uttered by an LDS general authority should be regarded as infallible. The problem is when we think that everything to come from the mouth of a prophet or apostle is part of the doctrine of the church. Were this the case we would have to believe several contradictory things. The question then comes up of what could be trusted from authorities to be authoritative? Millet answers that true doctrine should have something that he calls "sticking power."

Millet uses the example of the 1978 revelation enabling blacks to receive the priesthood and the attempts before the revelation to justify the prohibition. He cites Dallin H. Oaks's 1988 interview to the effect that, more often than not, commandments from God do not come with reasons explaining them, the reasons are often added by us. We should have faith in the command and not the reasons, even if those reasons were supplied by LDS general authorities.

Millet next considers the famous but also infamous doctrine among Mormon opponents: the LDS notions of deification. He talks about theosis in orthodox Christianity and cites an abundance of passages in the Bible and Mormon scriptures claiming that these doctrines are essential parts of the restoration. Humanity is not a lower order than God. This is what bothers traditional Christian critics of Mormonism because it appears that we are trying to bridge the Creator/creature chasm. However, Joseph Smith, in *The*

Lectures on Faith, still indicated that the distance was still huge, in fact "almost infinite" (*Lectures* 2:2). The "almost infinite" may sound to non-Mormon Christian ears like one could be "a little bit pregnant," but it indicates that Mormons do fall on both sides of the almost infinite and in that sense that some Latter-day Saints are closer to traditional Christians while others are further away from them. Both would have good standing in the LDS Church. Millet's point is that this doctrinal point is not settled beyond this: that God was an exalted man. However, even this is *not* a central and saving doctrine, it does not pass the test of the three rules of thumb. Millet maintains it is important to know "what we do not know." Like Huff, Sherlock, and Faulconer, he thinks that this militates against the development of a final systematic theology.

A Final Remark on the Essays

The diverse points of view in this volume begin to indicate the array of philosophical and theological positions that exist and point to the vast possibilities that exist for debate and discussion of LDS doctrine—both within the tradition and beyond it. This project is yet in its infancy. Its foundations have not even begun to be sounded, and, if they are infinite, they cannot be. But this is the beauty of a living tradition. The conversations with each other, with others in their traditions, and with God should never end.

Thinking about Mormon History and the History of Mormon Thought

A "Communities of Discourse" Approach to Early LDS Thought

Grant Underwood
Brigham Young University

A half a century ago, Herbert Butterfield composed a classic essay entitled, *The Whig Interpretation of History.* Therein, he described the distortions that occur when historians impose a rigid point of view on their study of the past. Such an approach, he warned, constrains the historian to be "vigilant for likenesses between past and present, instead of being vigilant for unlikenesses."[1] It is the elucidation of *unlikenesses* that Butterfield felt was the chief aim of the historian. Given popular Mormon assumptions about the conceptual consistency over time of LDS theology, it is understandable why many LDS doctrinal histories tend to be "vigilant for likenesses." Yet, as Butterfield has pointed out, this is not good history, nor is it good theology. If Latter-day Saints believe that revelation and theological understanding come "line upon line," then some unlikenesses with the past are to be expected. With the aid of a "communities of discourse" methodology, several unlikenesses will here be examined, and, in the process, a more nuanced understanding of LDS thought in 1830s will be gained.

I am a historian and have a special interest in what the historical profession calls "intellectual history." This is not the history of intellectuals but the history of what comes from human intellects, or in other words, the history of thought. As a cohesive field within academia, intellectual history usually traces its beginnings to Arthur Lovejoy and the Johns Hopkins University-based History of Ideas Club in the 1920s and 1930s. The members of this group were interested primarily in the "great books" and grand ideas that have shaped western civilization. Their work amounted to biographies of ideas with little attention paid either to the personal or social contexts in which those ideas were articulated. In the second half of the twentieth century, such an approach fell increasingly out of favor. It seemed that Lovejoy and the "history of ideas" school viewed ideas as "autonomous abstractions which, in their self-propelled journeyings through time, happened only accidentally and temporarily to find anchorage in particular human minds."[2] Leading the revolt against such ahistorical readings were scholars like Quentin Skinner, John Dunn, and J. G. A. Pocock who argued that to properly understand both the words an author used and what he/she was using them to say (their illocutionary force,) required the meticulous reconstruction of the thought world of that particular time and place. This alone would identify the repertoire of possible meanings, which the author could have been intending. In other disciplines, the communal quality of communication was being emphasized by sociolinguist Dell Hymes with his notion of "speech community," by literary critic Stanley Fish with his idea of "interpretive communities," and through the concept of "discourse community" proposed in composition studies.

Today's intellectual historians have learned from all of this to pay special attention to historical "communities of discourse." As historians use the term, a community of discourse is a group of people who share a common purpose or who confront a common question and who have developed an identifiable set of language conventions for their conversations with one another. A community of discourse does not necessarily imply a shared physical or even social space. The commonality is the shared intellectual concern. In time, an entire language or "discourse" grows up around that particular interest. Examples of communities of discourse relevant to the study of Mormonism would include "millenarianism" and "primitivism" in the nineteenth century and "success" philosophies and "family values" in the twentieth. To the discerning, the ideals, the logic, and the linguistic conventions of these "languages" are apparent in Mormon discourse.[3] Being attuned to the relevant contemporary communities of discourse will not only result in a heightened awareness of how much the Saints shared with the world around them but, crucially, will also lead to a better appreciation of where and how they differed.

Consider, for instance, the relationship between the nineteenth century "anti-trinitarian" community of discourse and early LDS doctrine. Prior to significant clarifications in the final years of Joseph Smith's life, LDS comments about the nature of God had much in common with the popular anti-trinitarianism of the Stone-Campbell Christian movement, the Hicksite Quakers, and even the Universalists. This particular subset of nineteenth-century Christians was endeavoring to combat the popular perception of a triune God who was everywhere present, yet nowhere located. They not only argued that God was separate from Christ and the Holy Spirit but that he had his own body. While struggling to comprehend the earliest Mormon views of God, historians have sometimes been tripped up by wording which seemed to anticipate later LDS developments but which was actually part of this contemporary popular anti-trinitarianism.

The classic case in point is the word *body*. Mormons have long assumed that an affirmation in early LDS literature that "God has a body" implied flesh and bones, but anti-trinitarians actually used the phrase to refer to a spiritually corporeal deity. Here are some examples from non-Mormon, anti-trinitarian preachers: "[William] Kinkade has a chapter of fifteen pages to show that God has a body like man. [Jabez] Chadwick says he is 'prepared to defend' this sentiment; and Elder G. Fancher says, 'God has a body, eyes, ears, hands, feet, etc., just as we have'. . . . Kinkade says, 'ears, hands, and eyes are part of an intelligent ruler, and if God has none of these he cannot hear, handle, nor see us.'"[4] How similar these sound to LDS expressions! "A God without body or parts," wrote Mormon Apostle Parley P. Pratt, "has neither eyes, ears, or mouth, and can neither see, hear, nor speak." Therefore, Pratt declared, joining other non-Mormon anti-trinitarians in his affirmation, "we worship a God who has both body and parts: who has eyes, mouth and ears, and who speaks when he pleases . . . "[5]

What is lost on modern Mormons, however, is that these remarks had reference to a spiritual, not a physical body. One prominent study, for instance, quotes the same 1838 statement by Parley Pratt cited above and hails it as "the first printed description in Mormon sources of an anthropomorphic, corporeal God," and by corporeal the author means "a tangible body of flesh."[6] Upon closer examination, we can see that this is not what Pratt meant. Actually his words reflect a nineteenth-century community of religious discourse heretofore unexplored by Mormon historians.[7] Two years later in a tract written to defend Mormonism, Pratt declared: "Whoever reads our books, or hears us preach, knows that we believe . . . that the Son has flesh and bones and that the Father is a spirit." Lest his opponent misunderstand, he continued, "but we would inform Mr. H. that a personage of spirit has its organized formation, its body and parts, its individual identity, its eyes, mouth, ears, etc., and that it is in the image or likeness of the temporal body, although not composed of such gross materials as flesh and bones."[8] Unaware of early LDS participation in this particular community of religious discourse, it is understandable that modern Mormons accustomed to a later, fuller understanding have misconstrued the meaning of 1830s Mormon references to God's "body."

Erastus Snow was another who participated in that community of discourse before the Prophet in 1840s Nauvoo explicitly imbued the term "body" with fleshly corporeality. His 1840 pamphlet-length reply to a Pennsylvania antagonist makes crystal clear what early Mormons of antitrinitarian background meant (and did not mean) when they spoke of God having a body. Snow begins his discussion by posing a question that is startling because it is the unambiguous opposite of what modern Mormons would expect him to be asking. "What Mormon, understanding our doctrines, ever said that God the Father had flesh and bones?" He continues: "It is truly diverting to see you make so much noise, in trying to destroy a building of your own make, and shooting so much at a mark you have set up yourself but if you had ever read our books it would have saved you all that labor." Snow then quotes from the fifth Lecture on Faith: "The Father is a personage of spirit, glory and power" and continues:

> Your long bombast about the God of flesh and bones, reminds me very much of my father's old buck making a furious attack upon an old hat, which he supposed contained a man's head. Does it necessarily follow that because God is a spirit, possessing universal knowledge, that spirit has no form, shape, or bodily appearance as you would have it? *Vice versa*: Does it necessarily follow that because, as we affirm, he has a form and bodily parts, that form is composed of flesh and bones? Does not Paul say there is a natural body, and also a spiritual body? According to your logic, because your shadow resembles your body, it must be the body itself; or will you deny the existence of spirit altogether? That God has a form is evident from Phil. 2:6; speaking of Jesus "who being in the *form* of God, thought it not robbery to be equal with God.[9]"[10]

As surprising as such comments seem to Mormons today, we can understand these early convert Saints when we stop to consider the communities of Christian discourse from which they were in the process of emerging. Christianity had inculcated in their minds a respect for spirit as a celestial substance. From that perspective, to affirm that Heavenly Father's body was composed of such supernal material was to honor him and praise his transcendent power. Traditionally, Christianity associated flesh with mortality and disparaged it for its weakness and imperfection. To envision the perfect and almighty God entabernacled in such a substance was beyond their comprehension.

Only later in the Nauvoo period when the Prophet was able to lay before this group of converts the grand vision of eternal progression and the glorious truth of how literally and fully humans were children of God with the potentiality of becoming like their

Celestial Sire could the doctrine be comprehended. Perhaps it is the cumulative effect of the subsequent 150 years of rejoicing in this reality along with years of combating John 4:24 ("God is a spirit . . . ") that makes it hard for Mormons to peel back their assumptions and realize that there was a time before so wondrous a truth was comprehended among the Saints. In the 1830s, however, it was revolutionary enough to argue that God the Father was separate and distinct from the Son and that he actually had a body, albeit spirit, rather than being the incomprehensible essence or omnipotent force filling the universe that some other Christians assumed. The nature of Heavenly Father, the God of the Universe, is indeed so awesome that even today, who would dare say they have a complete comprehension of his physiology?

Let us now consider two other examples of how a community of discourse approach to LDS thought enables a better grasp of early understandings among the Saints. First is the term "apostle." Both in the early revelations of the D&C as well as in contemporary church literature, the word "apostle" referred to function more than to position. Early usage reflected the larger Christian community of discourse in which *apostle*, based on the Greek verb *apostello* (to send), was understood literally as "one who is sent," an envoy, a messenger, a missionary.[11] Not surprisingly, this was the meaning that was carried into the Church by the first LDS converts. The Church's foundational Articles and Covenants made it clear that all church elders sent out to preach the gospel and administer its ordinances were apostles (D&C 20:38). By 1835, when there were hundreds of elders in the Church, a dozen were selected, based on D&C 18:26–40, to receive a special designation as "twelve apostles." Gradually, thereafter, the application of the term "apostle" was restricted to members of that body, especially after Joseph Smith gave them general church administrative responsibilities in the 1840s. Representative of the earlier essentially synonymous understanding of apostle, elder, missionary, Jared Carter, after being ordained an elder, journalized: "I now commence to give some short sketches of a mission that I performed from Ohio to Vermont after I had been to Kirkland where I received the authority of an apostle commenced a mission to the east on 22nd day of Sept. 1831 with Brother Ebenezer Page."[12]

A final example of a community-of-discourse approach to early LDS thought is the understanding the first Saints had of confirmation. From the beginning, the Saints were instructed to confirm by the laying on of hands, but the connotations of confirmation are more fully unlocked by attending to its linguistic context. In several places in the D&C the expression "confirm(ing) the church(es)" is utilized (D&C 20:43; 24:9; 26:1). Today Latter-day Saints speak of confirming *members* of the church, but not of confirming *the* church. Church is used almost exclusively to refer to the overall organization, not to its constituent congregations. Yet the Lord told Joseph to confirm "the church at Colesville" (D&C 26:1). This reflects the older New Testament usage where *ekklesia* or "church" literally meant a congregation or an assemblage of people. Moreover, early Mormon phrasing mirrored the King James rendering of Acts 15:41 where Paul and Silas travel "through Syria and Cilicia, confirming the churches."

Additional insight is gained by noting that other translations of the Greek word *episterizo*, rendered "confirming" in the King James Version, include "strengthening," "establishing," and "consolidating." This hints at a richer understanding of the term "confirm" in the 1830s. To confirm someone was more than to ceremonially *affirm* their membership in the church. The link with an NT-based Christian discourse suggests that the 1830s usage retained the rich original connotation of confirmation as a means of spiritually strengthening and establishing the Saints through the conferral of the Holy Ghost. What happened when hands were laid on the head of a newly baptized convert was not the bestowal of two separate gifts, (formal membership status *and* the gift of the Holy Ghost) but rather a single gift, which was expected to open the door to spiritual strength and stability.

I close by offering some theological, even pastoral, reflections for Latter-day Saints who have assumed that complete doctrinal understanding was present from day one in the Church and that throughout LDS history Church leaders have always said and meant exactly the same things when discussing doctrine. Actually, as we have glimpsed through a "communities-of-discourse" lens, the beautiful monarch butterfly of the restored gospel gradually emerged from the cocoon of contemporary Christianity. Let me modify the metaphor a bit. Just as we can more understandingly praise God's miracle in the creation of human beings by better understanding the details of their embryonic development, birth, and post-natal growth, so we can more fully appreciate the restored gospel as we take cognizance of its growth and development. Indeed, much of the wonder of life would be lost, if humans or the Church sprang full-grown from the hand of God. This connects us to our own LDS community of discourse, the "line-upon-line" principle, which allows for a gradual unfolding and refining of doctrine based on both human capacity and divine design. To purse Paul's metaphor, the Church is like a body, and all bodies go through successive stages of development from infancy to adulthood. A wise and loving father does not immediately correct all his children's mistaken notions nor attempt to teach them all truth at once. Rather, he closely monitors their development, adding, subtracting, and refining until they reach maturity. Would a perfect Father in Heaven be less wise? Continuous revelation is merely his method, the light "that shineth more and more unto the perfect day" (Prov. 4:18; cf. D&C 50:24).

As a Mormon historian who for many years has closely studied LDS thought, I am profoundly impressed with how patient the Lord is, how he treats his chosen servants not as puppets or pawns but honors their agency and understanding and teaches them, according to the Doctrine and Covenants, "in their weakness, after the manner of their language (cultural as well as verbal) that they might come to understanding" (D&C 1:24). If here and there history isn't quite as neat or dramatic as we may wish to see it, we can be grateful. It is a witness that a loving Lord, as consummate teacher and caring father, has been more concerned with dealing wisely with his earlier servants than he was with how those dealings might later look to some of his children. As we would hope, God places people, his children, above image. Let us be careful that we do not unwittingly cherish, even worship, a particular construct or image of the past more than we do the living Lord whose historical ways are not always our ways, nor whose thoughts are our thoughts. Let us rejoice in the miracle of growth, spiritual as well as physical.

GRANT UNDERWOOD is Professor of History at Brigham Young University. He received his Ph.D. in History at UCLA and is author of *Millenarian World of Early Mormonism*, editor of *Voyages of Faith: Explorations in Mormon Pacific History*, and is lead editor for the first volume of the Documents Series in the new Joseph Smith Papers. He has also authored dozens of articles on Mormonism and delivered papers at more than eighty scholarly conferences.

Notes

1. Herbert Butterfield, *The Whig Interpretation of History* (1931; reprint, New York: Norton, 1965), 11–12.
2. Stefan Collini, *What is Intellectual History? What is History Today . . . ?* (Atlantic Highlands, N.J.: Humanities Press International, 1988), 106.
3. Richard T. Hughes and C. Leonard Allen, *Illusions of Innocence: Protestant Primitivism in America, 1630–1875* (Chicago: University of Chicago Press, 1988); Hughes, ed., *The American Quest for the Primitive Church* (Urbana: University of Illinois Press, 1988); and Underwood, *The Millenarian World of Early Mormonism.* The influence of relevant communities of discourse on Mormon belief in this century has yet to be teased out though such influences are regularly suggested. Relatively little Mormon intellectual history from any perspective has been done for the twentieth century. A noteworthy exception is the recent discussion of the influence of Anglo-Israelism on LDS views of race: Armand L. Mauss, "In Search of Ephraim: Mormon Conceptions of Lineage and Race", and Arnold H. Green, "Gathering and Election: Israelite Descent and Universalism in Mormon Discourse" in *Journal of Mormon History* 25 (Spring 1999): 131–173; 195–228.
4. Hiram Mattison, *A Scriptureal Defence of the Doctrine of the Trinity, or a Check to Modern Arianism as Taught by Unitarians, Campbellites, Hicksites, New Lights, Universalists, and Mormons; and Especially by a Sect Calling Themselves "Christians"* (New York: 1840), 44.

5. Parley P. Pratt, *Mormonism Unveiled: Zion's Watchman Unmasked, and its Editor, Mr. L. R. Sunderland, Exposed: Truth Vindicated: The Devil Mad, and Priestcraft in Danger* (New York: 1838), 31.
6. James B. Allen, "Emergence of a Fundamental: The Expanding Role of Joseph Smith's First Vision in Mormon Religious Thought," *Journal of Mormon History* 7 (1980): 48, 50.
7. Dan Vogel, "The Earliest Mormon Concept of God," *Line Upon Line: Essays on Mormon Doctrine*, ed. Gary James Bergera. (Salt Lake City: Signature Books, 1989), 17–33, cites several representatives of this "community" but neither recognizes them as such nor realizes their relevance for explaining LDS understandings of God's "body."
8. Parley P. Pratt, *An Answer to Mr. William Hewitt's Tract Against the Latter-Day Saints* (Manchester: 1840), 9.
9. Erastus E. Snow, *Snow's Reply to a Self-Styled Philanthropist, of Chester County* (Philadelphia: 1840), 6.
10. In 1836, Truman Coe, a Presbyterian minister and former Kirtland resident, wrote that Mormons believed "that the true God is a material being, composed of body and parts; and that when the Creator formed Adam in his own image, he made him about the size and shape of God himself." See Milton V. Backman, "Truman Coe's 1836 Description of Mormonism" *BYU Studies* 17 (Spring 1977): 347–55. Since 1977 when Backman reprinted Coe's statement, it has been variously interpreted. Some have seen it as proof that the earliest Mormons knew that God had a body of flesh and bone. See Backman, "Truman Coe's," 350; and Robert Millet, "The Supreme Power over All Things: The Doctrine of the Godhead in the Lectures on Faith," in *The Lectures on Faith in Historical Perspective*, ed. Larry E. Dahl and Charles D. Tate, Jr., (Provo, UT: Religious Studies Center, 1990), 223–28. Others, realizing that the Saints generally did not hold such beliefs until the 1840s, dismiss Coe's statement as distortion. (See Allen, "Emergence of a Fundamental," 49–50).

    The problem may be that both sides are failing to locate Coe's expression within its proper community of discourse. "Material" did not always mean "fleshly." A "material being" could also be a spiritual being since "all spirit is matter," an idea not unique to the Mormons. In support of this reading it is noteworthy that Coe uses the discursively meaningful phrase "body and parts" and comments on the "size and shape" of God rather than on the more radical prospect of a deity "with hair on his arms" which in the eyes of Coe's audience would have made Mormonism appear to be even more the unorthodox "gust of Fanaticism" he claimed it to be.

If Coe is not reflecting a spirit-as-matter community of discourse, then his use of "material" as fleshly should be seen as the same kind of anti-Mormon distortion that Pratt and Snow were combating in the statements above. What won't do is to use Coe as the sole *contemporary* support for the claim that Mormons in the 1830s believed God had a body of flesh and bones. If such were the case, how likely is it that Pratt and Snow, two of Mormonism's best informed advocates, would either be oblivious to or explicitly opposed to what was supposedly a commonplace LDS teaching?

11. Francis H. Agnew, "The Origin of the NT Apostle-Concept: A Review of Research," *Journal of Biblical Literature* 105 (1986): 75–96.
12. Jared Carter, Journal, 1831–1833; LDS Church Archives, 34.

The Modernism Controversy

William Henry Chamberlin, His Teachers Howison and Royce, and the Conception of God Debate

James M. McLachlan
Western Carolina University

Introduction

The turn of the nineteenth to twentieth century marked a difficult period of transition for most Christian denominations in America as they struggled to adapt to modernism. This was doubly so for the Mormons. For not only did they have deal with modernist science and historical criticism they were moving from a communal theocracy to becoming a part of the greater American society. Between 1889 and 1931 Mormons moved from polygamy to monogamy, theocracy to patriotism, communitarianism to individualism, and from radical political and economic experimentation to political and economic conservatism. In 1884 a fourteen-year old William Henry Chamberlin, reflecting a typical Mormon attitude, had written in his diary that the Lord would save the Saints from their federal persecutors.[1] To achieve statehood the Church had had to give up the Mountain West theocracy and at least outwardly enter the American mainstream. Mormonism passed from its communal nineteenth-century roots to the increasingly capitalist individualism of the twentieth century.

The intellectual history of Christian denominations in the nineteenth and early twentieth century is filled with conflicts like the one at BYU. The adjustment to modernism, be it theories of the origin of life and humanity or the historical approach to scripture, spawned various reactions amongst religious groups in Europe and

America. The reaction in Utah reflects these trends but also has its uniquely LDS twists. Modernism in its many forms disturbed not only church superintendent of education Horace Cummings and conservative believers but Chamberlin and his philosophical mentors George Holmes Howison and Josiah Royce. Howison and Royce developed philosophical explanations of evolution in part to counter the survival of the fittest social Darwinism of Herbert Spencer. One of the ironies of Chamberlin's difficulties at BYU during the controversy is that he basically agreed with the basic belief of Commissioner Cummings that morality should be at the basis of education. Like his teachers Chamberlin argued that morality was at the basis of reality. It is unfortunate that Chamberlin's LDS vision of the basis of reality of the moral world has disappeared from discussions of LDS theologies.

In 1910 philosophy professor William H. Chamberlin arrived at BYU a year after President George Brimhall had hired a group of Ph.D. scientists including the Peterson brothers and Chamberlin's brother Ralph to recreate the University. William, fresh from Harvard and Josiah Royce's lectures on the Blessed Community and *The Philosophy of Loyalty*, expressed to his students at the Brigham Young University his dismay at the increase of cut-throat capitalism among the Mormons. He presented them with both a critique and appropriation of modernism that influenced an entire generation of educators and intellectuals in Mormon country. What he taught them was a form of idealist philosophy called "personal idealism" which was critical of his Harvard mentor Royce. Chamberlin had become a personal idealist under his M.A. professor at the University of California, George Holmes Howison and Royce's comments on his papers at Harvard show that he held the position throughout his stay there.[2] Chamberlin saw personal idealism as the bridge between scientific modernism and the gospel. Modernism's two threats to traditional Christianity and Mormonism, Darwinism and higher criticism, could be seen in terms of the development of human persons in freedom toward godhood. Royce's and Howison's debate on the conception of God and how to appropriate modernism underlay Chamberlin's efforts at BYU.

Things did not work out as Chamberlin hoped. In a year the Petersons and Ralph were gone, casualties in Mormonism's version of the modernist controversy. William hung on until 1916 but then resigned his position when the philosophy department was dissolved and his classes removed from the catalog.

The story of William Chamberlin's life and career, and the BYU controversy that cut it short has been told elsewhere and I will not repeat here.[3] But Chamberlin influenced an entire generation of Mormon educators. He was still on the list of "most influential Mormon intellectuals" in 1969 when Leonard Arrington did a poll for *Dialogue.*[4] It says something about Chamberlin's ability as a teacher that 48 years after his death a man who really published nothing beyond pamphlets for his classes and articles in the school newspapers, out of print since before his death would still be regarded as important. However, by the time the survey was redone in 1993 Chamberlin's name had disappeared.[5] Chamberlin's disappearance from discussions of Mormon theology is unfortunate. Mormon philosophers like Sterling McMurrin and E. E. Ericksen thought Chamberin was the perhaps the best thinker the Mormons had produced, but he is probably the least read.[6]

Struggles of Religion and Modernism

Chamberlin's life and thought reflects an age of transition within Mormonism and highlights the ambiguous position of theology, philosophy, and biblical/scriptural studies in the Mormon tradition. But it also reflects the larger uneasiness in philosophy and religion at the turn of the century. Chamberlin's teachers Howison and Royce were both concerned with the rise of positivism and capitalism to the detriment of faith and community, and in many ways their famous 1895 debate on the problem of God was an attempt to stem off the flood of the latter. But they were also concerned with the conservative anti-intellectual reaction against positivism. Chamberlin's defense of both evolution and higher criticism at BYU reflects his effort to follow his teachers' attempt to find a middle way between a religiously and philosophically untenable biblical literalism and the scientism, capitalism, and positivism they sought to avoid. This led him, like many religious thinkers of the nineteenth century, to schools of thought like philosophical idealism, pragmatism, radical empiricism, and, for Chamberlin, personal idealism and its sibling personalism.

The intellectual history of Christian denominations in the nineteenth and early twentieth century is filled with conflicts like the one at BYU.[7] One of the key thinkers in the personalist movement and a key influence on Chamberlin's thought, the Methodist philosopher Borden Parker Bowne, was tried for heresy in 1904 after he came to the defense of a colleague in the Department of Old Testament at Boston University School of Theology who advocated "scientific findings about evolution, coupled with the higher biblical criticism." But Bowne was acquitted unanimously after arguing that free speech was the moral and spiritual thrust of the attempt to find the meaning of issues essential to religious integrity.[8] Bowne was very critical of modernism; he saw personalism as a way to accept the insights of modern historical and scientific scholarship while rejecting materialism and positivism, arguing that mechanism and impersonalism fail, not only morally, but metaphysically and epistemologically to explain the world of our experience.[9]

In the BYU controversy, the moral and religious question was the primary concern of Church superintendent of education Horace Cummings, President Brimhall, the committee, and, eventually, President Joseph F. Smith. President Smith's statement in the *The Juvenile Instructor* for February 1911 took the cautious position that the theory of evolution and modernism in general might be passing intellectual moments and the church should take no position on their truth or falsity. In this way one might avoid the problem of confusing the faithful.

> Some of our teachers are anxious to explain how much of the theory of evolution, in their judgment, is true, and what is false, but that only leaves their students in an unsettled frame of mind. They are not old enough and learned enough to discriminate, or put proper limitations upon a theory which we believe is more or less a fallacy. In reaching the conclusion that evolution would be best left out of discussions in our church schools we are deciding a question of propriety and are not undertaking to say how much of evolution is true, or how much is false . . . [10]

There is much to be said for the church not taking a position. Yet the ban on discussion really could not work, for one could not avoid thinking about modernism once the genie was out of the bottle. The evidence for this is the recurring battle throughout the 20th century on the meaning of modernism in terms of evolution and also historical criticism of scriptural tradition.[11] But another aspect of President Smith's statement is more particularly Mormon and centers on the LDS practice against a trained ministry. It also seems to be an observation on the widening gap in Protestantism, between highly educated theological liberals and biblical literalists, that created a class division among the faithful. President Smith argues that the church should avoid philosophical speculation for fear of developing a philosophical and theological aristocracy that would eventually destroy the community of the church by creating intellectual class distinctions. President Smith here tries to move the discussion away from metaphysical and theological speculation to liturgical and moral considerations. The main concern is serving God and not explaining the meaning of creation.

> The Church itself has no philosophy about the *modus operandi* employed by the Lord in His creation of the world, and much of the talk therefore about the philosophy of Mormonism is altogether misleading. God has revealed to us a simple and effectual way of serving Him, and we should regret very much to see the simplicity of those revelations involved in all sorts of philosophical speculations. If we encouraged them it would not be long before we should have a theological and scholastic aristocracy in the

> Church, and we should therefore not enjoy the brotherhood that now is, or should be common to rich and poor, learned and unlearned among the Saints.[12]

But this was also, in many respects, Chamberlin's fear. He believed that people had basic moral and spiritual intuitions that had been confused by modernism.[13] The philosopher's task was to disentangle the confusion. He thought that basic questions about reality were unavoidable and thought personalism provided a metaphysical view that set morality and religion at the basis of reality. In this sense, it provided an intellectually satisfying position for those who, beset with modernism, could not return to the religious explanations of their youth, and yet preserved the religion and its key insights. Chamberlin's creation of a Mormon theology in personalist terms is not at all as alien to Mormon sensibilities as many of the liberal naturalist theologies of the 19th and early 20th centuries. But, like those liberal theologians, Chamberlin's studies, first in the sciences and then in biblical criticism, led him believe that a philosophical articulation of Mormonism was necessary for Mormon students, who, like him, were confronting modernism.[14]

Mormonism and Idealism: Chamberlin's "Spiritual Realism" in Context

Chamberlin called his point of view "Spiritual Realism." Like his teacher Howison, he was a personal idealist. In this respect Chamberlin is a unique figure in the history of Mormon thought; Mormons are of course supposedly materialists. To rule Chamberlin out as an important LDS thinker because he is an idealist is both to misunderstand Chamberlin's idealism and Mormon "materialism." Chamberlin's idealism is based on the assumption that a Mormon view of the universe should be an ethical view in which matter is subject to moral and religious concerns. Roughly this means Chamberlin is an Idealist if one holds by idealism that mind is fundamental in the world and there is no reality that is not supplemented or connected with minds and wills. But if idealism is taken to be the denial of the objective world, then Chamberlin was not an idealist. For Chamberlin naive realism and traditional Idealism are half truths. Realism is right in asserting that the being of sense-data is not entirely dependent on their being perceived, but wrong in so far as it asserts that they are a type of objects whose being is quite independent of perception. Idealism, on the other hand, is right in maintaining that if sense-data are to *be* at all, they must be perceived, but wrong in maintaining their being perceived is the only condition of their being.[15] This two aspect view of reality as relational was true of the personalistic strains of idealism advocated by Romantics and vitalists like F. W. J. Schelling and Charles Renouvier in Europe and in America by the personalists Borden Parker Bowne at Boston University and Chamberlin's University of California mentor George Holmes Howison. In this respect, it is significant that Chamberlin was also drawn to some of the key pragmatists of the age, particularly William James and Henri Bergson who considered themselves radical empiricists.[16] In Bergson's classic *Matter and Memory*, Bergson puts forward a central notion of the *image*. Bergson sought to walk the tightrope between two ways of thinking of reality: realism and Idealism. In the former, *things* are what are ultimately real. In the latter, *ideas* are real. Bergson sees problems in both these ways of looking at the world. In the former we say things like ideas are in the brain but forget that the "brain" is also a name or idea. In the latter we forget the connection between ideas and physical realities. Bergson's "image" lies between these two. In it we recognize our talk as a human approximation of an external/internal reality that we intuit. For Bergson this is a more radical type of empiricism because it deconstructs the latent idealism of more naive styles of empiricism and materialism. For example, to assert an object is material is to forget that the notion of matter is also an idea. For Bergson this intuition of the inadequacy and creative capacity of language is at the heart of our intuition of freedom which is at the basis of morality.

This insight is at the basis of Chamberlin's form of personal idealism which he called *spiritual realism*. It is also the philosophical source of what many religious thinkers at the beginning of the 20th century saw as the great defense against the positivism and agnosticism of such thinkers as evolutionary "naive" empiricists Herbert Spencer, the founder of social Darwinism who advocated a "scientific" ethics based on individual egoism and the complete exercise of individualist "freedom" (although this freedom is itself metaphysically completely determined by causal realities of materialism). Social inequalities were explained and perhaps justified by evolutionary principles, the best rise to the top, nothing can or should be done about it. Notice here that the idea of "freedom" is fairly weak. Individuals should be allowed to pursue there self desires, but they don't choose their desires. These are hard wired into them by evolution. Thus they are not free in any strong sense of the term. Chamberlin saw social Darwinism and the cutthroat capitalism it justified as antithetical to Mormon community.

For personalists like Chamberlin, and like the pragmatists and radical empiricists, our views of reality are already shot through with mind, with interpretation to the point where it is impossible to completely disentangle them. What are called "simple facts" may be shot through with a good deal of human desire. For example, the Victorian anthropologist Edward Tylor's claim that the "systematic study of the religion of the lower races" led to a definition of religion as a pre-scientific description of the world that evolved from animism to science. But now Tylor's reading of the facts may have had much to do with his place as a reader in anthropology at Oxford, a privileged post in imperial England and a privileged country at the beginning of the 20th century. This idea placed value inquiry at the beginning not at the end of our study, and allowed Chamberlin to assert that our primary experience of the world is the experience of choice of valuing one thing over another. Thus ethics is not just something added to a theory of reality but is at the basis of reality itself.

In this respect, the tragedy of Chamberlin's clash with Church Education superintendent Horace Cummings and school authorities at BYU becomes clear. Chamberlin saw himself working in the same direction of the Church authorities. Following his personalist mentors, Chamberlin was seeking a way of providing philosophical support to the basic idea that Cummings had taken from his mentor Karl Maeser; education should be primarily moral and spiritual and that the foundation of reality was moral.

Boston and California Personalism

Chamberlin's Spiritual Realism is a form of American personalism, of which there were two predominant strains at the beginning of the century, one founded in Boston and the other in California. The theistic personalism of the Methodist Boston University philosopher Borden Parker Bowne would develop into a school that would later include Edgar Sheffield Brightman, Peter Bertocci, and Martin Luther King.[17] California personalism or personal idealism was founded by Chamberlin's teacher at Berkeley George Holmes Howison and continued by Sterling McMurrin's mentor at University of Southern California, Ralph Tyler Flewelling. Personalism is, in essence, the contention that persons are the fundamental metaphysical reality.[18] Among personalists evolution became a characteristic of Deity, and though Borden Parker Bowne remained, in many ways, a traditional theist, Edgar S. Brightman and Peter Bertocci radically modified their theism, moving to much more finite notions of Deity which they called a finite/infinite God. In struggling with the problem of evil Brightman argued that God struggled with real *dysteleological surds* within God's own nature that could not be seen as harmoniously fitting into a perfect universe. Thus, Brightman and his student Peter Bertocci challenged traditional notions of theodicy that emphasized God's omnipotence. Brightman asserted that there are things that happen that do not coincide with God's will. God is involved in an internal struggle within God's own nature which Brightman termed the "non-rational given." Somewhat similar to what would be familiar to Mormons in discussion of light and darkness and opposition in 2 Nephi 2, Brightman asserted that part of the reason for creation was for God's overcoming of the darkness in God's own nature. God is also restricted by the free choices of human beings. "God is a Person supremely conscious, supremely valuable, and supremely creative, yet limited both by the free choice of other persons and restrictions within his own nature."[19]

Howison's California personal idealism precedes Bowne's and Brightman's personalism but also has the conception of a finite/infinite God who must create under the restrictions posed by the real freedom of real others. In order to indicate how this move to idealism and radical empiricism worked in Chamberlin's case, I want to offer a very brief discussion of one of the most famous debates of the age, and then show how these ideas carry over into Chamberlin's writing and teaching: the 1895 *Conception of God* debate that took place between Chamberlin's two teachers, Harvard's Josiah Royce and California's George Holmes Howison.

The Conception of God Debate

The Conception of God debate took place at the Berkeley Philosophical Union in 1895. Howison had formed the union when he came to Berkeley in 1885. The plan of the union was simple: members would read one work by a philosopher who would then be invited to speak at the union. In 1895 this work was *The Religious Aspcct of Philosophy* by Josiah Royce. A little drama was added to the festivities by the fact that Royce and Howison had been rivals for the position at Harvard that went to Royce. The debate included two other participants and was a kind of a family affair of American idealists. Joseph LeConte, of the University of California, at seventy-two was a father figure. He had taught both Sidney Mezes and Royce as undergraduates.[20] Mezes, of the University of Texas, had been a student of both Howison and

Royce. At the time, the *New York Tribune* labeled the debate "the most noteworthy philosophical discussion that for many a day has taken place in this country." The *New York Times* called it "the great debate" and "the battle of Giants."[21] But the discussion afterwards focused on the disagreement between Royce and Howison.

In *The Conception of God* Royce's argument for the existence and character of God proceeds from the experience of human ignorance. The argument from ignorance is significant historically in its opposition to agnosticism. The philosophers in the debate were all opposed to positivism, and saw idealism as an antidote to Herbert Spencer. Howison's introduction to the published book based on the debate discusses the inadequacies of Spencer's position and sees Royce's arguments as devastating to Spencer and to positivism.[22] Basically, Royce uses Spencer's agnosticism about reality to argue for an absolute.[23] Royce had already introduced this argument in *The Religious Aspect of Philosophy*; the central chapter of that book dealt with "The Possibility of Error." The argument basically proceeds like this: Since error is possible, two questions arise,

1. What is the truth that makes error possible?
2. What is the nature of reality which this truth implies? Either there can be no error, or, as Royce thought, there is "an infinite unity of conscious thought to whom is present all possible truth."

Error is incomplete thought that, viewed from a higher ground, fails to describe adequately what it was intended to describe. Once you admit that error only exists relative to a higher and more comprehensive thought, there is no stopping place short of an infinite thought. Thus, "all reality must pretend to the Unity of the Infinite Thought" which is God.[24] Later in 1907, the year that Chamberlin was a student at Harvard, in his lectures on *The Philosophy of Loyalty*, Royce would use the argument to support his justification of an ethics of community based on loyalty.[25]

For Howison, however, there was a radical flaw in Royce's argument. It is that this method of argumentation does not bring us to a community of knowers. What Royce really proves, according to Howison, " . . . was that the individual thinker, upon reflection, must unavoidably affirm his or her own all-conditioning reality in and over the field of possible experience." In other words Howison claimed that, given Royce's argument, there is no logical justification for favoring idealistic monism or monotheism to solipsism. Unintentionally Royce is arguing for the omniscience of the individual knower (Royce) as much as he is for the existence of God since it is the individual knower who "knows" or doesn't know (in the case of Spencer's agnosticism) the truth. So there is no logically compelling reason not to accept solipsism. We are stuck with in the position that we must take our own view of reality as the best available. Royce really rejects the outcome, not for logical reasons, but because he has the right moral intuitions.[26]

If the only choice is between solipsism/agnosticism and belief in God, the choice cannot be made on logical but must be on moral and religious grounds. For Howison the choice is ultimately a moral one not entailed by the formal logic of the argument. Though Howison doesn't admit it here or elsewhere, he sees choosing God as something of an existential choice. It is our moral reason, or what Howison called our "complete reason," that helps us to make it. In other words our theoretical/objective reason cannot be called upon to make the choice between solipsism/agnosticism and belief in a community. This is an ethical choice. Howison seeks to develop a metaphysical vision of religion but on a personalist ethics of the absolute value of persons.

After some philosophical wrangling with Royce, it finally terminated in the publication of the debate in a volume entitled *The Conception of God.* Though the debate took place in 1895, *The Conception of God* was not published until 1898. During that time Royce and Howison exchanged letters and arguments. Royce responded to Howison in a lengthy piece of more than 200 pages entitled "The Absolute and the Individual: A Supplementary Discussion, with Replies to Criticisms." This response comprises the bulk of the volume that was finally published in 1898. (The four essays that made up the original debate only comprise 132 pages.) Royce thought that the essay *might* reconcile his and Howison's positions. Royce claimed Howison's critique could be reduced to the Kantian antinomy between the theoretical and practical reason. Thus, Howison's main objection to Royce's argument only counted insofar as it concerned ethics. Howison, however, did not think the essay reconciled their positions. He disagreed with Royce's characterization of his argument, and in September of 1898 published an essay outlining his much more fundamental disagreement with Royce. In that article, "The Real Issue in the Conception of God Discussion," Howison says that his point is not to set moral consciousness simply as a "categorical imperative" against theoretical reason, and simply " . . . have the heart breathe defiance to the intellect."[27] Howison says his aim in his critique of Royce's "Conception of God" was a theoretical justification of ethics; that our moral sense objects to theoretical monism is not sufficient—we need a metaphysical theory to support it. Howison says that his real disagreement with Royce can be summarized in two main premises:

> (1) That no conception of God can have any philosophical value unless it can be proved real, or, in other words, unless it is the conception that of itself proves God to exist; and (2) that the conception [offered by Professor Royce and other monists] is the only conception that can thus prove its reality. It is precisely denying the validity of this second premise that the vital point of my dissent consists.[28]

Howison agrees with Royce on the first premise. He believes that there is a conception of God that can be proven real. But he denies the second premise for moral reasons. He thinks that Royce's God annihilates the freedom of the creature and with it the reality of the creature.[29]

In 1895, after the debate, Royce wrote to Howison that he should " . . . put his multipersonalitarianism once and for all into its final argumentative rights by a complete and technical statement.

That would be one of the most fascinating books of the century, for us who love dialectics, as well as truth."[30] But by 1897 Royce's tone had changed to exasperation for what he regarded as the incomprehensibility of Howison's objections. Royce even accused Howison of advocating a type of pantheism/polytheism where anyone was God.[31] It is ironic that Royce's objection to Howison's pluralism, where anyone is God, is so similar to Howison's objection to Royce's pantheism where the thinker is as much God as God.

For Howison, it was a challenge to finally attempt systematically to set forth his pluralistic, personalistic, idealism. He finally did this in his only major work, a group of essays published in 1901 under the title, *The Limits of Evolution, and Other Essays Illustrating the Metaphysical Theory of Personal Idealism.* In it he offers description of the pluralist "City of God," and, in response to Royce's argument from ignorance, his own argument for the existence of God based on Howison's ideal of complete reason.

Howison created a pluralist idealism in which God is related to an eternal community of persons that is based on the primacy of ethical reason. In the preface to *The Limits of Evolution,* Howison set forth a ten-point outline of his personal idealism which Royce had dubbed "multipersonalism." First, that all existence is either the existence of minds or the experience of minds. All material objects are certain types of these experiences. Second, time and space owe their existence to the correlation and coexistence of minds. This coexistence is not to be thought of as spatial or temporal but must be regarded as an internal relation, each is a logical implication of the other. The recognition of each other as alike, and each as self-determining makes their co-existence a moral order. The world becomes a stage for the moral life. Third, these many minds form the eternal "unconditionally real" world. They constitute what Howison called the "City of God." Each has the common aim of fulfilling one rational ideal. God is the fulfilled type of every mind, the " . . . living Bond of their union, [and] reigns in it, not by the exercise of power, but solely by light; not by authority, but by reason; not by efficient, but by final causation.—" Fourth, the members of this "eternal republic" have no origin other than the purely logical one they have in reference to each other. This includes their relation to God. This means they are, like God, eternal. However, in his fifth point, he indicates that they are not independent of each other, but they exist only through the mutual correlation. They are the ground of all temporal and spatial existences. They are thus, in his sixth point, free in reference to the natural world and to God. Seventh, this pluralism is held in union by reason. The world of spirits is the genuine unmoved that moves all things. It is the final cause of all activity. Eighth, this movement of changeable things toward the goal of the common ideal is what is called the process of evolution. And the world of spirits, as the ground of the project, can therefore not be a product of evolution itself, nor subject in any way to evolution except that:

> . . . minds other than God, who have their differentiation from him in a side of their being which is in one aspect contradictory of their Ideal, this sense-world of their's is by its very nature, in its conjunction with their total nature, under the law of return toward the essential Ideal. In this world of sense, this essentially incomplete and tentative world of experience, evolution must therefore reign universally. . . . Every mind has an eternal reality that did not arise of change and that cannot by change pass away.

Ninth, all these conceptions are founded on the idea of a world of spirits as the circuit of moral relationship and they carry within them a profound change from the traditional idea of God. Creation is no longer an event, and is not an occurrence that happened at some instant in the life of God. Rather, creation is ongoing. God, who is a person, also represents the realized final cause, the ideal toward which the activity of the world of spirits is aimed. Without this goal " . . . they would be but void names and bare possibilities." Finally, tenth, the Final cause is here not merely the guiding principle but the grounding and fundamental principle of all other causes. The reference to every other mind brings us into relation to the divine mind. In this way, mutual recognition is essential to all minds. It is essential to the very existence of the individual. God is the type of all intelligence. God is the final Goal, the ideal by which all are influenced, which is the only causation in the moral world.[32] Universality is retained by the common goal of all persons. A person is a member of a manifold system of persons, all of them are self active centers of origination as far as efficient causation is concerned. God is the final cause persons are led by the attraction of the ideal vision, the vision of the City of God. The community is coeternal with God.[33]

It is this notion of the divine community that animated Chamberlin's Mormon idealism which he called "spiritual realism."

Chamberlin's Personal Idealism: "Spiritual Realism"

When Chamberlin chose to study with Howison at Berkeley in 1906 he must have known that Howison's "Personalist Idealism" would not be unsympathetic to his Mormon faith.[34] In *The Limits of Evolution* Howison gave a systematic statement of his position that persons were co-eternal with God which is similar to a basic Mormon doctrine of the eternal relation of persons and God. This is the position of his 1906 M.A. thesis, "The Unity of Thought Is the Society of Minds," the title of which seems to refer directly to one of Royce's claims in *The Conception of God* debate that, "all reality must pretend to the Unity of the Infinite Thought."[36] The difference being that Chamberlin has "Howisonized" Royce's claim by saying the unity of thought is to be found in a society of minds. The absolute ceases to be monistic and becomes a community in which the whole pervades each part. This insight will pervade Chamberlin's work for the rest of his life. It is the position that he thought could bridge the chasm between Mormonism and modernism. This is the respect that he saw himself working in the same direction as Joseph F. Smith and Brimhall at BYU.

In his M.A. thesis Chamberlin makes the classic idealist move and claims that unity is only possible for mind(s). Matter can only be an aggregate, is not a unity, nor does it even have parts except for a mind. The ultimate unity must leave nothing out; it must be complete. In order to do this each part must mirror the whole and be a microcosm of the whole.

> In the first place we are led to observe that our ultimate unity can find its concrete embodiment only in absolute reality. There must be absolutely no disturbing influence outside of it. It must connect together its parts and be completely in them. Beyond them there can be nothing. In searching for such a unity, then, we may assume that it lies in an individual which is absolutely self-sufficient, binding together and yet, in a sense, in each of its parts.
>
> In what way can a unity be conceived which binds its parts together and yet can be in each of its parts?

Usually this absolute unity has been thought in monistic terms as the absolute God of traditional theism or the One of monistic systems. In either case the One is regarded as real and essential, whereas the many are dependent and contingent. For example in the argument from error, Howison claimed that Royce pointed to the infinite knower/God as the ultimate reality and thus ended with a monism in which the individuality of the individual is lost in the cosmic mind. Chamberlin, like his teacher Howison, sought a way around this problem by posing the community as the unity. The concrete whole must be a concrete unity. The whole must bind together and yet also be in each of its parts. A rock, for example, is an aggregate and not a unity. It cannot distinguish the parts from one another. A rock pile is not in the individual rocks. Each rock would exist if it had never been a rock pile, and indeed no rock sees itself as one or many. In Mormon terms Chamberlin would refer to 2 Nephi 2. The "unity" of the rock pile is nothing alive. The parts do not interpenetrate one another. It is dead. It is only seen as a unity by an observer. But in most idealist conceptions of unity, the observer (God or Brahman) becomes the real that contains the part the parts lose their independent reality in the whole. In *The*

Conception of God debate Howison claimed that this was the problem in much of the mystical tradition. The otherness of the Other is lost in union with the one. Somehow the unity of both the whole and the individuality of the parts must be preserved for there to be a true unity. If the other is absorbed into the one there is no distinction to be aware of, let alone to love. Love and knowledge both require another beyond us as well as unity with the other. Chamberlin maintained that neither plurality nor unity can be fundamental: both must be fundamental, the part cannot exist separately from the whole, all things exist in relation, and the whole only exists as the unity of the parts.[38] Notice that the objection here is ethical, the parts cannot simply be the means to the whole's end. This was also Howison's objection to Royce and Hegel.[39] As an idealist Chamberlin places the weight on unity in consciousness, there is only one type of unity that reflected the mutually relative unity and that was the unity of conscious individuals. "Now there is only one unity known to us in experience or conceivable by us in which the unity can be for the individuals which are its parts, and that is the system of conscious individuals."[40]

Only in consciousness where I am aware of the other, only here is the other "in me." "Here, therefore the unity is at once the whole of which the individuals are parts, and also completely present in each individual."[41] Chamberlin goes on, "And although the whole is not in the individuals in the same way that the individuals are in it, the demand of the ideal unity is fulfilled in that the unit."[42] The more one reflects the whole, the more one becomes a self because the whole is to reflect the reality of all the others. Thus to become one with reality is not, as Plato thought, or as Pilgrim in *Pilgrim's Progress*, or the Hindu philosopher Shankara, or countless others in the history of philosophical and religious thought, to forsake the other person who exists in time for the ideal whole of eternity, but to empathize with the other as completely as possible.

This paves the way toward Chamberlin's ideal of God as being the most thoroughly real by being also the most related being.

While I do not contain the reality of my wife in the way God contains me in perfect love, I am on the way. The final creation of reality is obtaining that relation where the other is not distorted in me. For Chamberlin this is eternal perfection and it is an infinite task.

One of the more famous examples of internal relation is Hegel's discussion in *The Phenomenology of Spirit* of the relation between a master and slave. It's not just that I am placed in chains and beaten by another that has made me a slave, I am internally modified in my consciousness through my relation to another being. I am a slave in relation to my master. My master is also modified. He depends on having us slaves in order to be a master. The process world is interrelational, every being is what it is in relation to others. But notice also that each has a distorted image of the other and thus also of himself. The slave is more than a slave and the master is more than a master. *The Phenomenology of Spirit* is the working out of these distortions until we arrive at absolute knowledge which is the knowledge of God. Even God is modified by God's relation to a world and others. God is only God because of this relation to a world. Thus for Hegel, religion is often seen in terms of the master/slave dialectic. Our idea of God is often that God is a master and a tyrant, and the dialectic brings us to Christ and eventually to the religion of the holy spirit in which the worship of raw power is replaced by love and freedom. William Ernest Hocking, an American Hegelian and Royce's successor at Harvard, was present at *The Conception of God* debate and argued that Howison had carried the day.[43] Later in his magnum opus *The Meaning of God in Human Experience* Hocking described love as an example of internal relation. Hocking refers to his wife, his comrade, and the internal relation that overcomes the external relation of two objects.

> I have sometimes sat looking at a comrade, speculating on this mysterious isolation of self from self. Why are we so made that I gaze and see of thee only the Wall, and never Thee? This Wall of thee is but a movable

> part of the Wall of my world; and I also am a Wall to thee: we look out at one another from behind masks. How would it seem if my mind could but once be within thine; and we could meet and without barrier be with each other? And then it has fallen upon me like a shock—But I am in thy soul. These things around me are in thy experience. They are thy own; when I touch them and move them I change thee. When I look on them I see what thou seest; when I listen, I hear what thou hearest. I am in the great Room of thy soul; and I experience thy very experience. For where art thou? Not here, behind those eyes, within that head, in darkness, fraternizing with chemical processes. Of these, in my own case, I know nothing; for my existence is spent not behind my Wall, but in front of it. I am there, where I have treasures. And there art thou, also. This world in which I live, is the world of thy soul: and being within that I am within thee. I can imagine no contact more real and thrilling than this; that we should meet and share identity, not through ineffable inner depth (alone), but here through the foregrounds of common experience; and that thou shouldest be—not behind that mask—but here, pressing with all thy consciousness upon me, containing me, and these things of mine. This is reality: and having seen it thus, I can never again be frightened into monadism by reflections which have strayed from their guiding insight.[44]

For Hocking the relation is beyond mere sensual stimulation; I am in my very being changed by my relation to the other because I share the world of experience with the other. I am what I am, in part, through relation to the beloved. This is true of the many types of relations that make up the world I share with others. What is significant about this passage is that love is not merely an epiphenomenon. It is not merely my external relation to another who is the object of my desire but is an expression, perhaps the truest of the very nature of the universe. We are related to and modified by all others and especially by those to whom we are closest, not just physically but spiritually.[45]

Chamberlin writes, "We ourselves embrace the entire cosmos as far as it is known to us."[46] As with the quote from Hocking, there is no clear outside/inside, and as the pure ego is only an abstraction separated from the world, there is only an abstraction, whether we are talking about the individual consciousness or God. Chamberlin thinks that

> Although the world of phenomena is divided into subjective and objective realms, both are equally within each self, the images of the subjective realms, both are equally within each self, the images of the subjective merely representing the things in the objective world. But while we cannot say of any reality that it is outside of us, neither can we say of any reality that it is only inside of us. In thinking about anything in the world a distinction, is made between the known and the object of knowledge. All but the pure ego can thus be separated from it and in that case of separation it is a mere abstraction, or nothing. As I know a thing more perfectly, I have it more completely within myself. But it can also be said that the more thoroughly I know an object the more distinctly contrasted with myself does it become.[47]

Thus, the nature of the self is relational. It is not simply an atom locked in its skin. This is evident from a mere common sense understanding of eating, breathing, and thinking. The self is both inside and outside. Mind is the conscious recognition of this fact. The fundamental differentiations of reality are made by minds. Chamberlin claims that we can conceive of nothing else that makes these differentiations. Thus, he claims: " . . . from the fact that selves have certain characteristics which can be understood if they are some of these fundamental differentiations and in no other way, we may properly conclude that the Society of Minds is the Ultimate Reality."[48]

The implications of this claim give a pluralistic idealism. Chamberlin thinks the community of minds is, like Howison's divine democracy, responsible for time and space. "Minds, then, by virtue of their inherent powers are the authors of time and space and of all the phenomena that they embrace of all of what we commonly call experience."[49] This has always been one of idealism's most controversial claims. The "common sense" position is that persons/minds are in time and space. Howison, Royce, and Chamberlin claimed that time and space are the result of the relations between persons. As counter intuitive as this might seem, it is a common religious position. Theists like Augustine and Berkeley claim the world to be a creation of the ultimate mind, and that space and time are dependent on eternity. The classical Hindu philosophers Shankara and Ramanuja saw time and space as appearances that are overcome in ultimate Brahman. One of Chamberlin's contemporaries, on whom Chamberlin relied on heavily in his M.A. thesis, the Cambridge atheist J. M. E. McTaggart, became famous for his argument about the unreality of time seeing it as the creation of a community of immortal persons.[50] But Chamberlin and Howison did not go as far as McTaggart in claiming the unreality of time and space. For them time and space are real but still dependent on the plurality of beings. Time and space are products of the interactions between persons. From a religious and particularly Mormon point of view, the claim that persons are more primary than space and objects makes sense. The claim is that persons are the primary reality on which all other things are in some way dependent. Still there is a necessary reality in Chamberlin's and Howison's view of time and space. This relates to their pluralism. Time and space arise from the very fact that a plurality of persons interact with each other. Were separation in time and space to cease to exist, there could no persons.

Separation is required for personal existence. This claim for the importance of separate persons creating a common time and space is the basis of Chamberlin's argument for immortality. The immortality of minds is their relation to one another. "In order that the mind may maintain a permanent existence it must be a member of the ultimate unity, and in order to do so, it must contain within itself the entire system of minds and yet permanently contrast itself with all other members. It must be at once federal and individual."[51]

This claim that person are at once federal and individual is important to understanding Chamberlin's position. We are usually viewed as individuals for practical reasons but Chamberlin claimed this is an abstract and partial view of a person. If we really examine ourselves we see that we are related to other persons. Their influence, for good or bad, is in me. I am never completely separate. Chamberlin calls this the paradox of both a distinct and yet shared consciousness. The whole only exists in the freely developing activity of the parts. Here metaphysics and morality are one. The world is the manifestation of the activity of an eternal society of persons. To exist is therefore to be in relation others. Evil is associated with egoism, with the lie that one exists as an atomistic individual. Even God does not exist in this way. To attempt is to move toward the non-existence of the lie, because it denies the dependency on others that is the basic fact of existence. To coerce another is to deny the reality of her freedom and relationality. Chamberlin writes:

> The phenomenal world is only a phase in the existence of the self-active or free beings and can only be fully understood when viewed as a manifestation of the freedom or self-determination of the society of persons. Among these primary realities the category of cause and effect can have no meaning. Because of their eternal natures, coercion of one by another is impossible. Each can influence all or any of the others only as it expresses itself in the recognition of others in the common world and there manifests its ideal meanings. But such is the nature of the ultimate unity that the mutual or reciprocal recognition of its parts or members is necessary to the conscious existence and development of each. Every member is thus constituted an end, as well as an aid to all the others by means of which they can define themselves. But while absolute free-agency is possessed by all, the degree of self-definition or self-realization achieved by each is measured by the effort successfully put forth in the recognition of the other members of the society.[52]

Chamberlin's unity of persons combines Kantian and Hegelian elements. From Kant's moral philosophy Chamberlin has taken the ideal of the "kingdom of ends" for his heavenly city, each person is an end in herself and not merely a means to an end. Thus even for God it would be immoral to use another as a means. Chamberlin ties this Kantian moral philosophy to a Hegelian and personalist metaphysics. It is not merely a postulate of practical reason that there is a kingdom based on the moral law. Chamberlin, following his teacher Howison, claims this to be a metaphysical reality.[53] The reality of interdependence is the reality of our moral world.

Mormons should find this analysis appealing because it is so strikingly similar to the reason for the rejection of Satan, the father of lies, given in Mormon scripture. The power of evil is coercive. In Section 121 of the Doctrine and Covenants, coercion is ruled out as a possible righteous activity of either human beings or God. In The Pearl of Great Price, Satan advocates the assertion of raw power to coerce moral sanctity from humanity (Abr. 3). God and Christ reject this proposal in favor of persuasion and agency for all. There is a strong sense in LDS doctrine that Satan's coercive plan is a lie from the beginning because it is rejection of reality itself which is based on the agency, creativity, and co-eternality of intelligences. This idea of God as non-coercive is such an important part of LDS doctrine that in the Book of Mormon the prophet Alma states that were God to coerce our repentance, even though acting out of his mercy, mercy would rob justice and God would "cease to be God" (Alma 42:13, 22, 25). In Chamberlin's Mormon metaphysics the freedom or creativity of beings is the metaphysical ultimate. If Chamberlin had developed an idea of hell, this would be it: that the individual cut off from socicty ccascs to cxist. Satan's plan of coercion is a lie against the reality of existence.

Thus, every act of the mind has moral quality. In Chamberlin's view of reality, the reason for this fact is clear, for there is no act which does not ultimately affect the common world and this is but another way of saying that every act is in relation to every other mind. This is the fundamental moral fact in accordance with which anyone must act in order to be a person at all, or in order to be able to define or realize himself. The constant presupposition of all action is the existence of the actor in the society of persons. The ultimate realization of the self is ultimately then to more fully empathetically relate to the reality of the interrelated world. The society of all selves is not only the ground of all things but the most important good. Good acts move toward harmony, evil acts are selfish and false, and thus introduce an "unhealthy strife."

> The society of all selves is not only the Ground of all things but it is our chief Good and those actions which tend to realize it are, of course, right. The good act is organically related to the common world and tends to fulfill the requirements of the reason manifested in it whereas an evil act introduces unhealthy strife into it. This is the idea of the Good which, in spite of false theories of ethics, is potentially at the heart of every act to approve or condemn it. As our Good we are impelled by our very nature to seek to realize it, and the sense of duty and love of the Good are necessary and universal.[54]

The "unhealthy strife" contributes to the maximization of chaos. For although God creates from chaos and thus chaotic potentiality is necessary to freedom, chaos is not a state to which one would want to return. Thus evil has two separate but related manifestations in Chamberlin. Egoism is the chaos in which billions of little "gods" wish to see themselves as omnipotent potentates thus destroying harmony and creating strife and chaos, ultimately nonexistence, because of the denial of relation. Thus, egoism would be an overabundance of individualism. But the second would be where God forces order and eliminates all other wills in pure obedience to God's coercive power. Here there is no freedom only the unity and death that Lehi describes in 2 Nephi 2. Here would be an overabundance of unity. The two are closely related and both manifest the tyrannical desire to be God that is illustrated in the Mormon stories of the rebellion of Satan and Cain's murder of Abel. Both manifestations of evil lead to the same result, sameness, disharmony, and death.

An important and un-Kantian aspect of this personalist theory is that it is not based on rules. Where for Kant, I respect the other person out of respect for the moral law, Chamberlin thought that rules could never satisfy the spirit of moral action because each person, though related to all others, is also unique; thus the duties of each person are different. Each also legislates the moral law which grows out of the concrete situation that each person is related to all others. Law cannot emerge from one member of the society (God); for if that were the case, as in the master/slave relation, the possibilities of the master as well as the slaves are impoverished. Rather the moral law, such at it is, arises from the very facts of plurality and freedom. If each is infinitely valuable and must actualize herself so far as possible in relation to others, then respect for each by all is necessary. "Hence, the superiority of Jesus' conception of God as The Greatest Member of the society inviting all the others to fellowship with Himself, and the intelligibility and virtue of the teaching to be perfect as God is perfect."[55]

The infinite task of eternal perfection is the creation of the harmony of the kingdom of ends as a divine community. It is, for most of us, our ignorance of the good that keeps us from this harmony. We pursue many false goods not seeing that God is present in the other beings that surround us. Should we realize this, thinks Chamberlin, the kingdom of God would be attained. "All this means is that free, unhampered communication with eternal spirits is what we desire. They are the Supreme and Abiding Good and in them there is a fountain of everlasting good as a well of water forever springing up to satisfy eternal lives."[56] It is the society of persons itself that is the Supreme Good. Chamberlin quotes his teacher Howison to illustrate his point.

> But the Society of Persons is the Supreme Good. No greater good can be discovered by us in the entire universe and no greater good is conceivable by us. In truth, as we have seen, they as the Ground of all things and are the determiners of all value. They set up ideals and have the power

> to reach them. As Professor Howison says, "they alone will prove supreme, truly organizing, normative; they alone can introduce gradation into truths, for they alone introduce the judgment of worth, of valuation; they alone can give us counsels of perfection, for they alone rise from those elements in our being which deal with ideals and with veritable Idea."[57]

Chamberlin says Jesus laid down his life that he might lead us to becoming persons. We could not be forced, we must come to this freely. Jesus' act of self-emptying sacrifice shows us the way to the eternal city, the kingdom of ends. He laid down his life to win our hearts. This action could not be coerced we can only be invited. God through Jesus tried to enlighten the darkness of egoism in which we live from within. Chamberlin claims that since God does not coerce, the only way that God could call us into a more cooperative relation with our environment is to call us to such a relationship through example and self-sacrifice. If each member of the society of mind is of infinite worth, to coerce the other is exactly to devalue them—to see them as a mere objects for God's purposes. Chamberlin and Howison argued that not only is this morally wrong, it is metaphysically counter to the nature of reality and leads ultimately to destruction of the self. Jesus tries to show us the way to life, the fullest possible life. Jesus is the example of the ideal personality that appeals to the best in us. He gave his life to " . . . win the hearts of men to himself as an ideal Personality, he respected men in appealing to the best that is in man himself in his efforts to reveal the nature of one whom he worshiped and called our Father."[58] Thus for Chamberlin, God is God by example. God's superiority is only in love for the rest of us. This is also the meaning of intelligence, which is an identification with the real or the unity of the society of minds. Thus in the creation of the world God forms the world from chaos in relation "others and with us."

> And from the nature of reality his pre-eminence must be determined by the superiority of his intelligence and the intensity of his love for others and his achievements in their service. But although from his nature He

> would be the most potent factor in the formation (Cf. The Hebrew *Bara*) of our common world, He could only co-operate with others and with us in its formation; and so the "heavens" could not decisively reveal his handiwork or his existence. He could only reveal Himself to us as we reveal ourselves to each other, by operating in accordance with laws of nature through the common world. Our ideal unity requires a common world, common in some way to all the invisible spirits or persons in the vast society of minds, among which invisible spirits are we ourselves.[59]

For Chamberlin God is revealed to us most decisively, not through the power of world creation and formation, but in the lives of other persons; Jesus being the most perfect example of this movement from chaos to personhood. And thus also God is born in us when we choose to follow this same path toward creation and the overcoming of death and chaos. At one point Chamberlin seems to almost become a Platonist, saying that the highest human experience is to contemplate the perfect personality, God. But then he reverses, adding, "Another source of satisfaction there will be the fulfillment of duties to immature a developing spirits and this can, perhaps, afford us the most satisfaction and joy that will be possible."[60] So beyond the beatific aesthetic vision is the ethical project of the creation of the world through the creation and continual development of others. It is not eternal ideal that calls us but the love of concrete individual beings.

Chamberlin carried this position on with him through his studies with Royce at Harvard which is evident from Royce's comments on Chamberlin's papers on "The Conception of God," "The Highest Good," and "On the Nature of Truth," that Ralph Chamberlin writes that " . . . Professor Royce, according to the notes preserved with the papers, was much impressed by the Pluralism, or 'Socio-Ethical Idealism,' 'clearly and beautifully stated as a doctrine'. . . . "[61] It is apparent also in his published pamphlets, particularly his "Essay on Nature" published in December 1915 toward the end of his time at BYU. Here it is coupled with an obvious allusion to Doctrine and Covenants 130:1-2 in his discussion of reality as dependent on the sociality of intelligences that will eventually be perfected.[62]

Conclusion: Evolutions

The modernism controversy at BYU virtually ended Chamberlin's career. He died just five years after leaving BYU in his very early fifties. The irony was that his object was the same as President Brimhall and Chamberlin's nemesis in the affair, Commissioner Cummings. Chamberlin, like his teacher Howison, was an evolutionary thinker. He saw evolution as a principle that was part of Mormonism. Like the other personalists of his age Chamberlin opposed agnostic and non-teleological evolutionism (the title of Howison's major work was *The Limits of Evolution*). Personalism reacted against the "cut throat" evolutionism of Herbert Spencer and the cosmic evolutionism of John Fiske. Chamberlin saw natural history as God's painstaking effort to create the "Kingdom of God" as a society of minds. His effort to express his belief during the controversy at BYU culminated in his essay "The Theory of Evolution as an Aid to Faith in God and in the Resurrection" which was written at the height of the 1911 controversy. In this essay Chamberlin begins with a quote from Section 88 of the Doctrine and Covenants that Christ is in "all things" and that the universe is the visual image of God's effort to further the society of eternal beings. The creation of the human body is one of the culminating events of this evolution that makes communication and love between persons possible. Therefore, God would not have gone through all this painstaking effort merely to see love destroyed.

I conclude with Chamberlin's conclusion from that essay which ends in an ecstatic and very Mormon vision of the resurrection and heaven as a family community with our father and mother.

> There is nothing that science contends for in the way of an obstacle to belief in the resurrection of the body; and, through the above discussion,

we are helped to believe in future stages of activity in which we may "partake of the fruit of the vine" with the Lord Jesus and with the great and good of every age, and in the society of all those loved ones who have made life so sweet here and who have passed or shall pass to their glory in those happy worlds; and there we may hope to stand in the presence of the Ancient of Days, the Adamic Being who, perhaps, as we have suggested above, headed the race of man, and who, through his devotion to immortal spirits, his children, won the resurrection of the body and with our heavenly mother, presides in the celestial world from whence he secures with Christ the cooperation of the Holy Spirit, who is in and through all things to the end that we might win the fullest lives here and companionship with Him in the eternal world hereafter.[63]

Bibliography of William H. Chamberlin's Work[64]

I. Published

Special Collections Utah State University. Brigham Young College Papers

"President Joseph F. Smith," *The Crimson* 1 (June 1904): 4–5.

"The Highest Good," *The Crimson* 4 (November 1907): 30–34.

L. Tom Perry Special Collections Brigham Young University

(These pieces were assembled by Wilford Paulson)

An Essay on Nature. Provo: 1916.

The Study of Philosophy: An Outline. Salt Lake City: 1919.

The Life of Man: An Introduction to Philosophy. Logan, Utah: 1920.

"The Social Nature of Man," Transactions of the Utah Academy of Sciences (no date).

"The Theory of Evolution as an Aid to Faith in the Resurrection," in Supplement to *The White and the Blue* 19, no. 12 (Feb. 14, 1911): 206–210.

"The Parables of Jesus: Their Nature, Purpose, and the Interpretation of a Number of Them," *Brigham Young College Bulletin* 2 , no. 3 (January 1904).

Brigham Young University Microfilm Collection

"Christ's Gift to Man," *The White and the Blue* 19, no. 9 (Dec 20, 1910): 135–137.

"A Christmas Sentiment," *The White and the Blue* 16, no. 7 (Dec. 12, 1912): 133.

"The Significance of the Resurrection," *The White and the Blue* (Girls' Edition) 14 (March 21, 1913): 296.

"Gratitude," *The White and the Blue* 16 (Commencement 1913): 403.

"Thanksgiving," *The White and the Blue* 17 (November 19, 1913): 127.

"Aphorisms from Prof. Chamberlin," *The White and the Blue* 20, no. 28 (May 17, 1916): 525, 540.

"W. H. Chamberlain (sic) Offers Views on Evolution," *Deseret News* (Salt Lake City) March 11, 1911.

University of California at Berkeley

"The Ultimate Unity for Thought is the Society of Minds." M. A. Thesis, University of California, 1906.

"Use of the Word Elohim," Appendix to B. H. Roberts, *The Mormon Doctrine of Deity*, Salt Lake City: Horizon Publishers, 1976.

II. Unpublished

"Berkeley's Philosophy of Nature and Modern Theories of Evolution." Unfinished Ph.D. diss., Harvard, 1916. University of Utah Marriott Library Special Collections.

Letters and Papers. David C. Chamberlin Collection

"The Social Nature of Man." David C. Chamberlin Collection

"The Origin, Nature, and Destiny of Man." LDS Church Archives, Joseph F. Smith Papers, MS 1325 Box 45 FD7

Mission Journal from the Society Islands. LDS Church Archives.

JAMES M. MCLACHLAN is Professor and Chair of Philosophy and Religion at Western Carolina University. He received his Ph.D. in Religious Studies from the University of Toronto where he studied philosophy of religion and Russian religious thought. He is author of *The Desire to Be God: Freedom and the Other in Sartre and Berdyaev* and articles on the thought of Nicolas Berdyaev, Lev Shestov, and Fyodor Dostoevsky.

Notes

1. William H. Chamberlin Diary in the Ralph V. Chamberlin Collection at the Utah State Historical Society, Salt Lake City Utah.
2. Ralph Chamberlin, *The Life and Philosophy of William H. Chamberlin* (Salt Lake City: Deseret News Press, 1926), 118.
3. The most complete story is in his brother Ralph V. Chamberlin's 1925 biography *The Life and Philosophy of W. H. Chamberlin* (Salt Lake City: Deseret News Press, 1925). E. E. Ericksen, one of Chamberlin's students who became head of the Philosophy Department at the University of Utah and president of the Pacific Division of the American Philosophical Association, wrote a thoughtful essay: "William H. Chamberlin: Pioneer Utah Philosopher," *Western Humanities Review* 8 (No. 4, 1954). Ericksen describes Chamberlin's influence of his own philosophical career in his autobiographical essay. E. E. Ericksen, *Memories and Reflections: The Autobiography of E.E. Ericksen*, ed. Scott Kenny (Salt Lake City: Signature Books, 1987), pp. 24–25, 54–55, 205–207. Chamberlin's embroilment in the modernism controversy and its relation to his attitudes toward evolution and critical approaches to the Bible that shook Brigham Young University in 1911 has been recounted in several places. Ernest Wilkinson ed., *Brigham Young University: The First One Hundred*, Vol. I (Provo: Brigham Young University Press, 1975) and Ernest Wilkinson and W. Cleon Skousen, *Brigham Young Univerity: A School of Destiny* (Provo, Brigham Young

University Press, 1976). Richard Sherlock has two fine accounts of the BYU crisis and the problem of evolution in the church. "Campus in Crisis: BYU 1911: Evolution and Revolution at the Mormon University," *Sunstone* 4 (January–February 1979), 10–16 discusses the 1911 controversy that led to the firing of the Peterson brothers and Ralph Chamberlin and eventually to William Chamberlin's resignation in 1916. Sherlock's second article, "A Turbulent Spectrum: Mormon Reactions to the Darwinst Legacy," *Journal of Mormon History*, 5 (1978), 33–60 serves both as a excellent discussion of early reactions LDS leaders and educators to theories of evolution covering the spectrum from Joseph Fielding Smith to Nels Nelson and William H. Chamberlin; it also contains an excellent short introduction to Chamberlin's thought. Gary Bergera and Ronald Priddis, *Brigham Young University: A House of Faith* (Salt Lake City: Signature, 1985) gives a very complete account from all the primary documents. Phillip Barlow devotes an excellent chapter on Chamberlin and Mormon responses to higher criticism at the turn of the century in his *Mormons and the Bible* (Oxford: Oxford University Press, 1992), 103–147. For a short introduction to Chamberlin's life and theology, read James M. McLachlan, "W. H. Chamberlin and the Quest for a Mormon Theology" *Dialogue: A Journal of Mormon Thought* 29 (Winter 1996), 151–167.

Five years after Chamberlin's death in 1921, attitudes in the LDS church hierarchy had changed. Apostle David O. Mackay wrote to Ralph V. Chamberlin in a letter of Feb. 17 1926:

> That a lofty, sincere soul like W. H. Chamberlin's should have been compelled to struggle in our community and to have been misunderstood by those who should have known him best, seems to me to be nothing short of a tragedy. . . . I wish it had been my privilege to know him intimately. For one thing, however, I am thankful, namely, that I had no reservation in mind when it came my privilege to recommend that W. H. Chamberlin's services be again secured for the Church Schools. (David O. Mackay to Ralph V. Chamberlin, Feb. 17, 1926, David C. Chamberlin Collection)

4. Leonard Arrington, "The LDS Intellectual Tradition," *Dialogue* 4 (Spring 1969), 22.

5. Stan Larson, "Intellectuals in Mormon History: An Update," *Dialogue* 26 (Fall 1993), 188.
6. Remarks during a panel discussion "A Mormon Socrates: William H. Chamberlin" at the 1993 Sunstone Symposium. McMurrin thought Chamberlin a profound thinker as the LDS tradition had produced and planned to write a chapter on him in a proposed but unfinished work on Mormon theology.

> W. H. Chamberlin was a more competent philosopher than Orson Pratt or B. H. Roberts. I wonder what would have happened to the philosophy department at the University of Utah if he had taught here for several years—Chamberlin and Ericksen together. What a combination! Ericksen was primarily a moral philosopher with an interest in ethics, while W. H. Chamberlin was very much interested in metaphysics. He was the best chance the Mormon church had for cultivating a philosopher who wanted desperately—I mean, desperately—to develop a meaningful philosophical position for the Mormon people. Sterling McMurrin and L. Jackson Newell, *Matters of Conscience: Conversations with Sterling McMurrin* (Salt Lake City: Signature, 1996), 69.

See also E. E. Ericksen, "William H. Chamberlin: Pioneer Utah Philosopher," *Western Humanities Review* 8, No. 4 (1954), Ericksen describes Chamberlin's influence of his own philosophical career in his autobiographical essay. E. E. Ericksen, *Memories and Reflections: The Autobiography of E. E. Ericksen*, ed. Scott Kenney (Salt Lake City: Signature Books, 1987), 24–25, 54–55, 205–207.

7. An excellent discussion of liberal protestant reactions to modernism is found in William R. Hutchison, *The Modernist Impulse in American Protestantism* (Durahm, NC: Duke University Press, 1992). An excellent introduction to the development of liberal theology and personalism is Gary Dorrien, *The Making of American Liberal Theology: Idealism, Realism, and Modernity* (Louisville: Westminster John Knox Press, 2003), 286–355.
8. Peter A. Bertocci, "Bordan Parker Bowne and His Personalistic Theistic Idealism" in *The Boston Personalist Tradition in Philosophy, Social Ethics, and Theology*, ed. Paul Deats and Carol Robb (Atlanta: Mercer University Press, 1986), 56. Bowne himself was very critical of impersonal modernism;

he saw personalism as a way to accept the insights of modern historical and scientific scholarship, while rejecting materialism and positivism. Bordan Parker Bowne, *Personalism* (Boston and New York: Houghton, Mifflin and Co., 1908), 1–54.

9. See especially the chapter on "The Failure of Impersonalism" in Borden Parker Bowne, Personalism
10. Joseph F. Smith, "Philosophy and the Church Schools," *Juvenile Instructor*, April 1911, 208–09.
11. Barlow, *Mormons and the Bible*, 103–147.
12. Joseph F. Smith, "Philosophy and the Church Schools," 208–09; Joseph F. Smith, "Theory and Divine Revelation," *Improvement Era*, April 1911, 548–51. Quoted in Wilkinson and Skousen, *School of Destiny*, 211.
13. Immanuel Kant, one of the greatest but also most difficult philosophers of the modern period, and an ancestor of the personalist movement, had voiced the same concern. Kant felt that the basic principle of morality, the categorical imperative, was known in the hearts of average people. Philosophers had confused the issue. Unfortunately, it would now take philosophy to help disentangle what it had confused. Immanuel Kant, *The Groundwork of the Metaphysics of Morals*, tr. H. J. Paton (San Francisco: Harper and Row, 1948), 61–62.
14. As Ephraim Ericksen put it:

    > His spiritual realism is a reasoned statement of the Mormon concept of the spirits of men as co-existent and co-eternal with God. The personal nature of God and the social relations between God and men argued for in his philosophy are no different for Mormon conceptions. Nor, of course, is the concept of immortality, which, for both Chamberlin and Mormonism, is a logical consequent of the metaphysical ultimacy of persons. (Ericksen, "Chamberlin," 284)

15. In this sense Chamberlin's position anticipates phenomenology and process thought where "things themselves" are not simply discrete objects unrelated to a world of relationships but appearances, and appearances are shot through with conscious interpretation.

    Garland Tickmeyer argues that Chamberlin anticipated process theology and optimistically claims that Chamberlin is receiving more attention now than in his lifetime. Unfortunately, this latter observation has not yet proven as acute as his interpretation of Chamberlin as close to process thought. Garland Tickmeyer, "Joseph Smith and Process Theology" *Dialogue*, Vol. 17, No. 3, p. 83.

16. Chamberlin taught Dewey and James in his courses at BYU and taught a seminar on Bergson's creative evolution. *Brigham Young University Bulletin*, 1910–1916. Letter to Ralph Chamberlin, 1915, David C. Chamberlin Collection.
17. Edgar S. Brightman, *A Philosophy of Religion* (New York: Prentice Hall, 1940). Peter Bertocci, *The Person God Is* (New York: Humanities Press, 1970).
18. Bordan Parker Bowne, *Personalism* (Boston and New York: The Houghton, Miffllin and Company, 1908). George Holmes Howison, *The Limits of Evolution: and Other Essays Illustrating the Metaphysical Theory of Personal Idealism* (New York: McMillan, 1908).
19. Brightman's discussion of God is quite different from traditional theism. He locates pain and suffering directly within the divine being. God's creation of the world is, in part, to illuminate the chaos that exists within the nature of God and hence all things.

    > God is a conscious Person of perfect good will. . . . Therefore His purpose and his nature must be inferred from the way in which experience reveals them, namely, as being gradually attained through effort, difficulty, and suffering. Hence there is in God's very nature something which makes the effort and pain of life necessary. There is within Him, in addition to His reason and his active creative will, a passive element which enters into every one of his conscious states, as sensation, instinct, and impulse enter into ours, and constitutes a problem for Him. This element we call The Given. The evils of life and the delays in the attainment of value, insofar as they come from God and not from human freedom are thus due to His nature, yet not wholly to His deliberate choice. His will and reason acting on The Given produce the world and achieve value in it. (Edgar S. Brightman, *The Problem of God*, New York: The Abbington Press, 1930, p. 113)

20. Howison considered LeConte one of America's most important philosophers. George Holmes Howison, "Josiah Royce: The Significance of His Work in Philosophy," *The Philosophical Review* (May, 1916), 243.

21. Cited in John Wright Buckham and George Malcolm Stratton, *George Holmes Howison: Philosopher and Teacher* (Berkeley, University of California Press, 1936), 80.
22. George Holmes Howison, *The Conception of God: A Philosophical Discussion Concerning the Nature of the Divine Idea as a Demonstrable Reality*, (New York: Macmillan, 1898), xii.
23. Royce gives the most impressive form of this argument in *The Conception of God* debate. For Royce the question of God's existence is reducible to the question of the existence of an omniscient being. Basic to the proof remains Royce's conviction that humans are essentially ignorant of reality "as it is in itself." This reality could only be present to what is ideally defined as an Absolute experience. The nature of experience reflects the nature of reality. Our deepest sense it that the experience of our fellows is as genuine as our own. Apart from social consciousness we have no clear conception of truth. My fellow's experience supplements my own in two senses: as actual and as possible experience. In so far as consensus has been reached, it presents us an ideal. The appeal here is "from what the various men do experience to what they all ought to experience, or would experience if their experiences were in unity. . . . Such an ideally united experience, if it could but absolutely define its own contents, would know reality." The terms, *reality* and *organized experience*, are thus correlative terms on this equivalence Royce's whole argument for the existence of God depends. Royce says if we assume "there is no universal experience as a concrete fact, but only the hope of it," then the absolute finiteness and erroneousness of the real experience will still be "a fact, a truth, a reality, and, as such, just the absolute truth." But for whom would this supposed ultimate truth exist? Not for the finite experience because for finite experience there is nothing beyond fragmentariness. "If we know this, it would be *ipso facto* an absolute, i.e., a completely self-possessed, experience." Thus to assert that the whole world is a fragmentary and finite experience is an effort involving a contradiction. The assertion of such fragmentariness is only possible from the point of view of an experience which transcends it so experience must constitute "one self-determined and consequently absolute and organized whole."

    Now Royce comes to the final conclusion of his argument by asserting that "all concrete or genuine, and not barely possible truth is, as such, a truth somewhere experienced"; for truth is only "so far as it is known." Since our experience is only finite and fragmentary and is known to be such, there must therefore exist some other experience "to which is present the constitution (i.e., the actual limitation and narrowness) of all finite experience, just as surely as there is such a constitution" (Ibid., 35–48).

24. Josiah Royce, *The Religious Aspect of Philosophy*, (Gloucester, MA: Peter Smith, 1965), 384–435.
25. Josiah Royce, *The Philosophy of Loyalty* (New York: The MacMillan Company, 1908). John McDermott has claimed that Howison's objections to Royce's argument are a spur to much of Royce's later work on community. John J. McDerrmott, "The Confrontation Between Royce and Howison" in *Transactions of the Charles S. Pierce Society* 30 (Fall, 1994), 779–802.
26. Howison, *The Conception of God*, 106. W. E. Hocking, *The Meaning of God in Human Experience*, (New Haven: Yale University Press, 1912), 390.
27. George Holmes Howison, "The Real Issue in 'The Conception of God'," in *The Philosophical Review* 12 (September, 1898), 519.
28. Ibid., 520.
29. Ibid.
30. John Clendenning, *The Letters of Josiah Royce* (Chicago: University of Chicago Press, 1970), 339.
31. Royce writes:

    I may frankly add that what I least can yet make out about the "City of God," as you so far reveal its mysteries, is what God (viewed as in any sense an unique or Absolute Being), has to do with it. So far as I can see, your view appears to be a polytheism, where anybody is as much God as he is even Christian. Or else God is merely the collective name for your crowd of polytheistic monads. I know of course that you can't really mean either of these things but I indicate the helplessness of my mind by suggesting the question; and my helplessness may help to show you what some other readers must most desire to have added, by way of explanation, to the account that you have so far given. But at all events, I await, with keen curiosity, your outcome. (Ibid., 360–361)

32. James M. McLachlan, "George Holmes Howison. The Conception of God Debate and the Beginnings of Personal Idealism," *The Personalist Forum* 11,

no. 1 (Spring 1995), 1–16. George Holmes Howison, *The Limits of Evolution, and Other Essays Illustrating the Metaphysical Theory of Personal Idealism* (New York: Macmillan, 1901). Most of *The Limits of Evolution* is included in the anthology, *George Holmes Howison, Philosopher and Teacher: A Selection from His Writings with a Biographical Sketch*, ed. John Wright Buckham and George Malcolm Stratton (Berkeley: University of California Press, 1934).

33. Robert Lauder wrote an excellent article on the debate between Royce and Howison. Robert Lauder, "Howison's Post Hegelian Personalism and the 'Conception of God' Discussion," *The Owl of Minerva* 18, no. 2 (Spring 1987), 135–144. See also Steven Tyman, "The Problem of Evil in the Royce-Howison Debate," *The Personalist Forum* 13, no. 2 (Fall 1997). The Peronalist Forum also published a complete number dedicated to the debate. Randall K. Auxier ed., *The Personalist Forum* 15, no. 1 (Spring 1999).

    I have written three extensive articles on Howison and the Conception of God debate. "George Holmes Howison's 'City of God with the True God at its Head:' The Royce-Howison Debate over the Idealist Conception of God," *The Personalist Forum* 15, no. 1 (Spring 1999). "The Idealist Critique of Idealism: Bowne's Personalism and Howison's City of God," *The Personalist Forum* 14 (Winter 1998). "George Holmes Howison: The Conception of God Debate and the Beginnings of Personal Idealism" *The Personalist Forum* 10, no. 4 (Fall 1995).

34. Howison coined the term *Personal Idealism* in his famous debate *The Conception of God* with Josiah Royce at the University of California in 1895. The debate brought together four philosophers: Josiah Royce, Jacob Laconte, Edward Meyes and Howison. It was later published as a book. Howison's essay in *The Conception of God*, "The City of God and the True God at Its Head," criticized Royce's idealistic monism that Howison thought ended up in destroying the freedom of human being and thus the relation between God and humanity. George Holmes Howison, *The Conception of God* (New York: Macmillan, 1898).

35. Howison, *The Limits of Evolution.*

36. Royce, *The Religious Aspect of Philosophy*, 384–435.

37. William H. Chamberlin, "The Ultimate Unity of Thought Is the Society of Minds." (M.A. thesis, University of California at Berkeley, 1906), 7.

38. Ibid., 62.
39. In a June 8, 1892 letter to William Torrey Harris, a Hegelian who would become the U. S. Commissioner of Education Howison referred to Royce's system as a "hopeless pantheism." He thought Royce had no proper respect for human nature, that for Royce the infinite self was only a "transcendent self." Howison protested that Royce might as well say that " . . . we have no true self at all." Royce's view of the person was not just an alternate view for Howison: it violated his religious and ethical sensibilities, his deep regard for the sacred primacy of personhood:

    And the most depressing sign about his thinking is, that he seems perfectly aware how this makes no provision either for immortality or for real freedom, and yet he appears to have no uneasiness under it, but to contemplate this ghastly destiny of ours with a complacency even savoring of self satisfaction. (Cited in Ralph Tyler Flewelling, "George Holmes Howison: Prophet of Freedom," *The Personalist*, 10–11)

40. Chamberlin, "Unity," 13.
41. Ibid., 14.
42. Ibid.
43. William Ernest Hocking was at the time a younger colleague of Howison at Berkeley. He agreed with Howison's critique of Royce.

    In failing to penetrate through the blank otherness of Nature to the spirit that is its support, natural Realism falls short of the truth. Idealism corrects this error; and in correcting this error, falls as a rule into another--it refers the experience of nature to a spirit, which turns out to be only the solitary finite self. The logic even of "absolute idealism" usually fails here, as Professor Howison has well shown. ("City of God" p. 104) The corrective of both this natural realism and this solitary idealism must be found, not by changing the venue of the question to the moral consciousness, but by appeal from natural realism to a *realism of social experience*. (W. E. Hocking, *The Meaning of God in Human Experience*, New Haven: Yale University Press, 1912, 390)

44. Hocking, *The Meaning of God*, 265–66.
45. The doctrine of internal relatedness gives us one way to interpret those passages of LDS scripture where God is described as in and through all things,

and Christ as having become in and through all things. An example is one of Chamberlin's favorite LDS scripture passages, Doctrine and Covenants 88:6–13.

> He that ascended up on high, as also he descended below all things, in that he comprehended all things, that he might be in all and through all things, the light of truth; which truth shineth. This is the light of Christ. As also he is in the sun, and the light of the sun, and the power thereof by which it was made. As also he is in the moon, and is the light of the moon, and the power thereof by which it was made; as also the light of the stars, and the power thereof by which they were made; and the earth also, and the power thereof, even the earth upon which you stand. And the light which shineth, which giveth you light, is through him who enlighteneth your eyes, which is the same light that quickeneth your understandings; which light proceedeth forth from the presence of God to fill the immensity of space - the light which is in all things, which giveth life to all things, which is the law by which all things are governed, even the power of God who sitteth upon his throne, who is in the bosom of eternity, who is in the midst of all things.

In this passage we learn that Christ, because he descended below all things, ascends on high and becomes "in and through all things." Apparently, despite the famous Mormon materialism, matter in not impenetrable or even exterior to Christ who becomes in and through all things, but rather he is within them and the are within him. One way to understand this passage is to see the relation between Christ and others as internal as well as external; but this demands we move beyond a substance oriented metaphysics where Christ confronts various bits or unchanging matter and just reconfigures them in various ways to produce you, me, the chair, my dog Idefix, and the universe.

46. Chamberlin, "Unity," 15.
47. Ibid.
48. Ibid., 17.
49. Ibid., 19.
50. Chamberlin relied mainly on two of McTaggart's early works from the latter's Hegelian period. J. M. E. McTaggart, "Hegel's Treatment of the

Categories of the Idea," *Mind: A Quarterly Review of Psychology and Philosophy*, No. 34, (April 1900). J. M. E. McTaggart, *Studies in Hegelian Cosmology* (Cambridge: Cambridge University Press, 1901). Although McTaggart's idealism became less and less Hegelian as his thought matured, he kept and developed the idea of the community of immortal persons. McTaggart's magnum opus, *The Nature of Existence*, ends with these lines about the eternal community.

> We know that it is a timeless and endless state of love—love so direct, so intimate, and so powerful that even the deepest mystic rapture gives us but the slightest foretaste of its perfection. (J. M. E. McTaggart, *The Nature of Existence*, vol. 2, Cambridge: Cambridge University Press, 1927, 479)

51. Chamberlin, "Unity," 20.
52. Ibid., 24.
53. In their debate Royce claimed Howison's critique could be reduced to the Kantian antinomy between the theoretical and practical reason. Thus Howison's main objection to Royce's argument only counted insofar as it concerned ethics. Howison, however, did not think the essay reconciled their positions. He disagreed with Royce's characterization of his argument, and in September of 1898 published an essay outlining his much more fundamental disagreement with Royce. In that article, "The Real Issue in the Conception of God Discussion," Howison says that his point is not to set moral consciousness simply as a "categorical imperative" against theoretical reason, and simply " . . . have the heart breathe defiance to the intellect." Howison says his aim in his critique of Royce's "Conception of God" was a theoretical justification of ethics. That our moral sense objects to theoretical monism is not sufficient—we need a metaphysical theory to support it. Howison says that his real disagreement with Royce can be summarized in two main premises:

> (1) That no conception of God can have any philosophical value unless it can be proved real, or, in other words, unless it is the conception that of itself proves God to exist; and (2) that the conception [offered by Professor Royce and other monists] is the only conception that can thus prove its reality." It is precisely denying the validity of this second premise that the vital point of my dissent consists.

Howison agrees with Royce on the first premise. He believes that there is a conception of God that can be proven real. But he denies the second premise for moral reasons. He thinks that Royce's God annihilates the freedom of the creature and with it the reality of the creature. Howison, "The Real Issue," 519.

54. Chamberlin, "Unity," 34.
55. Ibid., 35–36.
56. Ibid., 40.
57. Ibid., 40–41.
58. Ibid., 41.
59. Ibid., 42.
60. Ibid.
61. Ralph Chamberlin, *Life and Philosophy*, 118. The essays on the "Conception of God" and "On the Nature of Truth" have been lost. An essay under the title "The Highest Good" appeared in *The Crimson*, the student newspaper of Brigham Young College. It is important to note also that Royce himself backed away from the absolute idealism of *The Religious Aspect of Philosophy* and *The Conception of God* after the debate with Howison. The eminent historian of American philosophy John McDermott sees the debate as so important for Royce that Howison's objections returned to him again and again throughout his philosophical career. McDermott noted that Howison's principal objection was that Royce was caught between pantheism and solipsism with no real reason to choose the one over the other.

> Howison says of Royce, that he is caught between pantheism and solipsism. I think Howison was right. And Howison says that so far--even given the "rich and crowded arsenal of his thinking"—so far Royce has not sustained the presence of a real, flesh and blood, erotic, neurotic individual existence, that is a me, a you, within the boundaries of his Absolute. Here also I think Howison was right; not for all the king's horses, nor all the queen's men, nor the "Supplementary Essay" to *The Conception of God*, not *The World and the Individual*, nor the never-ending supplementary essays to those massive volumes, nor System Sigma, could overcome Howison's critique and it echoes in Davidson, and Hadgson and Pierce and James. For a possible way out look to

> Royce from his book on loyalty forward, and look backward to the social, historical, religious and environmental essays. There, throughout, has to be sought material for a reply to Howison. (John McDermott, "The Confrontation Between Royce and Howison," *Transactions of the Charles S. Pierce Society* 30, no 4 (Fall 1994): 788)

It is interesting that when Chamberlin attended Harvard in 1907–8 Royce was working on his lectures that became *The Philosophy of Loyalty*.

62. William H. Chamberlin, "An Essay on Nature" (Provo, Utah: 1915), 49.
63. William H. Chamberlin, "The Theory of Evolution as an Aid to Faith in God and in the Resurrection," Supplement to *The White and the Blue*, February 14, 1911, p. 4.
64. I have attempted to collect Chamberlin's work over the years. I have listed the pieces I have found and where they can be found.

Theological Questions

Prayer and Divine Attributes

Richard Sherlock
Utah State University

The fundamental problem of all theology is its ground or foundation. Though frequently ignored, this is the first question of any theology. In my view there are four fundamental possibilities. Theology may be grounded in (1) philosophical reason, (2) scripture, (3) prophetic teaching, or (4) the beliefs and practices of the faith community. Relying first on philosophic reason results in natural theology or deism. This cannot be the whole story for a theology that must articulate the beliefs of a community led by revelation. Grounding theology first in scripture brings you biblical fundamentalism. The problem here is that scripture is not self-authenticating. Texts become scriptural because in them the community finds the revelation of God's desires and teachings for His people. A community interprets scripture and thus makes it come alive spiritually, not the reverse. Prophetic teaching as a starting point has the same problem. Communities sustain prophets because they first come to find eternal truth in their words. If we want to know the deepest meaning of prophetic teaching, and thus the ground of theology, look to the community that lives by it.[1]

Reading the generally acknowledged classics of Mormon theology, the Pratts, Roberts, Widtsoe, McMurrin, etc., there seems to be a pronounced preference for avoiding the foundational question and instead engaging in what I shall call ungrounded stipulative theology.[2] In stipulative theology the author simply states or declares a point of doctrine as being "Mormon theology," and proceeds to work out, sometimes with philosopher's tools, the nature and implications of such point of doctrine. Whether it be an

Anselmian view of the atonement, personal material embodiment in the afterlife, divine material embodiment, or most other parts of theology stipulative theology is extraordinarily common from laypeople to professionals, who ought to know better.

McMurrin's *Theological Foundations of the Mormon Religion* is almost completely stipulative and many of the stipulations, on examination, turn out to be wrong. Consider, for example, the claim that: "Mormon theology is a modern Pelagianism in a puritan religion," or further that "the history of Mormon theology, therefore, has been at many points a recasting of Pelagianism, Socinianism, and Arminianism."[3] This claim about Pelagianism will not do. A close reading of the texts of Pelagius as reconstructed by Robert Evans and Theodore de Bruyn will show that Mormonism is not Pelagian.[4] Pelagius had no serious theory of grace, and his movement represented by the likes of Caelestius even less, while Mormon scripture has a robust theology of grace, a point that Robert Millet has so recently made.[5]

Another example comes from Hollis Johnson's paper on the big bang, which came to us too late for inclusion on this program. At one point Johnson writes, "The Church of Jesus Christ of Latter Day Saints teaches the eternity of human spirits."[6] That such an astute observer should make such a mistake shows, I believe, the attraction of stipulation. If Johnson means that he and I and everyone else who will ever exist have always existed, the claim is wrong. Some Mormons, I have no idea how many, hold such a view thanks largely to the efforts of B. H. Roberts who at the first of the 20th century articulated it.[7] But one need look no further than Elder McConkie for a completely opposite position in which Hollis Johnson and Richard Sherlock and everyone else owe our existence as separate beings with continuous personal identity entirely to God's creative act.[8]

Stipulative theology's circular character assures that it sheds no light on crucial theological points and leaves theology as such cut off from the living community of faith. On the contrary, I argue that theology is grounded in the epistemic practices, a term I borrow from William Alston of the covenant community.[9] Theology on this view is an activity of the faith community by the faith community and for the faith community. The community which forms around what for it is sacred text, prophetic witness, and personal spiritual confirmation creates theology as an activity which gives form and structure to its convictions. The community creates theology not the other way around.

In this view the fundamental test for theology is coherence with the convictions of the covenant people as expressed in word and especially in deed. Coherence theory alone, as Quine and Davidson have shown, can give us a substantive view of truth.[10] This is the only view that can comprehend the testimony of the believer who firmly states: "I know the gospel is true" except in an inadequate approximate manner. Correspondence theory cannot provide any meaning to this statement.

This coherence must be carefully thought out, but at least in this view the liberal claim that theology must make the gospel plausible or available to modern humans, i.e. enlightenment reason, is rejected without apology. "Modern humans," whatever the phrase means, is not the template against which theology must be measured. Since we all live in a universe comprehended by modern science it helps if theology is at least consistent with what science has good reason to accept as being the case with the natural world. By living in the world of science and making use of its fruits, we implicitly admit our belief-acceptance of its well-established result. Hence, I would argue, we ought to try, insofar as possible to make theological beliefs coherent with what we, by implication, believe about the world. By the same token I think that our beliefs about the physical out be so revised that fundamental theological beliefs, like the belief in miracles, can be coherently maintained. But theology need not and will not probably agree with any of the fashions of the day from Marxism, to feminism, to what, in the 1950s, was called "Americanism."[11]

With this as a foundation I want to consider two fundamental practices of the community. My argument is that implicit in these practices are firm beliefs about the attributes of God that many writers on Mormon theology might not agree with, but which I think are bedrock convictions of the covenant community. These are beliefs that the members of the community are least likely to want to give up.[12]

Private Prayer

In a classic essay Eleanore Stump has treated petitionary prayer, where the believer asks for something from God. Though important, this is one of a larger set, which I will refer to as private prayer.[13]

Private prayer is crucial in the lives of the Saints, and it is, I think, the most illuminative of faith practices. There are many social and psychological reasons for public religious activity, e.g., see friends, feel wanted, meet potential marriage partners, etc. Moreover, praying or speaking in meetings follows naturally from the reasons for activity in the first place. A potential spouse would think twice if one refused to say prayer at the start of a meeting.[14]

Private prayer, however, seems clearly different in that it does not help someone make human friends, or feel wanted or needed by others. One meets no potential marriage partners, dates, or clients. For these reasons I believe that private prayer is a central test case for understanding the spiritual convictions of individual believers and, by extension, the community.

Broadly, as noted above there are two large sorts of prayer. The first is petitionary prayer in which the believer asks or petitions God for something like moral courage or health. The second is what is called in the tradition contemplative or more recently "centering" prayer, after the work of Thomas Keating.[15] Here the believer simply tries to bring his/her mind and heart as close to God as possible. The fundamental example of centering prayer is the most important prayer in the history of the planet, which is

Jesus's prayer in Gethsemane. From the text Jesus first asked for relief, but concluded with commitment: "My Father, if it is possible, may this cup be taken from me, yet not as I will but as you will." This same point is made in Luke's account of the same event. Furthermore, I note that in what is commonly called "The Lord's Prayer," believers are instructed first to acknowledge that God's will is primary: "Your will be done on earth as it is in heaven."[16] As will become clear, I think the second, "centering prayer," is the most crucial. Properly thought through, the first collapses into the second.

Petitionary prayer is a complex phenomenon but I think that the complexity can be comprehended if we parse out three fundamental things that believers ask of God.

I. Comfort

As an example: "God, my spouse just died. Get me through this difficult time." Here the believer asks God to metaphorically put His arms around him/her and surround him/her with His love.

II. Guidance

As an example: "I'm at a crossroads, Father. What should I do?" or "Father, I've studied my choices. Is this one the right one?" Here, the believer wants to know what he/she should do with his/her life. Should he marry this person? Should she take this job? Should they move their family across the country?

III. Intervention

As an example: "Father, will you remove this obstacle from my path?" or "Will you intervene with my family or my friends to help them out?" Here we want God to do something in the world such as soften a heart or cure an illness.

I shall concentrate here on II, guidance. This is not because I think that I and III, comfort and intervention, are less important, but because I think that guidance illuminates the fundamental characteristics of prayer, through which we can also see I and III.

Guidance is a large part of private prayer; perhaps the largest part, though I have no way of knowing except in my own case. But what is implied in seeking divine direction and following it without reservation as Saints in all ages have done? If you just want decent or good advice ask a friend or a neighbor. If you desire professional advice, say on playing golf or piano or thousands of other things, take direction from someone who teaches golf or piano, etc.

In the lives of Saints, however, guidance from God is qualitatively different. First, the guidance is about eternal things.[17] Second, the guidance frequently contradicts what rational calculation would conclude.[18] Thirdly, the believer or Saint seems compelled to follow the guidance without question, unlike the advice from friends. Comparing the cases of human and divine guidance there is an interesting reversal. In the case of divine guidance the question is whether we have actually had guidance directly and specifically from God, not whether we should follow such guidance. In the case of friendly advice, the question is not, have we received advice, but whether we should follow it.

In other words, in the case of friendly guidance or advice the problem is ontological. We are not sure that the friend is in any better ontological position to give advice or guidance than we are. In the case of divine guidance the ontological position of God secures the nature of the advice as perfect, but the very difference between God and humans that secures the character of the guidance gives us second thoughts about whether we have actually been explicitly guided by God. The epistemological problem is rooted in the situation of human beings as "natural man" who is opposed to God in every way possible.[19] Thus we frequently find ourselves wondering whether we have properly heard God's word to us, not whether the word is perfect but whether we have perfectly heard it.

I submit that believers who ask for such guidance are convinced that divine guidance, if given, is not open to question or debate.

Why not? It is because God's guidance is certain. Now the character of this advice follows from the character of the giver. We are more certain of a physician's advice about health or illness than that of a coworker because we have more confidence about the physician's knowledge of health. Trust is rooted in the confidence we have in the knowledge and ability of the other in whom we trust.[20] I submit that the complete trust of the Saints in God's guidance is founded on a core conviction that God's knowledge of the future does not consist of inductive predictions no matter how good. Rather, God's knowledge of the future is just that knowledge in the strong sense. God's knowledge of the future is what Ockham would call a hard fact. To use the language of logicians, "God knows that P" means that P is truth functional and for all logically possible P's God knows whether they are true or false. As such, he can give us complete and certain advice about any set of propositions describing what others will do, including future tensed propositions, which is the basis of His guidance about the future such as whether I should marry a certain person.[21]

I think that the scriptures plainly teach that God knows what we are going to ask for before we ask. "Your Father knows what you need before you ask Him."[22] Since God only does what is best for us, this implies that He knows what He is going to do before we ask. This point is implied in our asking in prayer for "those things we stand in need of." The implication is plain; I think that God knows exactly, more exactly than we do, what we need, and therefore, for what we are truly asking.

Second, God's guidance is not only perfectly wise; it is perfectly good. In committing oneself to following divine guidance, if given, the believer understands God as good without qualification. As such, his guidance should not be questioned about being correct for me. Divine guidance again, in this respect, is qualitatively unlike human guidance. If I ask a priest, a rabbi, or an LDS bishop whether I should keep my comatose mother alive on a respirator and a feeding tube, I may expect better advice than I might think of on my own. The religious leaders may have gone through this experience far more than I have. This would also be the case with a sensitive, experienced physician. Experience, in this respect, does expand one's moral competence as Aristotle pointed out. But at the most fundamental level I must recognize that though their advice may be an improvement on my unformed thinking, ontologically they are no closer to the complete and full standard of righteousness or goodness than am I. As human beings they are no more able to grasp or comprehend the good as such than anyone else. In my willingness to follow and accept divine guidance I presuppose my conviction regarding the complete or transcendent goodness of God in distinction from any human source.

The example of Joseph Smith's prayer is much too easy at this point so I shall use a non-Mormon example. In the fall of 1954 new PhD Martin Luther King moved his wife and daughter to Montgomery, Alabama, where he became Reverend Dr. King. At that point his career goal was to become a teacher in a protestant seminary or divinity school. However, he wisely realized that teaching others how to be ministers without ever being one was the equivalent of teaching medical students without ever having treated a patient. Soon after his arrival in Montgomery, the bus boycott began as the opening salvo of the civil rights movement in the South. A charismatic preacher with a doctoral degree from a northern university, he soon became a leader of the struggle and the target of hate groups. King tells the story that one night he came home late and had another ugly call threatening death. As his wife and daughter lay asleep, he could not. He tried to think of a way out without seeming to let the people down. Exhausted, he asked for divine guidance. What he really hoped for was divine acceptance of his wish to get out. In his own words: "I immediately felt the presence of the Divine as I had never felt Him before. It seemed as if I could hear a still small voice saying stand up for righteousness, stand up for justice and I will be at your side forever." He recounts that his fears immediately disappeared. Three nights later while at a meeting he is told that his house had been bombed. It does not worry him at all. Seventy-two hours earlier he and his family would have fled into the night, but not now.[23]

On what ground might King's response to the bombing be questioned? One might wonder if God actually spoke to King or if King actually heard him correctly. King himself does not so question. If the voice had said what King wanted to hear, then it might be more reasonable to question whether this was a divine call or just his desires speaking to him. What King heard, however, like Abraham, Joseph Smith, and Paul, was guidance against his desires and even against his own personal interests. He commits himself to it without reservation. In doing so I believe, he acknowledges God's complete knowledge and complete and absolute goodness. This is the conviction of the Saints expressed in private prayer and the confident following of such prayer in our individual lives. I think, though I shall not argue it here, that this same analysis can be given of personal commitment to the most unique of Mormon beliefs; continuous divine revelation. When we commit ourselves to a living prophetic teacher, we do so only because we are committed to the belief that God's guidance to the church is just like God's guidance to us individually.

Comfort, my first category, is equivalent to guidance. One seeks divine comfort because when a friend says, in our time of crisis, "everything will be all right," we hope he is correct, but we realize that he has no more assurance than we do about the future. God's assurance is rooted in his ontologically different position and as such his assurance actually and fully assures.

This observation requires analysis. When a specialist in a given field such as medicine says, "everything will be all right" after an event like a heart attack; I am surely justified in giving more credence to such a statement than I would to the same statement from a friend. My belief in the physician's greater competence grounds my greater confidence. But my confidence is, nevertheless, limited. While I do believe in the physician's knowledge and skill, I also believe that he/she is limited in both. The physician only predicts the future and cannot be assured concerning what will happen, nor can he/she be certain about the results of whatever treatments he/she employs. Thirdly, the physician, qua physician, is not concerned about my eternal destiny so he/she will have a limited perspective to conclude "everything will be fine." God's ontologically different position and existentially different concerns answer these three limits fully. His assurance will not be based on prediction. His complete power over nature guarantees success, not just the "likelihood" that the physician speaks of. Finally, God is completely concerned about my eternal destiny and my life here on earth only as grounding for that.

Petitions for intervention are equivalent. The witness of Saints, prophets, and scriptures of every era is the same. No faithful prayer for intervention is ignored. Our problem is that God's intervention is frequently not what we wanted to hear. True prayer must be like true blessing: "If it be Thy will, remove this rock, nevertheless not my will but Thine be done."

Though I shall not develop it here, there is another implication of prayer, the openness of the human being to divine revelation. Metaphorically we are beings that can "hear" a divine call and respond to it. Much work needs to be done on what this implies for a theological anthropology. Important material might be developed out of Heidegger's later work and Karl Rahner's *Hearer of the Word*,[24] along with other works exploring how human beings are open to the transcendent.

Temple Commitment

Along with continuous prophetic witness, the other most unique part of Mormonism is the temple ceremony. At the center of the endowment is a personal covenant that each Saint makes with God to give or consecrate everything that the person is, has, will have, or will become to God. Like the case of prayer, this commitment is qualitatively different than any human commitment.

Even the marital commitment is not the same. God can release us from the marital covenant for reasons of abuse or abandonment. But there is no divine release from the temple covenant. We may abandon it but we are never released from it.

Consider this eternally binding commitment. What makes such a commitment at all plausible? Is it not because of a firm conviction that God cannot possibly change the nature of the contract or be unable to fulfill his part of the covenant? Again, there is nothing new that God can learn that would require renegotiation of the terms. Furthermore, God has complete power to do whatever he has committed himself to do in the agreement. The agreement lasts for eternity and in every conceivable set of conditions, including any possible world. There is no possible world in which God cannot act decisively to bring us to his ontological position. Following this logic out, God must have all power over any obstacle. Since we do not know the obstacles in the cosmos, from our perspective it must be the case that God is in the classic sense omnipotent. Following George Mavrodes, I think the implication is that any act, which does not involve a logical contradiction, God can perform.[25]

Whether this concept of God implied in prayer and covenant is the so-called "god of the philosophers" I leave for others to decide. In my view, it is the God to which the vibrant community of faith and individual members commit themselves. It helps that this view of God is a superior response to the theodicy problem, as Marilyn Adams has so well argued, in contrast to our usual wholly insufficient collection of character building or free will claims.[26] It also helps that this view allows for a God who stirred the initial energy pot at the moment of the big bang and that we do not need to limit God's creative activity to this universe alone.[27] It helps that on this view the fine tuning of the constants at the start of the universe, the so called anthropic cosmological principle acknowledged by theists and non-theists alike, can be part of a robust design argument. It also helps in my view that this concept of God follows from the perfectly valid formulation of the ontological argument by Leibniz.

This general position is not perfect and it represents only one strand of Mormonism. There are many issues that would need to be developed to see this view to fruition. I have only tried to present what I believe is a genuinely Mormon view of God. The convergences with design theory, with the big bang in any form, and especially as an approach to the problem of evil I am prepared to defend extensively.

Though these convergences are important, the most crucial point is that this view of God articulates the faith of the community of Saints better than any other. For this, any theologian must be grateful.

RICHARD SHERLOCK is Professor of Philosophy at Utah State University. He received his Master of Theological Studies and Ph.D. at Harvard University. His philosophical interests include the concept of conscience, early modern arguments for religious toleration, and ethical and conceptual issues in biotechnology. He served as president of The Society for Mormon Philosophy and Theology from 2004 to 2006.

Notes

1. This tradition is known as post liberal theology, most closely associated with the work of George Lindbeck and Hans Frei. See especially George Lindbeck, *The Nature of Doctrine* (Philadelphia: Westminster Press, 1984).
2. John A. Widtsoe, *A Rational Theology* (Salt Lake City: Deseret Sunday School Union, 1917); Parley P. Pratt, *The Essential Parley Pratt*, ed. Peter Crawley (Salt Lake City: Signature Books, 1990); B. H. Roberts, *The Mormon Doctrine of Deity*, (Salt lake City: Deseret News Press, 1903); Idem, *Seventy's Course in Theology* (Salt Lake City: Deseret News Press, 1912); Sterling McMurrin, *Theological Foundations of the Mormon Religion* (Salt Lake City: University of Utah Press, 1965).
3. McMurrin, *Theological Foundations*, pp. x, 67.
4. Robert Evans, *Pelagius: Inquiries and Reappraisals* (New York: Seabury, 1968); *Pelagius, Commentary on St. Paul's Epistle to the Romans*, ed. and trans. Theodore de Bruyn (New York: Oxford, 1998).
5. Robert Millet, *Grace Matters* (Salt Lake City: Deseret Book Company, 2003).
6. Hollis Johnson, "Mormon Cosmology and the Big Bang"; also see Keith Norman, "Mormon Cosmology: Can it Survive the Big Bang?" *Sunstone* 10 (1986): 19–23. If Norman means, "Can the Roberts-Widtsoe cosmology survive the big bang?" the plain answer, which he tentatively suggests, is no; nor should it. What I am disputing is the implied premise, that there is some one authoritative "Mormon cosmology" articulated somewhere.

7. The finest statement after Roberts is Truman Madsen, *Eternal Man* (Salt Lake City: Deseret Book, 1966); also see McMurrin, *Theological Foundations*, 49.
8. Bruce McConkie, *Mormon Doctrine* (Salt Lake City: Bookcraft, 1958) see the entries on "Intelligences" at p. 354 and "Spirit Element" at p. 678. Also see Paul Hyde, "Intelligences" in Daniel Ludlow ed. *Encyclopedia of Mormonism* 4 vols. (New York: Macmillan, 1992) 2: 692–693. Hyde states that there are two views held in Mormonism, the "eternal man" view articulated by Roberts and Madsen and the view that "intelligence" is a sort of primal undifferentiated "stuff" out of which God made individual human beings.
9. William Alston, *Perceiving God* (Ithaca: Cornell University Press, 1991). Alston's is a fine treatment of the way beliefs are embedded in practices, but he is not a coherence theorist as am I.
10. W. V. O. Quine, *From a Logical Point of View*, 2nd ed, (Cambridge: Harvard University Press, 1980); The seminal statement is Donald Davidson, "A Coherence Theory of Truth and Knowledge," in Donald Davidson, *Subjective, Intersubjective, Objective*, 2nd ed. (New York: Oxford University Press, 2002): 137–154. For a powerful theological application see Bruce Marshall, *Trinity and Truth* (New York: Cambridge University Press, 2000).
11. Coherence theory is not committed to epistemic or scientific relativism of the sort associated with certain forms of deconstructionism or with paradigm theory in the philosophy of science. Since in any plausible view of human existence, we as humans share an extraordinary number of beliefs, our "overall" epistemic sets or "webs of belief" are almost certain to be remarkably similar. The most cogent critique of radical Kuhn-style paradigm views comes from Davidson himself. Donald Davidson, "On the Very Idea of a Conceptual Scheme" in Donald Davidson, *Inquiries into Truth and Interpretation* 2nd ed. (New York: Oxford University Press, 2001): 183-198.
12. The single most powerful statement of the Roberts-Widtsoe position is Blake Ostler, *Exploring Mormon Thought* (Salt Lake City: Greg Kofford Books, 2001).
13. Eleanor Stump, " Petitionary Prayer," *American Philosophical Quarterly* 16 (1979): 81–91.

14. Christ agrees that prayer should be private. Matt. 6:5–6; 3 Nephi 13:5–6.
15. Thomas Keating, *Intimacy With God* (New York: Crossroad Books, 1994); Idem, *Centering Prayer in Daily Life and Ministry* (New York: Crossroad Books, 1998).
16. Matt. 26:39, 42; Luke 22:42; Matt. 6:10.
17. What I mean is this. The goal or telos of human existence is eternal life, life with God and like God. This is God's goal for us. As such, any advice that he gives us will be advice that helps us in achieving this goal.
18. The scriptures are rife with examples, such as Abraham and Isaac. But the best example is Alma the Younger and the Sons of Mosiah in Mosiah 27. The people, including Alma the Elder, had been praying for the repentance of these young men. Nothing in the text suggests that they had any reason to expect such a transformation, absent divine action. The message given by the angel contradicts both the character of the "Sons of Mosiah" and the rational hopes of the community.
19. Mosiah 3:19; Alma 41:11.
20. Work on trust has recently been substantial. Richard Holton, "Deciding to Trust, Coming to Believe," *Australasian Journal of Philosophy* 72 (1994): 63–76; Karen Jones, "Trust as an Affective Attitude," *Ethics* 107 (1996): 4–25; Onora O'Oneill, *Autonomy and Trust in Bioethics* (New York: Cambridge University Press, 2002); Piotr Sztonkpa, *Trust: A Sociological Theory* (New York: Cambridge University Press, 1999); Elinor Ostrom and James Walker, eds., *Trust and Reciprocity* (Los Angeles: Russel Sage, 2003); Russel Hardin, *Trust and Trustworthiness* (Los Angeles: Russel Sage, 2002).
21. Much has been written on this topic. See, for example, a classic account by Alvin Plantinga, *God, Freedom, and Evil* (New York: Oxford University Press); also see the molinist accounts of William Lane Craig, *The Only Wise God* (Grand Rapids: Baker Books, 1987) and Edward Wierenga, *The Nature of God* (Ithaca: Cornell University Press, 1989); my own thinking has been decisively shaped by Linda Zagzebski, *The Dilemma of Freedom and Foreknowledge* (New York: Oxford University Press, 1991). I also note that James Faulconer's review of Mormon thinking on this issue concluded that "historically most Latter-day Saints have taken the first general position: everything is foreseen, yet freedom remains." See James Faulconer,

"Foreknowledge of God," in Daniel Ludlow ed., *Encyclopedia of Mormonism* 4 vols. (New York; Macmillan, 1992) II: 521–522.

22. Matt. 6:8; 3 Nephi 13:8.
23. Martin Luther King, *Stride Toward Freedom* (New York: Harper and Row, 1958): 132–135.
24. Karl Rahner, *Hearer of the Word* (New York: Continuum, 1994).
25. George Mavrodes, "Some Puzzles Concerning Omnipotence," *Philosophical Review* 72 (1963).
26. Marilyn Adams, *Horrendous Evils and the Goodness of God* (Ithaca; Cornell University Press, 2000). Character building, or, as Hick calls it, "soul making" theodicies are incapable of giving an account of natural evil, e.g. earthquakes, floods, hurricanes, etc. that might cause great harm to sentient creatures. But most importantly they fail in the face of horrible or "horrendous" evils that leave a person with no chance to develop their character. Rapes of a child or an earthquake that leaves a child severely brain damaged are examples. As Adams has so well shown, the answer is not to find some rational solution but to have faith despite the horror. What makes this possible is a belief that God is so good, wise, and powerful, that one can have faith in God's redemption, even when all the evidence of reason points against it. Job is the example. The three friends and later Elihu want to play the theodicy game. They want to answer the query: why evil? Job's response is the correct one: "Though He slay me, yet will I trust in Him" Job 13:15.
27. The idea of limiting God's creative activity to this world and after the moment of creation at that comes from the Hollis Johnson paper referred to earlier.
28. John Barrow and Frank Tipler, *The Anthropic Cosmological Principle* (New York: Oxford University Press, 1986); Also see Del Ratzsch, *Nature, Design, and Science* (New York: SUNY Press, 1999).

Theological Method and the Question of Truth

A Postliberal Approach to Mormon Doctrine and Practice[1]

Brian D. Birch
Utah Valley State College

Introduction

From its beginnings, Mormonism has had an uncomfortable relationship with theology. Unlike most Christian denominations, Latter-day Saints do not rely on a theological tradition to shape the development of doctrinal discourse, but look instead to continuing revelation through recognized authorities, religious experience, and communal practice for guidance in matters of theology. The ministry is not academically trained in philosophy or theology, and many in the tradition see little or no value in theological inquiry arguing that such an enterprise results in the bastardization of LDS beliefs by mixing doctrines of God with the philosophies of men. One frequently hears the charge that mainstream Christian theology has enslaved itself to intellectual methods that distort the truth of the gospel and a correct understanding of God.[2] For example, an important theme in LDS scholarship of late has been the critical appraisal of modernism and its continued influence in the study of religion. The term modernism is commonly used to refer to a cluster of theoretical positions including positivism, materialism, objectivism, and rationalism. Despite the historical dominance of modernist methodologies in the academic study of religion, the past few decades have witnessed a strong challenge to many of the abiding assumptions of modernism by thinkers who appeal to concepts and methods that have come to be labeled "postmodern." Although a near hopelessly fluid term, postmodernism is famously characterized by Jean-Francois Lyotard as "the incredulity towards metanarratives," those modes of discourse that seek to totalize human knowledge according to a common method of theoretical reflection.[3] This importantly includes the rejection of philosophical or scientific claims to objectivity and the attendant authority of reason characteristic of much of modernism. Given Mormonism's emphasis on continuing revelation and the role of religious experience in belief formation, several LDS thinkers have utilized postmodern insights to respond to these approaches that are said to minimize, redescribe, or dismiss important aspects of Mormon thought. Because postmodern thought has opened up new ways of thinking about knowledge and truth that had for so long been dominated by a set of shared assumptions, a new way of engaging the wider intellectual community has emerged and proven fruitful in certain respects. The use of postmodernism in LDS intellectual life has been utilized primarily in the service of apologetic endeavors in the context of debates regarding scriptural exegesis, historiography, theological method, and the historicity of scripture. There is much of value in these critiques of modernism and this paper is an attempt to argue in favor of an approach to theology that shares many of these insights. I will begin by offering a sketch of this position as a response to alternative approaches within contemporary mainstream Christian theology. Second, I will address some implications of this method for LDS scholarship by examining specific works in the areas of scriptural exegesis and historiography. An important aim of the paper is to show how postliberal theology has both apologetic and critical implications that have not been adequately explored in the Mormon courtship of postmodern thought.

Postliberal Theology

Postliberal theology as a distinctive approach has its origins in the mid-1970s in the work of Yale theologians Hans Frei and George Lindeck, whose respective books *The Eclipse of Biblical Narrative* and *The Nature of Doctrine* made a huge impact on the theological community.[4] It is influenced philosophically by the work of the later Wittgenstein and theologically by certain aspects of neo-orthodoxy, most notably the confessionalism of Karl Barth. The postliberal project situates itself between the traditional divide of so-called conservative and liberal approaches to theology that has characterized the discipline since the mid-nineteenth century.[5] Liberalism has generally been described as an attempt to reconcile the claims of modernity with Christian belief. While it has not been the case that liberal theologians have agreed on "how to reconstruct Christian beliefs in the light of modernity, they agree on the necessity of that ongoing project as the fundamental task of theology."[6] This approach has its origins in the work of nineteenth-century German theologian Friedrich Schleiermacher and became influential in the United States in the work of William Ellery Channing and Harry Emerson Fosdick. On the other hand, conservative approaches tend to harden the divide between science, reason, and the Christian gospel and emphasize traditional doctrines of Biblical inerrancy and literalism against what Walter Lippmann called "the acids of modernity."

Postliberal theology accuses both liberal and conservative approaches of being enslaved, to varying degrees, by modernist assumptions. Hans Frei, for example, has argued that conservative approaches to biblical interpretation, in their reliance on traditional propositional-realist accounts of truth, are as much a product of modernist thought as their liberal counterparts. According to this approach, "the metaphors and narratives of scripture carry meaning as religious truths only if they are restated in propositional form."[7] George Lindbeck describes this approach as the attempt to understand religious beliefs and doctrines as "informative propositions or truth claims about objective realities."[8] Hence, both the truth-value and meaning of religious doctrines are ultimately determined by their correspondence to the reality they seek to describe.

This approach is well represented in the tradition of systematic theology and Anglo-American philosophy of religion. A paradigmatic example of this position in evangelical theology is the influential work of Carl F. H. Henry, who argues that biblical narratives and metaphors must be grounded in clearly stated propositions.

> Christianity's very claim to truth collapses unless truth can be affirmed of certain core-propositions inherent in it and integral to it. If the logical-propositional truth of Christian revelation is ignored, and is even to be disowned, on the pretext that the efficacy of personal faith can be preserved only in this way, we shall needlessly and disastrously sacrifice what superbly distinguishes Christianity from other religions, viz., the truth of certain specific propositions that cannot be affirmed by rival faiths. . . . Faith divorced from assent to propositions may for a season be exuberantly championed as Christian faith, but sooner or later it must become apparent that such mystical exercises are neither identifiably Christian nor akin to authentic belief.[9]

This position is also to be found in the work of Latter-day Saint thinkers and their interlocutors. For example, two papers presented at the 2003 Mormon theology conference at Yale University argued explicitly for a propositional-realist method of inquiry.[10] In "The Future of Mormon Philosophy," Dennis Potter argued for its appropriateness by claiming that apologetics and the exclusiveness of Mormon claims require such an approach. Drawing on Rudolf Carnap's distinction between internal and external questions, Potter states that "internal questions are asked within the context of a practice, form of life, or language-game," while external questions "are questions about the relationship between our practices and/or language-games with external reality."[11] The point of his paper is to argue that the propositional-realist approach, which focuses on external questions, is in a better position to explain the exclusiveness of Mormonism. "When confronted with the fact of diversity, Mormons respond by saying that all religions have some truth, but that there is only one true church. This is a claim that necessarily compares practices with practices, an external question. Hence, our exclusivism entails Realism."[12]

Another advocate of a propositional approach is Paul Owen, an evangelical Christian theologian and friendly interlocutor for Mormon philosophers. Owen argued, similarly to Potter, that Mormons need a systematic theology to enter into genuine and meaningful dialogue with other faith traditions. He states:

> After all, it was Joseph's desire to overcome the chaos of multiple theological traditions that were making incompatible claims, all at the same time pronouncing themselves as the guides of religious truth. . . . The question that plagued this young man was not, how can religious truth be systematized; but which version of systematic doctrine is objectively true, and how can I know it?[13]

Potter and Owen agree that the most appropriate way to address the question of religious truth is to compare doctrinal beliefs (or sets of beliefs) with reality, and this is presumably done by means of subjecting incompatible beliefs to some objectively valid method of adjudication in order to establish correspondence with reality or lack thereof.

Implied in this approach is the idea that religious beliefs and doctrines have the epistemological status of hypotheses. But to meaningfully call something a hypothesis requires that there be some agreed upon method for its confirmation, and this is precisely what is lacking across religious lines in the effort to determine the truth of the matter. Hence, the appeal to "reality" in settling disputes leaves both parties with a set of beliefs and yet without a context of adjudication, which leaves the concept of reality employed to settle the dispute as a meaningless philosophical abstraction. This is seen in the practice of what D. Z. Phillips calls "philosophy by italics."[14] According to Terence Penelhum, a person advocating a realist position "would hold that the supernatural facts which he thinks faith requires must indeed *be* facts for faith to be true, so that if they are not facts, but fantasies . . . then faith is unjustified."[15] But from a philosophical standpoint, of what theoretical value is italicizing the word "be"? Examples abound in the literature in which someone will assert that faith is empty unless God *actually* exists, or that God's existence is a *fact*, or that God is *there* to be worshipped. The point is that emphasizing these words does not do any theoretical work. In fact, far from clarifying matters, it appears to me that the need to italicize these words actually reveals their questionable status. For this reason, the so-called "external questions," especially when applied to theological questions, are idle, and hence meaningless. Far from Mormon apologetics requiring realism, I would maintain that the realist approach serves to obstruct productive dialogue across theological boundaries. How does the appeal to objective reality aid in the discussion as to whether or not God has a body? "Well," one might say, "there is a fact of the matter as to whether God does or does not have a body." But where would the conversation proceed from there? Any appeal to the "sober facts of the world," to use Alvin Plantinga's phrase, will be necessarily informed by the criteria of truth and meaningfulness present in the specific faith-tradition of the interlocutors. Consider the following quote from Peter Winch in his essay "Understanding a Primitive Society":

> Reality is not what gives language sense. What is real and what is unreal shows itself in the sense that language has. Further, both the distinction between the real and the unreal and the concept of agreement with reality themselves belong to our language. . . . We could not in fact distinguish the real from the unreal without understanding the way this distinction operates in the language. If then we wish to understand the significance of these concepts, we must examine the use they actually have in language.[16]

In short, what counts as correspondence to reality can take as many different forms as there are different uses of language. Hence, what correspondence *means* cannot be assumed prior to an investigation of its employment in a particular context; nor can the concept of reality be usefully severed from the epistemic practices through which it is understood.[17] Carl Sagan and Jerry Falwell may agree that reality is what it is independent of human beliefs, languages, and practices. However, despite the fact that they employ the same words, they mean distinctly different things because their beliefs in this regard are tied to entirely different conceptual communities. These criticisms should not be mistaken for a metaphysical thesis in the service of a certain type of nihilism; rather the argument presented here is a grammatical insight regarding the status of propositions or beliefs in their appeal to reality.

The propositional-realist may retort that this issue has nothing whatsoever to do with the status of reality itself, but rather with differences as to how it is conceived. It does not follow from a diversity of beliefs, they may add, that there is no objective fact of the matter. I would rejoin that the very employment of this concept in the service of a philosophical resolution is empty and meaningless because it cannot be filled in apart from referential practices that may fundamentally differ depending on context. To continue to appeal to the "facts" or "reality" or the "world" as the arbiter of truth once this insight is recognized is an exercise in theoretical futility. In short, to separate the ontological status of reality from its grammatical status in language results in a vacuous distinction for purposes of inquiry. As Hans-Georg Gadamer points out, "Language is not just one of man's possessions in the world; rather, on it depends the fact that man has a *world* at all. . . . [F]or there is no point of view outside the experience of the world in language from which it could become an object."[18] However, this is precisely what is implied in propositional-realist conceptions, most of which rely on a correspondence theory of truth in which the appeal to reality functions as little more than a metaphor for the hope of resolution between diverse belief systems. It has no content of its own and is thus made sublime in the interest of theoretical convergence.

Despite the attempts of very talented philosophers, I do not believe that the different variants of philosophical realism have escaped the difficulties described above.[19] For this reason, if the appeal to objective reality is a theoretically misguided enterprise analogous to greyhounds chasing wooden rabbits, we need to look elsewhere for a method adequate to the task of theological inquiry.

Postliberalism and The Task of Theology

George Lindbeck summarizes three problems with the propositional approach that are particularly relevant to doctrinal issues in the Latter-day Saint community:

> The conceptual difficulties involved in the traditional propositional notion of authoritative teaching have contributed to discrediting the whole doctrinal enterprise. They have helped legitimate unnecessary and counterproductive rigidities in practice because, first, propositionalism makes it difficult to understand how new doctrines can develop in the course of time, and how old ones can be forgotten or become peripheral. Second, propositionalist accounts of how old doctrines can be interpreted to fit new circumstances are unconvincing: they have difficulty in distinguishing between what changes and what remains the same. Third, they do not deal adequately with the specified ecumenical problematic: how is it possible for doctrines that once contradicted each other to be reconciled and yet retain their identity.[20]

Drawing on the distinction between what he calls "extratextual" (read realist-propositional) and "intratextual" approaches to religious doctrines, Lindbeck argues in favor of an intratextual account for which religious meaning is located within the symbolic relations of the community rather than being severed from it. "Thus the proper way to determine what 'God' signifies, for example, is by examining how the word operates within a religion and thereby shapes reality and experience rather than by first establishing its propositional or experiential meaning and reinterpreting or reformulating its uses accordingly."[21] This amounts to a kind of conceptual ethnography with regard to religious beliefs and practices.[22] One must look to see how concepts function in relation to one another in order to render them meaningful for purposes of verification and correspondence. Rather than comparing scripture with a non-scriptural concept of reality, "intratextual theology redescribes reality within the scriptural framework. . . . It is the text, so to speak, which absorbs the world, rather than the world the text."[23] The importance of this approach lies in the recognition that both the truth value of religious claims and the criteria for establishing their truth are necessarily tied to the practices of particular religious communities in their relation to text, ritual, etc. Because religious communities make contrasting claims about the nature of reality and possess incompatible methods by which their truth is established, the task of the theologian is to offer a faithful account of the doctrines, rituals, and norms of the community in how they function in relation to one another. In doing this the aim is to provide a coherent and meaningful account of how this community understands reality. Lindbeck quotes Clifford Geertz approvingly as follows: "What the theologian needs to explicate 'is a multiplicity of complex conceptual structures, many of them superimposed or knotted into one another, which are at once strange, irregular and inexplicit, and which he must contrive somehow first to grasp and then to render.'"[24] This requires waiting on the lived practices of the community to show the meaning of doctrine, ritual, and scriptural text rather than imposing a theoretical method that distorts their character. Hence, religions can be understood as sets of shared linguistic and ritualistic practices that show the character of the absolute and the nature of human life. To understand a religion is not to understand a set of propositions. Rather, it is akin to learning a language. One becomes competent in the various ways in which words and actions are tied together in the various practices of religious adherents.

For example, appropriate distinctions between literal, figurative, and metaphorical applications of scripture can only be understood by means of their use in a community of believers.[25] In fact, Joseph Smith describes his own religious crisis as a problem of which criteria to apply to biblical interpretation.

> In the midst of this war of words and tumult of opinions, I often said to myself: What is to be done? Who of all these parties are right; or, are they all wrong together? If any one of them be right, which is it, and *how shall I know it*? . . . for the teachers of religion understood the same passages of scripture so differently as to destroy all confidence in settling the question by an appeal to the Bible.[26]

The direct appeal to the Bible, as we have seen from the history of Christianity, has not yielded consensus on the meaning of scripture. Martin Luther and other reformers were confident that a direct appeal was possible and could result in consensus, if not unanimity, under the direction of the Holy Spirit. However, one lesson of Christian history is that the guidance of the Holy Spirit was itself understood in divergent ways resulting in the variety of Christian communities we observe today. From the standpoint of an intratextual approach, without the practices of the community in relation to the text, one would not know where to begin in terms of determining the propositional status of the passages in question. Evangelical Christians appeal to, among other factors, a long tradition of established Christian practice as carrying authoritative weight in matters of biblical dispute while Latter-day Saints appeal to continuing revelation by means of recognized authorities. Both communities appeal to the witness of the Holy Spirit as confirming the legitimacy of the criteria in question. Where does one go from here? Wittgenstein states that:

> Where two principles really do meet which cannot be reconciled with one another, then each man declares the other a fool and a heretic. I said that I would 'combat' the other man,—but wouldn't I give him reasons?

> Certainly; but how far do they go? At the end of reasons comes persuasion. (Think what happens when missionaries convert natives.)[27]

It is not that religious communities are without recourse with regard to scriptural and theological interpretation, but, as with Joseph Smith, disputes are very likely to develop into disputes over *criteria* for establishing *how* to read scripture rather than over specific content.[28] The point is to illustrate that one must ultimately appeal to a communal practice for guidance and that appeal to the text *itself*, the world *in-itself*, or the historical *facts* is an exercise in futility.

Criticisms of Postliberal Theology

Nancy Murphy and James McClendon summarize the task of the postliberal theologian well:

> The question of truth arises in two ways in a cultural-linguistic approach. One is that of the consistency or coherence of each part of the system with the rest—first-order community practices and beliefs must be consistent with second-order theological and doctrinal statements and vice-versa. Such consistency measurements are intrasystematic or "intratextual." Second, one may raise a question about the "truth" of the religion itself, but this is better expressed as a question about the *adequacy* of the system as a whole to conform its adherents in the various dimensions of their existence to what is "Ultimately Real."[29]

This emphasis on internal coherence and meaning has led to vigorous debate regarding the merits of postliberal theology as the means of overcoming the conservative/liberal split that had come to dominate Christian theology. Since its introduction to the Christian community, postliberal theology has been accused of many things including antirealism, protectionism, relativism, fideism, and conservatism. Both first and second generation postliberal theologians have responded to these accusations differently and with varying degrees of effectiveness.[30] However, one very serious concern from both a theoretical and practical perspective is that postliberal theology isolates Christian beliefs such that they become cut off from broader intellectual and ethical discourse. The result is that Christian belief is forced into a conceptual ghetto where it is insulated from criticism. One example of this criticism is found in the work of David Tracy, who in his very influential book, *The Blessed Rage for Order*, argues that:

> [C]ontemporary Christian theology is best understood as philosophical reflection upon the meanings present in common human existence and the meanings present in the Christian tradition. . . . Therefore, Christians cannot appeal simply to the Bible or distinctively Christian experience or the Christian tradition; they have to show what they say at least addresses questions and makes some kind of sense in terms of experience all human beings share, and they have to be willing to submit the "cognitive claims" they make to investigation by the methods of philosophy. . . .[31]

For Tracy, postliberal theology does not meet these conditions and risks rendering theological voices irrelevant in public discourse on important intellectual and social issues. This charge of fideism has been leveled by others including James Gustafason, who maintains that "the practical theology of 'postliberal' Christianity has to do one of two things: either a) show the falsity or at least inadequacy of nonbiblical explanations and interpretations of events or b) become explicit about the relationships between biblical theological interpretations of the events to those which are not explicitly biblical."[32] William Placher, in his book *Unapologetic Theology*, responds to these charges by arguing that the appeal to common theoretical or experiential grounds may actually serve to distort the character of the beliefs in question.

> All that we ever have is the common ground that happens to exist among different particular traditions. If I am right, then *pretending* that some such contingent ground is in fact a provable universal standard of human morality [or absolute truth or human rationality] is a dangerous business:

> socially dangerous because it dismisses all those who do not share one set of cultural norms as primitives to be forcibly educated or lunatics to be locked up, and theologically dangerous because it turns into a form of idolatry in which these cultural standards become the norm according to which we judge our faith.[33]

Getting someone to see the world in a new way does not require the appeal to a common rationality or universally shared human experience. Rather, it is more like helping someone appreciate the rhythm in a song they could not pick up on their own, or recognize a pattern in a painting that was hidden from their view. There is an aesthetic quality to our understanding of the world that is often overlooked in the attempt to capture and understand the meaning and application of religious beliefs.[34] Placher states, "A Christian sees the universe as the creation of a loving God. A Buddhist sees a pattern of striving and suffering, to be escaped only by enlightenment. An atheist, perhaps, sees a different pattern. . . . For most observers, some features come to the foreground, and the whole patterns itself around them."[35] Within this approach, interreligious dialogue would consist of the sharing of "patterns" wherein absolute claims about the nature of the whole would certainly be proffered, but they would not be made by means of an appeal to a common theoretical method. Absolute truth is relocated *in* the pattern of phenomena.

For this reason, the rejection of metaphysical realism or epistemological foundationalism does not entail that religious believers cannot make absolute claims. The acknowledgment of the relativity of criteria does not end in the denial of religious truth. Rather, it takes away the false foundation upon which both religious beliefs and criticisms of religion have traditionally rested. It serves to give perspicuous representation to their function in the life of the religious community with no attempt to unify religious practices within a philosophical method. Utilizing Wittgenstein's later philosophy, postliberal theologians argue that the meaning of absolute truth claims can only be understood from within a particular form of life.[36] On this account, conversion from one religion to another is to appropriate a different form of life, a different way of looking at the world. It is the appropriation of the relations, distinctions, concerns, passions, commitments and attitudes befitting another way of living life. Sue Patterson summarizes the point well: "We read all truth-claims through the entire Christian form of life but not as requiring a justification from beyond that form of life, for there is no beyond in this world and whatever may await us eschatologically will also take place in Christ."[37]

Postliberal Theology and Mormon Studies

The attempt to develop a coherent doctrinal account that is adequate to its own categories is an important undertaking and one I would argue requires further exploration in Mormon studies. For this reason, the last section of this paper will consist of a brief examination of two approaches to LDS scholarship that share important features with the arguments presented above. An important aim of this section is to raise questions and explore some ramifications of other theoretical treatments of Mormon belief and practice. It is important to note that the intratextual theological method is not to be mistaken as an apologetic defense strategy. There are critical as well as apologetic implications for LDS doctrine that require more careful study.

Scriptural Interpretation

James Faulconer's essay, "Scripture as Incarnation," argues in favor of an approach that understands scripture as "an enactment of history rather than a representation of it."[38] He describes modernist approaches to history and scripture as maintaining that historical events and religious objects exist independently of their meanings as they are expressed in the language of the community. In this view, religious texts are judged according to their descriptive abilities with regard to the events or objects in question. Faulconer points out, however, that:

> If, as modernism suggests, the words that refer to God and divine things were mere signs, tools for thinking *about* or referring *to* something else, then for them to function as signs, we would also have to have direct access to the referent, to God, which is impossible. Merely referential signs require that what they refer to be available to the person who understands them.[39]

Furthermore, the analysis of a narrative in the interest of such a separation often results in an irreplaceable loss of religious meaning. In Faulconer's account, the meaning of scripture goes far beyond its referential function. Thus, it should not be read as a series of propositions about a chronology of discrete events. Rather, it is more like a poem in which the truth is *embodied* in the narrative such that the meaning of a story or the significance of events in relation to one another serves religious ends. In this account, the use of symbols in the practices of religious community is what it means to speak of religious truth. Faulconer states that " . . . to say that scripture or an ordinance is an incarnation is to say that in the material existence of these things—as scripture and ordinance rather than as abstracted to merely so-called objective qualities—we are given an orientation to the world: relations to things, meanings and values of things, the existence and non-existence of things."[40] The sacred is thus revealed in the symbolic ordering of scriptural narrative and other ritualized forms of religious discourse and practice. A critic may respond by asking "symbolic of what?" Doesn't the same argument used against words as mere signs apply to language as symbolic ordering? Must not there be a literal reality that allows one to see the symbols precisely as symbols? The idea of scripture as incarnation, however, is to problematize the literal/symbolic disjunction. "For premoderns, reading the story of Moses and Israel typologically, figurally, analogically, or allegorically is not what one does *instead of* or *in addition to* reading literally. Such readings are part and parcel of a literal reading."[41] The significance of the events as part of a sacred story is what gives them relevance precisely as scripture. Thus, by reassessing how we approach the text, we can presumably avoid the theoretical crisis involved in subjecting it to rational modes of discourse that do violence to depth, richness, and religious significance of the narratives we find there.

"Scripture as Incarnation" is a valuable contribution to the divide between the simplistic literalism and the dismissive naturalism that has come to characterize much of the work on Latter-day Saint scripture. Faulconer's work here and elsewhere represents a theoretical advance beyond most of the literature on these issues by raising challenging questions that deserve more careful attention. Nevertheless, I believe there are subtle weaknesses in his argument that point to even deeper issues as we strive to do justice to the meaning of the text. For example, in the latter part of his essay, Faulconer qualifies his position by pointing out that his approach

> . . . is not to deny that the scriptures tell about events that actually happened. They are about real people and real events. What I propose is not a way to reduce the premodern understanding of history to a modern view, to one that denies the historicity of scripture by taking scripture to refer to a transcendent, nonhistorical reality by means of only *seemingly* historical stories. Premodern interpreters of the Bible understand the scriptures to be about actual events. For them, what the scriptures say includes portrayal of and talk about real things. However, premodern interpreters do not think it sufficient (or possible) to portray the real events of real history without letting us see them in the light of that which gives them their significance-their reality, the enactment of which they are a part—as history, namely the symbolic ordering that they incarnate. Without that light, portrayals cannot be accurate.[42]

The major point of his argument is meant to show that one cannot separate "real events" from their significance as part of the symbolic ordering of the narrative in which they occur. This appeal to the real, as he indicates, is intended to defend against his view being confused with an account of scripture in which the narratives of scripture are reducible to moral archetyes or instructive myths. According to the latter approach, " . . . scriptures are not about historical truth, they are about religious truth, these people argue. Thus, according to them, though scripture takes the guise of history, it is actually about something else, such as a transcendent or archetypal reality."[43] While it is important for Faulconer to distinguish his approach from an archetypal account, it appears as if the way he is using the word "real" in the above quote has subtly slipped back into its modernist use that his whole argument was trying to avoid. In other words, the grammar of "actual" and "real" has shifted from *real only within a symbolic ordering narrative* to *real within a wider common sense use* that could be understood outside of the narrative. This can be seen by comparing the above quote to a point made earlier in the essay where he is arguing for the theoretical vacuousness of "bare events." Faulconer states in a footnote that " . . . reference is inherently unstable, not only in its inability to be explained by any theory of reference, but also over time. As the context of an event changes over time (and the event has temporal as well as momentary context) *so too does the event. . . .* "[44] If this is the case, then reference to "real events" and what "actually happened" has lost its theoretical purchase. An account in which reference is "inherently unstable" cannot talk about "real events" without reference to the particular way in which those events are taken up in some narrative or other as it is understood *at a particular time.* The ship has sailed as they say and there is no tether back to the "actual" or "real" that has any application outside of this unstable, temporally evolving symbolic understanding. Thus, the appeal to the historicity of scripture must be severely qualified in a way that renders problematic most LDS appeals to a commonsense conception of historicity as do several of the essays in the volume in which Faulconer's essay appears.[45] Hence, far from providing a philosophically sophisticated defense of their use of historicity, "Scripture as Incarnation" actually serves to undermine their attempts to offer the robustly realist account of the events reported in scripture. Although it provides an excellent critique of the methodological presuppositions of the modernist approach, it also serves, perhaps unwittingly, as a critique of the accounts presented in most LDS apologetic defenses of the historicity of scripture.

Historiography

In his essay, "Unfounded Claims and Impossible Expectations: A Critique of the New Mormon History," David Bohn calls into question the methodological approach of historians who believe (1) that the Mormon past consists of a series of facts or events that could be assembled in such a way so as to recreate the past "as it really was," and (2) that scholarly detachment is possible and desirable in the interest of faithful recreation of the Mormon past.[46] He describes the situation as follows: "The detachment or neutrality called for by apologists for the New Mormon History rests on the assumption of a certain transparency in understanding the past; it demands a presuppositionless or objective vantage point—one above passion and polemic—which, we are told, allows the reality of the past to reappear as it really was, uncolored or undistorted by personal longings and biases."[47] Utilizing the insights of hermeneutic thinkers such as Paul Ricoeur and Hans-Georg Gadamer, Bohn attempts to show that this kind of scholarly objectivity is impossible to achieve and is thus a misleading ideal for those who attempt to write history, religious or otherwise. Every historian, he asserts, brings to the data a set of biases, assumptions, methodological ideals, and scholarly conventions that necessarily affect the way in which the past is presented. This approach is based upon the idea that there is a necessarily interpretive aspect to human experience that shapes the way in which we understand ourselves, our environment, and our past. This interpretive "horizon" is informed by the structure of our language and the conventions of our culture. These "prejudices" are not barriers to understanding, so the argument goes, but are its necessary preconditions. Because there is no such thing as a state of being free from prejudices, to see them as barriers is to misunderstand how it is we come to understand anything at all. If this account is correct, then the idea of the neutral and objective vantage point from which to understand history is a chimera based upon a misleading picture of human knowledge. Bohn states, "Clearly, efforts of historians to ground their conceptual language objectively on claims to having discovered a universal methodology, underlying laws, core social structures, or essential human nature fail to own up to the historically situated conventions that make possible and necessarily prejudice their historical accounts."[48] The implication is that there is a necessary "emplotment"[49] that structures the historical narrative and gives it meaning according the values, ideals, and aims of the narrator. This situation applies to secular approaches to the Mormon past as well as those which acknowledge the reality of angels, visions, and prophetic gifts. Bohn accuses the new Mormon historians of an emplotment based upon naturalistic assumptions regarding human nature, the source of religious experience, and the influence of environmental factors on religious ideas and practices. For this reason, he characterizes this approach as "revisionist"[50] in that it does not provide an "authentic" account of the Mormon past as told by those who experienced it. Instead, secular theories serve to structure the story in ways that are repressive of, and hostile to, "language that is open to the sacred and sympathetic to belief."[51] For this reason, Bohn believes that, because traditional Mormon historians work within a horizon of belief that does not seek to hide their biases and commitments, theirs constitutes a more "honest and straightforward approach" that "seeks to authentically re-create our common past."[52] By using categories and causal relations internal to LDS belief and practice (i.e. those that are faithful to the experience and self-understanding of the Latter-day Saints), Bohn believes that traditional histories are more accurate and meaningful and ought to be free of many of criticisms brought to bear by the new Mormon historians.

There is certainly much to be valued in Bohn's approach. He calls our attention to the dangers involved when, as we saw above, alien forms of discourse and their methodological presuppositions are used to characterize a faith tradition with its own criteria of intelligibility that are mediated in the life of the community. Nevertheless, important broader questions remain regarding the implications of Bohn's account of Mormon studies. For example, if Bohn's appeal to universal hermeneutics is correct, and the use of external theories and categories in accounting for Mormon history does violence to the narrative, this has important implications for LDS scholarship in a variety of disciplines in that one may give pause regarding the value of the natural and social sciences, literary criticism, textual analysis, etc. to the extent they reflect on scripture, religious social practices, etc. In more pointed terms, Bohn's universal hermeneutic appears to destabilize the moorings upon which talk about cause and effect in history rests such that the application of his theory, if applied consistently, could serve to undermine other areas of LDS apologetics that utilize the methodological assumptions of secular scholarship in the service of, for example, demonstrating the historical plausibility of the Book of Mormon or the textual integrity of the Bible.[53]

In response to the apparent fideism implied in his arguments, Bohn qualifies his position in a way that raises crucial questions regarding the utilization of secular scholarship in Mormon studies more broadly. He argues that a strictly secular or "logocentric" view of rationality,

> would deny much of the richest scholarship found in the traditions of both East and West where rational discourse worked out its arguments from within a horizon of belief. It would deny rationality to the prophets of Israel and the Rabbinic tradition in their efforts to get clear on the meaning of the *Word*; to much of what constitutes the history of philosophy; indeed to our own Mormon tradition in which we are enjoined to seek wisdom through both Spirit and Reason.

> Clearly, Latter-day Saints understand rational discourse in a much broader way. They are willing to explore all modes of discourse, even those that are blind to spiritual things in order to get clear on their past; but they realize that all "worldly" ways of understanding work within limits and are thus insufficient.[54]

So it is clear that Bohn does not reject the appeal to reason altogether, but that it must operate within the constraints of spiritual categories such that "the plenitude of reason is obtained only in a space opened up by the Holy Spirit."[55] This is certainly consistent with the scriptural mantra that Latter-day Saints "should seek wisdom by study and also by faith." The particular way this has been taken up into the curriculum and discourse of Latter-day Saints is that the criterion for choosing between the two seems to be that when the findings of reason are inconsistent with, or otherwise call into question, the teachings of the scriptures and the prophets, they are to be rejected. Elder Dallin Oaks, in his book *The Lord's Way*, articulates this position well:

> Study and reason also have an important role in learning the things of God. Seekers begin by studying the word of God and the teachings of his servants and by trying to understand them by the techniques of reason. Reason can authenticate revelation and inspiration by measuring them against the threshold tests of edification, position, and consistency with gospel principles. But reason has no role in evaluating the content of revelation in order to accept or reject it according to some supposed standard of reasonableness. Revelation has the final word.[56]

However, if reason is trumped by revelation such that rational arguments and secular scholarship are valid only to the extent they are consistent with revelation, reason ends up serving *only* apologetic ends. The problem is this: Many accounts of Mormonism suffer from the difficulty of, on the one hand, using secular categories and methods to validate a particular interpretation of history, scripture, etc., while on the other hand, rejecting this same methodology to the extent that it yields conclusions at odds with this interpretation. This is not scholarship. In order for scholarship to maintain its integrity *as such*, the methods used must be applicable to all data under consideration and carry the same weight. Otherwise, this "scholarship" serves a purpose inconsistent with its own self-understanding and, hence, ceases to be scholarship. Scholarly methods cannot justifiably be applied in patchwork fashion that depends on what the outcome of the inquiry will be. As I have argued above, there certainly may be "internal standards"[57] by which data are selected, categorized, and assessed. However, the moment at which one appeals to an external theory or argument form reflecting on Mormon history, theology, or ritual, one must allow the theory or argument to be applied to *all* relevant data. By "relevant" is meant the set of data that would appropriately fall within that field of investigation as determined by the discipline.

One very important example is the debate regarding "environmental explanations" of human events. Robert Millet articulates the point well in his description of historical criticism of the New Testament:

> One obvious presupposition of this perspective is that an event or a movement is largely (if not completely) a product of its surroundings, the result of precipitating factors in the environment. Though it is certainly valuable to be able to look critically at the setting—for nothing takes shape in an intellectual or religious vacuum—and though it is true that many elements impinge upon a moment in history, we need not suppose a causal connection between any two factors in an environment. Simply because A precedes B, we need not conclude that A caused B; we need not be guilty of the logical fallacy of *post hoc ergo propter hoc.*[58]

As we have seen, this type of criticism is commonly employed in LDS scholarly circles as a way to preserve the religious integrity of a Latter-day Saint understanding of history and scripture against causal explanations for events that depend upon naturalistic methods of inquiry. However, this same "environmental argument" has been repeatedly employed in LDS scholarship to argue that Christian doctrine was co-opted by Greek philosophy such that it became theologically misguided.[59] The implication seems clear. Critical methods cannot only apply in one direction and maintain any *scholarly* respectability. One must employ a kind of theoretical "golden rule" in these cases: Apply only those critical methods to others you are willing to be subjected to yourself.

Conclusion

The implications of the above arguments importantly include the idea that Latter-day Saints are theoretically justified in speaking on their own terms without the need to provide philosophical or scientific foundations for their beliefs. However, the method for which I argue also necessitates critical assessment of the coherence of both LDS beliefs themselves and second-order accounts of these beliefs by theologians, historians, social scientists, and philosophers of religion. Obviously, much more can be said on these issues. My purpose in raising them is to set before the intratextual theologian selected methodological questions that require further examination in the interest of a coherent understanding of LDS belief and practice.

BRIAN BIRCH is Director of the Religious Studies Program and Associate Professor of Philosophy at Utah Valley State College. He received his Ph.D. from Claremont Graduate University and specializes in philosophy of religion and comparative theology. He is also the editor of *Element: The Journal of the Society for Mormon Philosophy and Theology.*

Notes

1. This paper is a greatly revised and expanded version of a presentation given at the first annual conference of the Society for Mormon Philosophy and Theology, March 2004 at Utah Valley State College.
2. See, for example, Louis Midgley, "No Middle Ground: The Debate over the Authenticity of the Book of Mormon" in *Historicity and the Latter-day Saint Scriptures* (Provo, Utah: Religious Studies Center, Brigham Young University, 2001); Louis Midgley, "Directions that Diverge: 'Jerusalem and Athens' Revisited" review of *The Ancient State: Rulers and the Ruled* by Hugh Nibley, ed. Donald W. Parry and Stephen D. Ricks (Salt Lake City: Deseret Book Company, 1991); and Stephen E. Robinson, *How Wide the Divide: A Mormon & an Evangelical in Conversation* (Downers Grove, IL: InterVarsity Press, 1997).
3. See Jean-Francois Lyotard, *The Postmodern Condition: A Report on Knowledge*, trans. Geoff Bennington and Brian Massumi (Minneapolis: University of Minnesota Press, 1984).
4. Hans W. Frei, *The Eclipse of Biblical Narrative: A Study in Eighteenth and Nineteenth Century Hermeneutics* (New Haven: Yale University Press, 1974); George A. Lindbeck, *The Nature of Doctrine: Religion and Theology in a Postliberal Age* (Philadelphia: Westminster Press, 1984).
5. As is the case with most academic labels, postliberal theology refers to a range of arguments with important common features having a relationship of family resemblance. There are important disputes within this scholarly

community that defy a tidy definition of the position. Hence, a statement of qualification is necessary in the interest of "truth in labeling" with regard to the arguments presented in this paper.

6. Roger E. Olsen, *The Story of Christian Theology: Twenty Centuries of Tradition and Reform* (Downers Grove, IL: InterVarsity Press, 1999), 539.
7. Gary Dorrien, "The Origins of Postliberalism," *The Christian Century*, July 4–11, 2001, 16–21.
8. Lindbeck, *The Nature of Doctrine*, 16.
9. Carl F. H. Henry, *God, Revelation, and Authority: God Who Speaks and Shows*, vol. 3 (Nashville: W Publishing Group, 1979), 486–87.
10. The conference was entitled "God, Humanity, and Revelation: Perspectives from Mormon Philosophy and History" and was organized by Kenneth West. The papers referenced here were delivered in a panel discussion entitled "The Future of Mormon Theological Studies."
11. R. Dennis Potter, "The Future of Mormon Philosophy," unpublished paper delivered at the "God, Humanity, and Revelation Conference" at Yale University, March, 2003, 2–3. Used with permission. See Rudolf Carnap, "Empiricism, Semantics, and Ontology" in *Meaning and Necessity: A Study in Semantics and Modal Logic*, 2nd edition (Chicago: University of Chicago Press, 1956).
12. Potter, "The Future of Mormon Philosophy," 6.
13. Paul Owen, "Can Mormon Theology Be Systematic?" Unpublished paper delivered at the "God, Humanity, and Revelation Conference" at Yale University, March, 2003, 3. Used with permission.
14. See D. Z. Phillips, "Religious Beliefs and Language-Games," in *Wittgenstein and Religion* (New York: St. Martin's Press, 1993).
15. Terence Penelhum, *God and Skepticism: A Study in Skepticism and Fideism* (Boston: D. Reidel Publishing Company, 1983), 151. Quoted in D. Z. Phillips, "Religious Beliefs and Language Games."
16. Peter Winch, "Understanding a Primitive Society," in *Religion and Understanding*, ed. D. Z. Phillips (New York: MacMillan Press, 1967), 13.
17. See, for example, the arguments of Wilfred Sellars in "The Structure of Knowledge," in *Action, Knowledge, and Reality: Critical Studies in Honor of Wilfred Sellars*, ed. Hector-Neri Castaneda (Indianapolis: Bobbs-Merrill

Co., 1975), and *Science, Perception, and Reality* (New York: Humanities Press, 1963); Charles Taylor, "Overcoming Epistemology," in *Philosophical Arguments* (Cambridge: Harvard University Press, 1995), and Rush Rhees, "Remarks on Reality and Religion," in *Rush Rhees on Religion and Philosophy*, ed. D. Z. Phillips (Cambridge: Cambridge University Press, 1997).

18. Hans-Georg Gadamer, *Truth and Method*, 2nd ed. rev., trans. Joel Weinsheimer and Donald G. Marshall (New York: Continuum Publising Co., 1994), 443, 452.
19. For example, William Alston and Alvin Plantinga offer exceptionally powerful arguments that serve to defend forms of philosophical realism. For more, see William Alston, *Perceiving God* (Ithaca: Cornell University Press, 1991); Alvin Platinga and Nicholas Wolterstorff, eds., *Faith and Rationality* (Notre Dame: University of Notre Dame Press, 1983); Alvin Plantiga, *Warranted Christian Belief* (New York: Oxford University Press, 2000). This work is the final installment in Plantinga's trilogy on warrant. See also Plantiga's *Warrant: The Current Debate* (New York: Oxford University Press, 1993) and *Warrant and Proper Function* (New York: Oxford University Press, 1993).
20. Lindbeck, *The Nature of Doctrine*, 78.
21. Ibid., 114.
22. In addition to the philosophy of Wittgenstein, the work of anthropologist Clifford Geertz plays an influential part in Lindbeck's thinking on these matters. See, for example, Clifford Geertz, "Religion as a Cultural System," in *The Interpretation of Cultures* (New York: Basic Books, 1977).
23. Lindbeck, *The Nature of Doctrine*, 118.
24. Ibid., 115.
25. Familiar examples abound. Latter-day Saints often interpret Acts 7:55–56, in which Stephen reports seeing Jesus standing on the right hand of God, as evidence of the literal separateness and spatiality of the two. Mainstream Christians, on the other hand, are likely to offer a more figurative reading of the passage on account of their reliance on a traditional understanding of God as articulated in the creeds and the relative weight of the passage in relation to others. However, certain passages in the Book of Mormon seem to

imply a more traditional trinitarian understanding of God. For example, Ether 3:14 reports God saying "I am the Father and the Son." And yet, Latter-day Saints believe, as noted above, that Jesus and God the Father are separate beings. Certain Latter-day Saints thinkers have responded to this and other similar passages such that the attribution of the term "Father" in these cases applies to Jesus Christ figuratively. This ascription, of course, is not clearly gleaned from the text itself and, to an outsider, could just as easily be interpreted literally as the above biblical passages were so interpreted.

26. Pearl of Great Price, Joseph Smith—History 1:10, 12.
27. Ludwig Wittgenstein, *On Certainty*, trans. and ed. A. J. Ayer (New York: Harper & Row Publishers, 1972), 611–12.
28. This discussion raises extremely interesting questions regarding (a) the justificatory relationship between religious experience and religious belief, and (b) the criteria for establishing doctrinal authority within the LDS community. I am currently working on both of these issues and plan to present on them in forthcoming papers. For the moment, however, I must acknowledge their relevance and avoid the temptation into further digression.
29. Nancy Murphy and J. William McClendon, "Distinguishing Modern and Postmodern Theologies," *Modern Theology* 5:3 (1989): 191–214, 206.
30. For example, Lindbeck's description of religions as "super-propositions" amounts to pushing the issue of correspondence one level higher and is thus theoretically inconsistent with his own valuable insights. See Lindbeck, *The Nature of Doctrine*, 63–69.
31. David Tracy, *The Blessed Rage for Order: The New Pluralism in Theology* (New York: Seabury Press, 1975), 34. Quoted in William Placher, *Unapologetic Theology: A Christian Voice in a Pluralistic Conversation* (Louisville: Westminster/John Knox Press, 1989), 155–56. It must be noted that Tracy's more recent writings offer more nuanced accounts of the "public character of theology," most notably in his distinction between fundamental and systematic theologies. See David Tracy, *The Analogical Imagination* (New York: Crossroad Publishing Co., 1986).
32. James M. Gustafason, "Just What is 'Postliberal Theology'?" *Christian Century*, March 24–31, 1999, 355.
33. Placher, *Unapologetic Theology*, 168.

34. For more on this issues, see Wittgenstein's discussion of aspect perception on Part II of the *Philosophical Investigations*, trans. G. E. M. Anscombe (New York: MacMillan Publishing Company), 1953; Stephen Mulhall, *On Being in the World: Wittgenstein and Heidegger on Seeing Aspects* (London: Routledge, 1993); and John Wisdom "Gods," in *Philosophy and Psychoanalysis* (Oxford: Basil Blackwell, 1953).
35. Placher, *Unapologetic Theology*, 124.
36. See Brian Birch, "The Limits of Pluralism and the Primacy of Practice: An Epistemological Inquiry into Religious Diversity," (Ph.D. diss., Claremont Graduate University, 1999), 272–74.
37. Sue Patterson, *Realist Christian Theology in a Postmodern Age* (Cambridge: Cambridge University Press, 1999), 38.
38. James Faulconer, "Scripture as Incarnation," in *Historicity and Latter-day Saint Scriptures*, ed. Paul Y. Hoskisson (Provo, Utah: Religious Studies Center, Brigham Young University, 2001), 30.
39. Ibid., 37.
40. Ibid. 41.
41. Ibid., 48.
42. Ibid., 44.
43. Ibid., 19.
44. Ibid., 52 ff. (italics added)
45. See, for example, Paul Hoskisson, "The Need for Historicity: Why Banishing God from History Removes Histortical Obligation," and Louis Midgley, "No Middle Ground: The Debate over the Authenticity of the Book of Mormon," in *Historicity and the Latter-day Saint Scriptures* (Provo, UT: Religious Studies Center, Brigham Young University, 2001).
46. David Bohn, "Unfounded Claims and Impossible Expectations: A Critique of the New Mormon History," in *Faithful History: Essays on Writing Mormon History* (Salt Lake City: Signature Books, 1992), 231. Other essays by Bohn dealing with the same subject matter include "No Higher Ground: Objective History is an Illusive Chimera," *Sunstone* 8 (May-June, 1983): 26–32; "The Burden of Proof," *Sunstone* 10 (June, 1985): 2-3; and "Our Own Agenda," in *Sunstone* 15 (June, 1990).
47. Ibid., 230.

48. Ibid., 233.
49. This term is coined by Paul Ricoeur to describe the process of configuring events in a story to give it intelligibility and meaning.
50. Bohn, "Unfounded Claims," 248.
51. Ibid., 253–54.
52. Ibid., 249.
53. This point is made by Malcolm Thorpe in "Some Reflections on New Mormon History," in *Faithful History: Essays on Writing Mormon History* (Salt Lake City: Signature Books, 1992). See pp. 271–4.
54. Bohn, "Unfounded Claims," 253.
55. Ibid.
56. Dallin H. Oaks, *The Lord's Way* (Salt Lake City: Deseret Book Company, 1991), 73.
57. See Bohn, "Our Own Agenda," *Sunstone* 15 (June, 1990), 47.
58. Robert L. Millet, "The Historical Jesus: A Latter-day Saint Perspective," in *Historicity and Latter-day Saint Scripture*, 176. op. cit.
59. See, for example, Craig L. Blomberg and Stephen E. Robinson, *How Wide the Divide? A Mormon & an Evangelical in Conversation* (Downers Grove, IL: InterVarsity Press, 1997); and James E. Talmage, *The Great Apostasy: Considered in Light of Scriptural and Secular History* (Salt Lake City: Deseret Book Co., 1968).

The Relation of Moral Obligation and God in LDS Thought

Blake T. Ostler

In his contribution to *The New Mormon Challenge*, Francis Beckwith argues that the LDS view of God(s) cannot explain the existence of objective moral obligation and that the "classical" view which he purports to defend can.[1] Beckwith is not alone in making this type of criticism of LDS thought. Richard and Joan Ostling assert:

> [Traditional Christianity] provides a theology of God being. Mormon theology has more in common with "process theology": it is a theology of becoming. One difficulty is in satisfactorily tying a theology of becoming to an ethic of moral absolutes. . . . [Mormonism] does not resolve the problem of how a philosophy of becoming can posit a moral philosophy of absolutes or normative ethics. . . . [I]f a finite God with limits who did not create the world out nothing—is off the hook on the question of being responsible for the existence of pain and evil, this leaves open another question: from where do we derive the principle of moral good? It is a difficult question if . . . Mormonism favors the principle of an absolutist or normative ethic. With a finite god, and a philosophy of progressive becoming, how does one introduce the idea of universals? How does one define moral goodness without the moral sovereignty of God?[2]

They are joined in this critique of LDS thought by Rex Sears. He argues that Kant's moral argument for the existence of God cannot be adopted in LDS thought because "Mormonism's God is a part of nature, rather than a causality underlying it, so whatever the merits of Kant's moral argument in other contexts, it does nothing for Mormon apology."[3]

Such arguments are based on meta-ethics and not ethics proper. That is, such arguments are based on the theoretical underpinning of moral obligation—"what is the source and explanation of the fact that we have objective moral obligations?"—and not on the practical ethical question: "what are we morally obligated to do?"

However, I believe that such judgments are fundamentally shortsighted with respect to the LDS view of the relation between ethics and God. The revelations of the Restoration point to a profound and thoroughly Christian view of ethical obligation that is not available to creedal Christians. In addition, I argue that creedal Christians cannot adopt the view that moral law is grounded in God's nature given the constraints of an adequate moral theory. I argue that Beckwith's position is *necessarily* false because he takes all moral laws to be logically necessary. Moreover, I argue that the moral law cannot be the result of a rational mind if it is grounded in God's nature. I also argue that if God is necessarily good, as the argument implies, then God is an amoral being in whom we cannot repose interpersonal trust. Finally, I argue that the view of God which Beckwith critiques is not necessarily the LDS position.

Beckwith's Argument

Beckwith begins his elucidation of the LDS view of God by observing:

> According to *a prominent stream* of LDS theology, God the Father is a resurrected, "exalted" man named Elohim, who was at one time not God. He was a mortal on another planet who, through obedience to the precepts of *his* God, eventually attained exaltation, or godhood, through "eternal progression."[4]

Beckwith contends that given this view of "God" it follows that: "the Mormon God is not the being in whom morality ultimately rests, for the moral law is something that he had to obey in order to achieve his divine status."[5] That is all that Beckwith needs for his argument against the LDS view, for he claims that, given this view, it follows that God is not the source of moral law but subject to it:

> Just as our wills, desires, and interests are independent of the existence of moral law, so are God's will and decrees [in the LDS view]. That is, if God's decrees and acts are good, they are only good because they are consistent with an unchanging moral law that exists apart from him. God's decrees are not good merely because they are God's. For God was himself once a man who, through obedience to certain eternal principles and laws, eventually became God.[6]

In contrast, he argues that there is a neat explanation for the existence of the Good and moral obligation in classical thought. He claims that God's commands are necessarily good and morally obligating because: "God's nature (or character) is such that it is eternally and perfectly good. That is, God's commands are good, not because God commands them, but because God is *good.* Thus, *God is not subject to a moral order outside of himself,* and neither are God's moral commands arbitrary. God's commands are issued by a perfect being who is the source of all goodness."[7]

Beckwith begins by observing that both Evangelicals and LDS are committed to the existence of objective moral absolutes: "the LDS Church teaches that there is an unchanging moral law that all humans are obligated to obey."[8] Beckwith then outlines five conditions of "moral laws" which he maintains must be met by any adequate moral theory. First, moral laws are capable of being known; otherwise, we would have to be moral skeptics about our ability to conform to the moral law. Second, moral laws are such that they are necessarily capable of taking a linguistic form of a command that conveys the content of the law "to another mind." Third, moral laws have an incumbency or "oughtness" about them that obliges us to act in conformance with them though we are free not to do so. Fourth, a moral law is capable of inducing feelings of guilt in us when we violate them—though we can resist that feeling. Fifth, moral laws are not physical in the sense that they are material or extended realities—they are purely ideal realities.

Beckwith then contends that the LDS view is incapable of giving an adequate account of moral obligation and laws. To make this argument, he suggests that the LDS view does not fit well with Platonism or the philosophy that there *are* simply ideal moral absolutes. His arguments at this point are not really against the LDS view but Platonism. He suggests that Platonism fails because it does not fit well with his list of requirements for moral theory. For example, Platonism fails to explain why violation of moral principles engenders guilt. He argues that Platonism must be false because we cannot owe any obligation to ideal absolute principles, for obligation arises only toward other persons. Finally, there is "no purposing agent or mind behind" such moral principles; but it seems to Beckwith that moral principles and laws are such that they must be the result of mind or purposing agent.

He also reviews the divine command theory (the view that an act is good or evil solely because God wills or commands it), a "Rawlsian" social contract theory (which bases moral obligation on voluntary and implied contracts among "ideal" persons in the social context of the society in which they reside), Aristotle's theory of final causes (which bases moral theory on the fulfillment of human nature) and a theory of moral properties emerging from physical realities (the view that moral obligation arises from the natural environment and supervenes in physical states of affairs analogous to the way that complex properties such as mind arise from biological complexity in the theory of evolution). He suggests that each of these theories is not a good fit with his set of criteria that any moral theory must meet—and that this ill-fit is especially true for LDS thought. He thus concludes (rather hastily) that Mormons cannot avail themselves of any explanation for the source of moral obligation and should therefore be rejected: "The above options seem to be the most viable alternatives to classic Christian theism that Mormonism could appeal to, but they all fail."[9]

Why Beckwith's Argument is Necessarily Unsound

In contrast to the LDS view, Beckwith contends that the classical view of God easily accounts for the existence of moral laws and obligation. Beckwith asserts:

> The moral law does depend on God, but not because God issues moral commands and is the all powerful Creator of the universe. Rather, it is because God's nature (or character) is such that it is eternally and perfectly good. That is, God's commands are good, not because God commands them, but because God is *good.* Thus, God is not subject to a moral order outside of himself, and neither are God's moral commands arbitray. God's commands are issued by a perfect being who is the source of *all* goodness.[10]

Beckwith maintains also that there is "an unchanging moral law that is true in every possible world . . . "[11] Of course, it follows that in Beckwith's view God must also exist in every possible world. Remember that a possible world is a maximally inclusive description of the ways things can possibly be. If God exists in every possible world, it means that, no matter how we conceive things, it is impossible to consistently think of any way the world could possibly be without including God. However, this latter proposition is dubious at best.

Thus, there is a very simple reason why Beckwith's position regarding the relationship between the "classical" God and moral law cannot be accepted. In Beckwith's view, moral laws and principles are metaphysically necessary in the sense that they obtain in every possible world. It is indeed impossible to imagine that there is some possible world where it is morally right to torture children just for fun. However, as I have shown in response to Parrish, the notion that God exists of logical necessity in the sense that God exists in every possible world is false.[12] God (as conceived classical tradition defended by Beckwith) does not exist in those possible worlds where there are vast amounts of unjustified evils. It follows that there are possible worlds where God does not exist but the moral laws still obtain in those possible worlds because they are necessary truths. Thus, it also follows that moral law cannot be dependent on God, or be included within God's nature, because they can exist even if God does not exist.

It seems to me that Beckwith, and others who locate necessary moral truths in God's nature, have simply substituted necessary truths about moral goodness with truths about God. However, necessary moral truths have a different logical status than God, and thus we run into an incoherent view. The view that moral goodness must be independent of God's existence in some sense is strongly supported by our moral intuitions. Consider the following conditionals:

P. If God did not exist, no one could be morally good or bad.

Q. If God were not loving and just, no one could be morally good or bad.

These conditionals seem obviously false to me.[13] Consider the proposition which Beckwith presents as an example of a truth which must be objective and obtain in every possible world: "It is morally objectionable to torture little babies." If God did not exist, would there be some possible world in which "it is not morally objectionable to torture little babies" is true? Hardly. In fact, it seems to me that the proposition: "It is morally wrong to torture little babies" is analytically true because what we mean by "torture" is "a morally wrong action."[14] An analytic truth is one that is known to be true by virtue of the meaning of the words used, such as: "this wife is married." By *wife* we mean a married woman, so saying that "a wife is married" is necessarily, though vacuously, true. In the same way, the assertion that "it is morally wrong to torture babies" is necessarily true. Now with the exception of Descartes, no theologians in the creedal tradition have maintained that logically necessary truths are created by God. Indeed, logically necessary truths are logically prior to God's existence and thus cannot depend on God.

Beckwith would undoubtedly counter that a possible world where there are sentient beings but where God does not exist is impossible because God exists of logical necessity and any world with sentient beings can only exist if God creates it (assuming that he agrees with Parrish). However, such a view requires us to alter the nature of logical space to assert that possible worlds where there are unjustified evils are not really possible. Such a view is a very large stretch of logic to make room for a logically necessary God. In any event, until we have some compelling argument to support such a revisionist system of logic, the assertion that God exists of logical necessity is dubious at best.

Are Moral Laws Logically Dependent on God's Nature?

Beckwith also attempts to save his view of God from two compelling objections. My objections to Beckwith's view are versions of Plato's *Euthyphro* dilemma. In its standard version, the dilemma is posed as follows: Is an act good because God commands it, or does God command it because it is good? To take the first horn of the dilemma is to adopt the view that moral laws are arbitrary. For God could then command us to kill innocent children just for the fun of it and that act would be our duty because it is good. On the other hand, if we assert that God commands an act because it is good, then we acknowledge that there are moral standards independent of God's command by which we judge the goodness of God's command. Beckwith wisely realizes that any divine command theory that bases moral principles on God's commands is inadequate:

> Like many classical Christians, I do not find the [divine command theory] (or its modified version defended by Adams) to be an adequate justification for moral law. But that does not mean that God is not the ground of the moral law. It simply means that it is not his commanding that gives the

> moral law its authority. . . . That is, God's commands are good, but not because God commands them, but because God is *good.*[15]

But does locating goodness in God's nature rather than his commands solve the problem? I stated two objections to this supposed solution. First, I argued that it makes God's commands arbitrary: "If God's nature is logically prior to God's will, then God is stuck with whatever his nature happens to dictate—and in this sense moral values are clearly arbitrary."[16] Beckwith responds by guessing: "What Ostler seems to be saying is that God's nature is a sort of impersonal, undirected force to which his will is subject." He goes on to conclude:

> Thus, if God commands, "Don't torture babies for fun," because he *wills it in every possible world* "torturing babies for fun is wrong," and that principle is the result of a good nature, then God's command is "arbitrary" because he has no control over the nature that apparently directs his will.[17]

First, note that Beckwith has shifted the grounding of moral goodness from God's nature to God's will. He answers my objection by asserting that moral laws are grounded in what God *wills* in all possible worlds. But isn't this response an abandonment of the very position he seeks to defend? After all, if moral laws are grounded in what God wills rather than in God's nature, we have a form of divine command theory which Beckwith expressly rejects as inadequate to explain the existence of moral laws.

Moreover, Beckwith attempts to answer my objection to *his* view by asserting that my objection "doesn't help the LDS worldview . . . [because in the LDS worldview] moral law does not have its source in a mind, nor is it under the direction of any being."[18] Hold on a minute. My point was that Beckwith's view is deficient. In defense, he then turns and asserts that somehow LDS doctrine holds that moral law is mind independent so it can't solve the problem either. But this won't do. Beckwith's response is simply the assertion that two wrongs make his view right. In fact, Beckwith is correct that

I reject his view (that moral goodness is a constituent of God's nature) because I accept (as does Beckwith) that the moral law arises only in the context of interpersonal relations among persons. If the moral law is located in God's nature, then it does not arise solely in the context of interpersonal relations. God's nature obtains prior to any interpersonal relations on Beckwith's view of God. I also accept Beckwith's suggestion that the moral law requires a personal mind to give it existence and content. Yet if the moral law is located in God's nature then it cannot be the result of a rational mind because God's nature is logically prior to any rational thought by God.

Beckwith can't respond to my argument against *his* view by saying that the *LDS view* can't respond to the criticism either. Because God's nature is logically prior to his will, it follows that the moral law is arbitrary in the sense that it arises from an impersonal universal that is neither the product of a mind nor arises in the context of interpersonal relations. It also follows that God has no say or control over the moral law at all because it is given in his existence in the same way that "humanness" is given in my nature. Thus, such "goodness" in Beckwith's view becomes merely a surd given that it is logically prior to God's will and mind.

This argument is doubly telling against Beckwith, *ad hominem*, because he explicitly argues that the moral law must be the product of a rational mind and arises only in the context of interpersonal relationships. Beckwith can't accept his own view given the criteria for moral laws that he has elucidated. God's nature is logically prior to God's decisions and mental acts. Thus, if the moral law is based on God's nature rather than his commands, then the moral law already obtains logically prior to anything God can do or think. God's nature is logically more basic than any of God's rational acts because, in Beckwith's view, God's rational acts must conform to God's prior nature. Therefore, the moral law cannot be the result of a personal mind given Beckwith's assumptions about God's nature, for the moral law is what it is prior to any thought or rational input on God's part.

Equally problematic for Beckwith is the fact that locating moral goodness in God's nature rather than God's commands only moves the *Euthyphro* problem back one step. What is it to have a nature? It is commonly thought that a person's nature is that set of properties which she possesses in every possible world in which she exists. If God is good by nature then he has properties of goodness in every possible world in which he exists. Thus in every possible world in which He is located, God has properties such as being perfectly benevolent, loving, kind, etc. But if we identify moral goodness with God's nature, as Beckwith does, then we must ask: Is God good because he has these properties, or are these properties good because they are God's? If God is good because he has these properties, then we imply that there is a standard apart from God by which we judge his goodness. That is, God isn't the ultimate standard of moral goodness; rather, the moral content of his properties is thus the standard of moral goodness. On the other hand, if properties such as being generous, loving, kind, etc., are good merely because God has them, then their content is not important; what is important is that they have a certain "owner" rather than a certain moral content. But then it seems that moral goodness is arbitrary and loses its meaning. Don't generosity, loving kindness, and faithfulness have moral value regardless of who has these properties? It seems to me that they do.

However, Beckwith further argues that the moral law is not arbitrary because moral values obtain in every possible world:

> But to paraphrase Ostler's critique of my view, if the moral law is logically prior to God's will, then God is stuck with whatever the moral law happens to dictate—and in this sense, moral values are clearly arbitrary. . . . But Ostler would clearly reject this. He would deny that an unchanging moral law *that is true in every possible world* is arbitrary. I would agree.[19]

I would indeed agree that a moral law that obtains in every possible world is not arbitrary because such a moral truth is *logically necessary*. But what has that got to do with locating moral law in

God's nature? What convinces me (and I propose Beckwith also) that truths like "it is morally wrong to torture babies for fun" are logically necessary is that such moral truths are true in virtue of the meaning of the words we use—not that they are constituents of God's nature. What we mean by "torture" is a morally wrong act. Thus, such moral truths are logically necessary in the same sense that "this bachelor is not married" is logically necessary. Indeed, as I argued above, the fact that such truths are logically necessary only shows that they cannot be dependent on God's nature. Such necessary moral truths obtain even in possible worlds in which God does not exist and therefore they cannot be dependent on God for their nature. Thus, Beckwith can respond to my arbitrariness objection only by impaling himself on the other horn of the *Euthyphro* dilemma—if the moral law is not arbitrary then there must be moral standards independent of God's nature. In this case, the moral standards are established by the meaning of the words used and not by God's nature.

Is God a *Morally* Perfect Being?

Beckwith also seeks to defend his view of God against the argument that if God is perfectly good by nature rather than by choice, then God is an amoral being. The argument is essentially that if God is perfectly good by nature, then he is not a moral agent because a being who must, of logical necessity, do what is good is not free to do what is wrong and therefore is not free in a morally significant sense. Now Beckwith admits that his God who is perfectly good by nature is in fact not a moral being in the sense that he is subject to moral obligation because: "God is necessarily good, and because to have a duty to do something implies that one has the ability *not* to do it, God, strictly speaking, does not have a duty to obey the moral law."[20] Note that Beckwith maintains that "God is good" even though it is impossible in his view that God be subject to any moral obligation. Thus, the type of goodness exemplified by God cannot be "moral goodness." It follows that we have a being that cannot be called "morally good" without a vicious equivocation; and yet this amoral being is supposed to be the source of all moral goodness. How can that be? God is not morally praiseworthy in Beckwith's view.

In response, Beckwith suggests that most people would find the view of a God who could go wrong much more difficult to swallow than the view that God is not morally praiseworthy. He argues that God need not have every great-making property; rather, he needs only the greatest set of properties that are compossible or jointly possible together. He admits that "no being can have both the ability to choose good and evil and necessarily always choose the good. . . . Thus, these are not compossible properties."[21] Given the choice between moral freedom and perfect goodness, Beckwith argues that we should give up moral goodness. He quotes Katherine Rogers who observes that if God's "choices simply flow from his character and disposition, if there is something that forecloses evil as a really viable option, how is there choice and hence morally significant freedom involved? If it is possible for God to be tempted by evil and choose against His character, then it is not unthinkable that He would do so."[22] The point seems to be that if God really could do evil, then such a thought is very discomforting because we must admit the real possibility that he will do evil.

I agree that if God is free in a morally significant sense then it cannot be logically impossible that God would do evil; what I deny is that the logical possibility of God's doing something evil is a reason for failing to trust or have faith in God. Indeed, I claim something profoundly more important and significant for religious faith: In the absence of genuine ability to go wrong, we cannot genuinely trust or have faith in God in any significant sense.

The Hebrew *emunah* is translated as both "faithful" and "trust," but its essential sense is interpersonal in nature. It is the type of trust that means a person is faithful to his or her word, or faithful to his or her spouse. In fact, it is the way that God is faithful to his covenant.[23] This type of interpersonal trust is essentially such that it presupposes that the person who is trusted has the ability to refrain from doing as trusted. Suppose that we are in a room together and you have a gun in a safe in that room. You know that I don't know the combination and I'm not strong enough to rip the safe open. In this situation, would it make any sense to say that you trust me not to get the gun and shoot you with it? Or that you morally commend me for not getting the gun and shooting you? Hardly. A part of the meaning of the word "trust" is the ability of the trusted person to act contrary to the trust.

The notion that God is good by nature entails that we cannot truly trust him. A nature is not a person, nor can a nature enter into interpersonal relationships. Nor can we praise and express gratitude to God for doing what is good in this view because he simply can't do otherwise. Could I trust my wife to be faithful to me if it were impossible for her to be unfaithful? Suppose that she were in a vegetative state, or suppose that she has a mental disorder that caused her to remain faithful to me no matter what. In these latter cases, could my surety that she will remain faithful to me be called "faith" or "trust" in any sense? Would the outcome be any different if, for some reason, she were incapable of being unfaithful to me because of the makeup of her nature? Say that she were, by nature, an immaterial spirit incapable of engaging in unfaithful conduct. Could we call it trust when I am sure that she won't engage in unfaithful conduct? Surely not. Epistemic warrant or certitude is not the same thing as trust. I may be certain that an immaterial spirit is such that, by nature, it will not engage in certain acts that require a body to perform. But my certitude that this immaterial spirit won't engage in such acts isn't based on trust; it's based on logical meanings and usage.

It also follows from the fact that trust presupposes the ability to refrain from doing as trusted—that trust is essentially interpersonal in nature. Trust can arise only in a relationship where the other is a Thou—a person whom we encounter in reciprocal and mutual trust. We cannot trust a rock to abide by the law of gravity even though, necessarily, it will do so. We cannot trust a machine, the weather, or a law of nature. We may depend or rely upon them; but we cannot repose our trust in them. Nor can we trust logical necessities. We can only trust persons when we repose faith in them to do as they say they will. Moreover, we cannot trust a person if we know that she is not good for her word. Trust arises only in the context of interpersonal faith in the trusted person.

Trust is the essential act that we must engage in as the necessary starting point of every truly interpersonal relationship. Trust is essentially an act of commitment and openness to the other. I trust my wife to remain faithful to me even though it is logically possible that she will not be. If I knew or suspected that she would break her word of faithfulness to me, then I really don't trust because of this suspicion. But I trust that she will be. However, it is no less trust simply because it is possible that she won't be faithful—in fact, it is trust only because it is possible for her to be unfaithful. What is wonderful in our relationship is that she is free to choose out of it at any time but she freely chooses to love and remain faithful. Such freely given love is more valuable to me than any love that would be impossible for her to refrain from giving. It means that her love for me is a choice, an expression of who she is and what she chooses to give.

I propose that such examples show that we trust persons, but we cannot trust natures or logical necessities. In fact, my greatest concern about the so-called classical God presented by Beckwith is that such a being is sub-personal. My concern about "faith" in such a being is that it is not "faith" at all unless guaranteed by logical necessity—and what faith is needed when it is guaranteed by logical necessity? I suggest that those who believe in the classical God do not repose trust *in Him*; rather, they repose their trust in logical necessities and semantic guarantees.[24] They say, in effect, "I trust God only so long as I can know of logical necessity that he will always act in conformance with his logically perfect nature"—which is to say that they don't trust *him* at all. Their faith is in logic and necessity rather than God.

There is therefore a very important reason why a Christian cannot give up the view that God is a morally free being. The importance of God's ability to violate our trust, even though we trust that he won't, is essential to our ability to trust and have faith in God. In addition, it is of surpassing importance to see that such moral freedom is also essential to God's ability to love. Both trust and love are a gift that is freely given—the gift of one's self to the beloved. When we open up to trust another we necessarily speak to a Thou, and in the act of trusting we speak with our entire being: Thou art *worthy* of trust. In trusting another we give ourselves to them in the sense that our well-being is tied up with their faithfulness to us. Thus, to trust another is to make a free choice to be vulnerable in relation to the trusted Thou. We stand in a vulnerable relation to a trusted Thou because we give ourselves freely when we are not compelled to do so. Moreover, the trust we repose in the other makes us vulnerable because in a sense we have placed ourselves at the mercy of that person to do what we trust is best - knowing that it is possible that it will not be so. Trust is a very valuable gift to give to another. As Ted Gulesserian stated: "Trust is a highly precious and significant gift of love....Can love be given without being freely given? If it can, I think that we can all recognize that such love would not have *nearly* the intrinsic value of love that is freely given."[25]

Thus, I suggest that faith in logical necessities and a perfectly good nature, rather than trust in the Holy Thou who is a morally perfect person, is a shallow faith. We can trust God because we know of his moral excellence. Moreover, we trust that God, as a perfectly rational being, will not do any act inconsistent with his perfect knowledge. We can be perfectly confident that God will not do anything wrong out of sheer stupidity as we mortals so often do. We can rest assured that God will not do something wrong out of lack of consciousness. We can be sure that God will not do anything wrong because of weakness of will or because of bodily urges that are difficult for him to control. Thus, he will never violate a moral law out of stupidity or failure to be conscious of the best for us. Moreover, our trust in God arises from a knowing that surpasses mere excellence in logic, but involves our entire being in the most profound interpersonal sense possible—his light and truth shine in our hearts at our very core. If we can ever truly trust God, then we must know him in the intimacy of our hearts where he dwells in us. We know of his love because it is made manifest to us at the core of our being. It is logically possible that such a being could do something wrong; but in the presence of his love, trust in him is the only meaningful response. While it is logically possible that God could perform a morally wrong act, it is not a practical concern that we can have in relation to God if we know him. Merely knowing *about* him—merely knowing about the logical qualities of his nature—will never suffice for the demands of religious faith.

An Overview of an LDS Theory of Ethics In Alignment with the Gospel of Christ

I want to outline a "pre-theory" of moral obligation in LDS thought, for the Restoration has the resources to provide a profound basis for a Christian ethic. The starting point for an LDS ethic is the realization that whatever we are essentially is uncreated. Our eternal nature defines our inherent capacities. The next step is the recognition that the purpose of life is to advance and learn so that we can enjoy "eternal life," or the very kind of life that God lives. As Joseph Smith stated:

> The relationship we have with God places us in a situation to advance in knowledge. He has power to institute laws to instruct the weaker intelligences that they may be exalted with himself, so that they might have one glory upon another, and all that knowledge, power, glory and intelligence which is requisite in order to save them in the world of spirits.[26]

The most natural view of ethics in LDS thought, it seems to me, is one that grounds moral obligation in the eternal nature of uncreated realities and our inherent capacities for progression and growth to realize our divine nature. Moral laws define the conditions that are necessary for the growth and progress of intelligences to partake of the divine nature to be pure as God is pure (See 2 Peter 1:4). Thus, the most basic moral law is that each person ought to act so that each shall have the best life possible within the constraints posed by eternal conditions necessary for mutual self-realization. Moral laws are grounded in our eternal divine nature, for the good is whatever leads to realization of our humanity in a fulness of divinity. However, because the realization of our nature is to be divine, the good is also defined by the nature of God. Indeed, only by being as God is can we become fully human. As Truman Madsen noted:

> Now, Joseph Smith taught that absolutes derive from the ultimate constitution of two things: the self (including the divine self), and the cosmos. The permanent, undeviating aspects of these provide the foundation. . . . What then is absolutely good [in LDS thought]? A godlike condition of existence—the fulfillment of destiny.
>
> At this point the Prophet is close to the views of stoics, aristotelians, and thomists, viz., in maintaining that all men have an "essence" or "nature" or potential, and that "good" consists in the fulfillment, and "bad" in its frustration. There is also similarity to self-realization theories such as in Bradley and Green. But the "perfection" Joseph Smith envisioned is superlative. It is literally godlike.[27]

We must next ask what laws define the conditions of mutual self-realization that we must abide to partake of the divine nature? The answer is that there is one eternal law that defines this possibility: the law of love. God, as a unity of divine persons, is love. The Father, the Son and the Holy Ghost share an interpersonal relationship of indwelling unity and, in virtue of this relationship, they are one God. They share a relationship of interpenetrating love where they live their lives "in" each other because of the type of love they share. Because the divine persons are divine by virtue of their love one for another, it follows that "God is love" in a literal sense.

However, this divine "nature" is one that is freely chosen to the extent it arises from loving relationships. The Godhead would cease to be God if the divine persons ceased to love. Thus, *theosis* is necessarily a *mutual* self-realization of divine potential, for divinity is a mutually and perfectly loving relationship.

The Father, the Son, and the Holy Ghost share the attributes of godliness because they have the relationship of divine love. Their love is a free choice to be in such a relationship, for love by its very nature is freely chosen. Thus, this view of ethics is possible only if the divine persons are in fact distinct in the sense that they are separate, individual personalities each having a distinct mind and will. The type of love we are discussing is a freely chosen love that expresses the personality of the lover for the beloved. We have been invited to share this divine relationship and thereby to be glorified. (See John 17 and 3 Nephi 27.) Thus, by learning to love one another, we learn to be as God is. The purpose of life is to learn—and it is to learn one thing in particular—to love one another. As we progress in knowledge, as we learn to love, we reflect the image and likeness of divinity in our countenances. The purpose of the moral law is to challenge us to so act that we love others as we love ourselves.

Thus, good and evil can be defined solely in terms of the law of love. Love itself is intrinsically valuable, for love is the fullest expression of who we are in relationship with one another. In terms of this ethic, good is whatever leads to greater love and unity in interpersonal relationships. Good acts are acts that arise out of and express our love—and our expressions of love are revelations of who and what we really are in our eternal being. A good act is one that leads to healing a broken relationship or growing in intimacy and meaning in existing relationships. I would add that those choices and acts which lead to personal growth are the same as those acts which lead to interpersonal growth. Personal growth entails an increased capacity to love and to be loved. Such personal and interpersonal growth are also intrinsically valuable as ends in themselves. However, there is a byproduct of love that also makes love worth pursuing for its own sake—happiness.

In contrast, an evil act is whatever injures or destroys a relationship—or alienation. The relationships at issue can be broader than relationships between persons, for it is evil to torture animals just as it is to torture humans. It is evil to destroy the environment. The relationships at issue thus include the broadest array of relationships, the relation we have with each other, the relation I have with animals, with the earth and with myself. An evil act is one that injures relationships or which leads to alienation or separation. The alienation, destruction, and separation that result from acts injurious to relationships make us miserable. These terms seem to me to capture the views of good and evil described in scripture much better than the metaphysical view that the Good is God's nature.

Paradoxically there is only one way to realize our nature, only one path to actualize our potential to be as God is—that is to *be* as God is. How can that be, that to realize our potential to be as God we must be already as God is? By being loving, for that is how God is. Thus, the love command is the clearest expression that God's purpose for us is *theosis*, to give us commandments to guide us to be what He is. The fact that love is commanded is also a clear recognition that our true nature is divine and that *theosis* is the fullest realization of human potential. Indeed, the love command is a recognition that God seeks the best life possible for us, and to provide that life to us He must work within the constraints necessary for interpersonal growth and self-realization. The love command points to the deep truth that the best possible life is mutual self-realization made possible only in loving relationship. The "laws of ethics" are the conditions and constraints necessary for beings having our eternal nature to realize that reality. The law of love defines the means of obtaining the best life possible within the constraints of mutual self-realization. However, it is of paramount importance to see that the best life possible, the fullness of self-realization, is achieved only through loving relationships with the people in our lives. Moreover, for love to be genuine, our entire end in acting for others cannot be merely our own self-realization, our own happiness alone, but must include love for our neighbor as its ultimate purpose, for anything less is not truly love. Thus, love is not only the means of achieving the best life possible, it is also the only possible end that allows its achievement. In other words, we must act out of love for others as an end in itself; otherwise, the moral ideal of the best life possible within the constraints of mutual self-realization is impossible.

All of the commandments are given to us by God to teach us how to love one another, for all commandments are summed up in the great command to love God with all of our heart, might, mind and strength and to love our neighbor as we love ourselves. Now God's purpose in giving us the commandments is also to lead us to exalted happiness and joy unalloyed. God has given us the law of love to guide us to happiness. Now this law is one that obtains independently of God, for God is divine by virtue of the fact that he is love; he is not love by virtue of the fact that he is God. Not even God can make it so that hate and alienation lead to human happiness. We are so constituted that by our very eternal nature we are fulfilled and find our greatest joy in committed, meaningful, and eternal relationships of love one for another. We realize our inherent divinity by eternal, loving relationships. Neither can God bestow salvation on us without our abiding by the law of love, for not even God can force us to love if we choose not to. Love cannot be coerced or forced or manipulated—it must be freely chosen as a choice of the heart. If we love God, then we keep his commandments because we trust that what he has commanded us to do leads to joy, happiness, eternal life in the presence of God and eternal increase. We keep his commandments because we respond to his love for us.

Ultimately, it is only through the healing love of the atonement that any moral act is possible, for without the atonement we would be incapable of any morally good act. That is, without the atonement we would be slaves to our past and unable to break free of the barriers and walls we create. The atonement is what allows us to let go of the past, to break down the walls that imprison us, and to be free to love.

Now this law of love cannot be formulated easily, for it is known only through the spirit rather than the letter of the law. Yet this law is near to us, for it is written in our hearts precisely because it is an expression of who and what we are eternally. We know the moral law of love because it is a part of us. To the extent that it can be defined, this law can be formulated simply as the practical law of the harvest: what we give, we receive—what we sow, we reap—what we send out returns to us. Therefore, do unto others as you would have them do unto you, for as we judge others we shall be judged. This is the eternal law decreed by God before the world was and by which we shall be judged. The judgment simply declares the natural consequences that necessarily follow from the law of love: The love that we give shall be returned to us and the love that we fail to give shall be withheld from us. We cannot have the joy and happiness that naturally arise from loving relationships if we choose not to love. God cannot save us if we do not freely choose to give our love and to receive his love. Love is expressed by giving ourselves to the beloved, and receiving the beloved into our lives without condition.

The law of love is objective and universal in two senses. First, the force and effect of the law of love cannot be escaped. The results of failing to live the law of love follow naturally. If we refuse to open up and love, there is no power in the universe that can give us the joy that is known only in intimate, loving relationships. In this sense, the law of love is not a law instituted by God, although it is a law expressive of who and what God is. We cannot enjoy loving and intimate relationships if we choose not to love—it is that simple. On the other hand, living the law of love as one's entire way of being in the world inexorably results in the happiness and joy that can come only from being in intimate and loving relationships. The law of love is universal also in another sense: it is the same for everyone though its expression is as individual and unique as each of us is. The law of love is "objective" in the sense that we cannot choose to define love as something other than what it is, although we can choose whether and how we will express our love.

There are eternal moral principles which condition even God, and these principles are found in the constraints inherent in intelligences to mutual self-realization as divine persons. These eternal principles are based on the very nature of godliness or divine love. Thus, an outline of moral theory in LDS thought ties together the moral intuitions that underlie several ethical theories. Like Aristotelian and Thomist theories, the good is defined in terms of what fulfills our human nature to the extent such fulfillment leads to mutual self-realization. Like utilitarian theories, the good is what leads to the greatest happiness and joy. Like Kant's theory moral obligation is a duty that arises out of our nature as rational agents. Like social contract theories, the good is not something imposed on us by another but something to which we mutually agree, for the choice to love is certainly an autonomous choice that expresses our deepest being. Like Platonic theory, the law of love is not open to a point of view or merely a subjective judgment, for there truly is conduct that is not loving no matter how we judge it.

How well does this cursory outline of an ethic of love in the LDS tradition line up with Beckwith's list of requirements for moral theory? First, the law of love is capable of being known because it is written in our hearts. It is known through revelation in the form of commandments when our hearts are too hard to get it. It can be stated in the form of commands or imperatives of the type we find in the Bible and other scriptures—indeed, that is precisely where it is given as a command! The law of love has an incumbency or "oughtness" because when we violate it we betray who we are at the deepest level of our being. We feel the incumbency because when we violate the law of love we act against ourselves and everyone else by damning them and us in our eternal progression. We know that violating the law of love is a foolish choice to be miserable rather than to experience happiness and joy—and it is utter stupidity of the silliest sort to choose misery when we could choose joy. Thus, the law of love explains why we appropriately feel guilt—we know that we have betrayed ourselves, God, and our neighbor. We know that we are choosing against our real interest because we know that what we really want, above anything in the world, is to love and to be loved. The law of love arises only in the context of interpersonal relationships. In fact, it defines the nature of our interpersonal relationships. Finally, the law of love is not "material," for a relationship cannot be reduced either to me or to you; it arises in between us. However, such a view is fully consonant with LDS commitments because it follows that love must supervene on persons, and all persons are material. Thus, this view of ethics more than satisfies Beckwith's list of desiderata for a moral theory. In fact, it fulfills these requirements far better than his own theory that the Good is grounded in God's necessarily good nature.

BLAKE T. OSTLER earned his Juris Doctorate at the University of Utah. He has published widely in philosophical journals such as *Religious Studies* and *International Journal for Philosophy of Religion*, as well as journals dedicated to Latter-day Saint interests. He is the author of the four volume series (two of which have been published to date) *Exploring Mormon Thought.*

Notes

1. Francis Beckwith, "Moral Law, the Mormon Universe, and the Nature of the Right We Ought to Choose," *The New Mormon Challenge*, eds. Francis Beckwith, Carl Mosser, Paul Owen (Grand Rapids: Zondervan, 2002), 219–41.
2. Richard N. Ostling and Joan K. Ostling, Mormon America: The Power and the Promise (New York: HarperSan Francisco, 1999), 301–02.
3. Rex Sears, "Philosophical Christian Apology Meets 'Rational' Mormon Theology," *Dialogue: a Journal of Mormon Thought* 33:3 (Fall 2000), 78.
4. Beckwith, "Moral Law," 222. Italics added.
5. Ibid., 232.
6. Ibid., 226.
7. Ibid., 232.
8. Ibid., 226.
9. Ibid., 239.
10. Ibid., 232.
11. Ibid., 234.
12. See my response to Robert Parrish, "Necessarily, God Does not Necessarily Exist," *forthcoming.*
13. I derive these conditionals from Wes Morriston, "Must there be a Standard of Moral Goodness Apart from God?" *Philosophia Christi* 3:1, (2001):127–138.
14. See T. J. Mawson, "God's Creation of Morality," *Religious Studies* 38 (2002): 1-25.

15. Beckwith, "Moral Law," 232.
16. Blake T. Ostler, "Review of The Mormon Concept of God: A Philosophical Analysis by Francis Beckwith and Stephen Parrish," *FARMS Review of Books*, 8/2 (1996), 125.
17. Beckwith, "Moral Law," 233.
18. Ibid.
19. Ibid., 234.
20. Ibid., 235.
21. Ibid., 236.
22. Katherin A. Rogers, *Perfect Being Theology* (Edinburgh: Edinburgh University Press, 2000), 123. Quoted in Beckwith, "Moral Law," 234–5.
23. Robert Girdlestone, *Synonyms of the Old Testament* (Grand Rapids: Eerdmans, 1897), 102–03; See, Dt. 32:4; Ps. 33:4; 98:3; 100:5; 119:30.
24. Evangelical theology in its entirety is shot through by a lack of trust, all the way from the assurance of the elect and of guaranteed salvation by grace alone to guaranteed goodness by logic alone. This same lack of trust in God as a person is demonstrated when Evangelicals refuse to pray and get a response from God because they don't trust their relationship with God enough to trust him when he speaks to them; rather, they repose trust in biblical and philosophical scholars and their own ability to interpret dead prophets.
25. Ted Guleserian, "Can God Be Trusted?" *Philosophical Studies* 106 (2001), 301–02.
26. Joseph Smith, *Teachings of the Prophet Joseph Smith*, ed. Joseph Fielding Smith (Salt Lake City: Deseret Book Co., 1977), 181.
27. Truman G. Madsen, "Joseph Smith and the Problems of Ethics," in *Perspectives in Mormon Ethics: Personal, Social, Legal and Medical*, ed. Donald G. Hill (Salt Lake City: Publishers Press, 1983), 33.

Theology in the One-Room Schoolhouse[1]

Benjamin Huff
Randolph-Macon College

It is natural for me to think about my religious beliefs systematically. Yet many Latter-day Saints have doubts about whether it is appropriate to take a systematic approach to theology. They see this approach as prone to certain serious problems. In particular, critics suggest that systematic theology seems inherently closed to continuing revelation, that it involves an overly intellectualized notion of faith, and neglects the plurality of meanings to be found in scripture. I believe these are real problems where they occur, but not problems with the systematic approach itself. Rather, they stem from presuppositions and attitudes that are sometimes associated with the systematic method. In this paper I sketch what I have in mind as a systematic approach to theology and explain these alleged problems with it. I explain what I see as the real sources of these problems, and then describe a context of presuppositions and attitudes, expectations and goals in which I argue systematic theology can be appropriate for Latter-day Saints. I compare the church to a one-room schoolhouse.

Theology and the Systematic Method

By theology I mean a disciplined study of God and his teachings. This study is an ongoing activity, an activity that one should not expect to reach an end in this life. For now, we see darkly, as through a glass. Still, diligent study will pay rich dividends and yield a real increase of knowledge. The term "theology" can also refer to a particular account of God. While the study of God will involve considering and producing accounts of God, writings, talks, and conversations about God, I regard any particular account of God as subordinate to the larger activity of striving to know God. It is a primary goal of this paper to clarify how I believe particular theological accounts should fit into the activity of theology within the LDS community.[2]

One way to approach theology is to approach it systematically. A theological system aspires to be a comprehensive and consistent account of God and our relationship to him. To approach theology systematically is to approach it with the goal of building a theological system—to aspire to include all major points of faith in a single, cohesive account; showing how they fit together, how they are logically related, with some of them serving to explain or clarify others. Ideally, when we see our beliefs as parts of a coherent system we understand them better.

In some ways an LDS understanding of faith and spiritual knowledge seems amenable to a systematic approach to theology. Brigham Young said that the plan of salvation "takes from the right and the left, and brings all truth together into one system."[3] We believe that truth harmonizes with truth,[4] that when the revelations given to one nation are brought together with those given to another, that the two will agree, and confirm each other[5] and further, they will illuminate each other. We believe that by reading the Book of Mormon together with the Bible, we will understand both better.

Indeed, it seems that often we stand to gain a great deal by taking a systematic approach to learning from the scriptures, reading the many texts we have to build a fuller account than any one passage provides. As an illustration, I will consider some scriptures on the judgment of the wicked after the resurrection.

In the book of Matthew, Christ says that at the last day he will say to the wicked, "Depart, into everlasting fire." The book of Revelation mentions fire in a similar way, but without much explanation (e.g. Rev. 19:20, 20:14-15). What are we to understand by this fire? It seems hard to avoid the idea that this fire is intended to have an effect on our motives, to reduce our desire to sin and strengthen our desire to be righteous. It also indicates something about what God's justice is like. Surely it is worth some effort to understand it.

In Matthew, the fire appears to be a punishment for the wicked. Mosiah 2:38 refers in similar language to "an unquenchable fire, whose flame" ascends "up for ever and ever." Yet here, fire is a simile used to characterize the torment of the wicked, not the cause of that torment. We are told in 2 Nephi 9 that in the resurrection we will not only receive perfect bodies, but also a perfect knowledge of our righteousness or our wickedness, and that we will be ashamed if we have not repented. Likewise in Mosiah 3:28 we learn that the demands of divine justice will awaken in us a sense of guilt and shame that is like an unquenchable fire. Mormon tells us the wicked would be more miserable to stay in the presence of God than to be among the damned, and so the wicked shrink from the presence of God.

So it appears that the fire mentioned in Matthew and Revelation, which torments the wicked, is a keen sense of shame that arises from a perfect knowledge of one's guilt in the presence of God, who is perfectly righteous. This is a shame that leads the unrepentant to depart, or at least wish to depart, of their own accord, though the shame apparently is only diminished, not extinguished, by leaving God's presence. God gives this perfect knowledge, and the chance to stand in his presence, to both the righteous and the wicked, but the righteous feel it as a blessing while the wicked feel it as a curse. This pattern of judgment fits beautifully with Christ's teaching that God sends rain upon the just and the unjust alike, and stands in contrast to a common conception of divine judgment as consisting in righteous vengeance. By reading these passages together, assembling a more complete account, we see a much fuller picture than by reading them one by one. Not only does understanding accumulate by bringing together more passages; the full meaning of some passages becomes clear only in light of others. Clearly we stand to gain by drawing together the insights offered by the writings of all the prophets. A systematic approach to theology aims to do just that: draw all that we know from revelation into a single, unified account.[6]

Objections to the Systematic Approach

Despite its attractions, some aspects of a systematic approach to theology may seem to fit badly with a proper approach to faith. I will consider three problems in particular that have been associated with systematic theology.

I. Rejection of continuing revelation

Latter-day Saints believe that many important religious truths are yet to be revealed. Yet historically, Christians doing systematic theology have typically believed that God's work of revelation was complete long ago, in the New Testament period. A similar idea accompanies essentially all well-known examples of systematic theology; hence one might think they are inseparable from it. However, the belief that revelation is complete is hardly unique to systematic theologians. Rather, all major Christian groups before the establishment of the Church of Jesus Christ of Latter-day Saints have rejected continuing revelation. I suggest that the idea that revelation had ceased is a presupposition they held independent of any practice of systematic theology, and hence our association of the two is mostly based on a mere historical coincidence. Since we do not share their presupposition, we are quite free to do systematic theology while remaining open and even looking forward to continuing revelation.

Setting history aside, however, there is another reason Latter-day Saints might suspect that systematic theology is inherently closed to continuing revelation. This is its aspiration to compose a complete account of revealed truth. So long as important truths remain unrevealed, the goal of constructing a complete theological system is unachievable. On the other hand, to say one's system is complete would be to claim that everything important *has* already been revealed, and therefore to close oneself off to further revelation. It is important to acknowledge this fact.

However, the *aspiration* to a complete and coherent understanding of God and our relationship to Him is quite a separate matter from a *declaration* that one's present understanding is actually complete. For a Latter-day Saint, the aspiration for a complete understanding should simply lead one to look forward to the time when more will be revealed. Thus, rather than conflicting with it, the goal of a complete account only makes the doctrine of continuing revelation sweeter. I suggest that an interest in completeness is only a problem when it overpowers one's interest in knowing the truth.[7]

Certainly there have been many people who have clung to some systematic theological view, leading them to reject the truth or to neglect other key aspects of faith. Certainly there is a human tendency to want to have all the answers. There is a danger that someone who is more eager to have all the answers than to have the truth may cling to a theological system in resistance of the truth, whether truth that is new to the world, or merely truth that is new to that person.

However, it seems to me these mistakes are entirely optional, and even incidental to systematic theology. Indeed, these mistakes seem perfectly common among those who do not approach theology systematically. For example, claiming that the closing passage of Revelation declares the scriptures complete seems quite sufficient for many to close themselves to further truth. Someone reluctant to admit ignorance may be drawn to systematic theology. Yet such a person may just as well be drawn simply to avoid any careful theological inquiry. By avoiding or dismissing difficult questions, one can avoid having to answer them. Ignorance supports complacency at least as well as pretended knowledge does. Thus rejection of continuing revelation is rightly seen as a result of ignorance or pride (or both), not a result of systematic theology.

II. False conception of faith

Another concern one might have about systematic theology is that it implies a false conception of faith. The systematic approach focuses on intellectual understanding, yet there is much more to faith than understanding. Faith requires a willingness to trust even when one does not understand; it also requires action and the offering of one's heart. One may worry that systematic theology neglects these other, arguably more important aspects of faith.

Here again, history contributes to this concern. A number of Christian groups in history have overemphasized belief, particularly certain Protestant groups with a strong presence in the U.S., with whom Latter-day Saints are familiar. These groups, coincidentally, often hold to a system of theological views Latter-day Saints do not accept. Further, when other Christian groups criticize Latter-day Saints they often focus on certain narrowly understood doctrines that we don't share with them, as though these fine points were crucial to faith in Christ. We are right to be wary of an overly intellectualized approach to faith. However, a construal of faith as a mere matter of belief, despite the poor fit of this notion of faith with the scriptures, is also common among those who eschew systematic theology. At times the focus on belief may also have been attractive to those wishing to excuse their sins, or simply to those taking excessive pride in their intellectual talents. It would not be surprising if many of the builders of theological systems suffered from this sort of pride. Still, it again seems to me that the problems here are a mistaken notion of faith, and sometimes pride, and that the association of these errors with systematic theology is largely a matter of coincidence.

Belief is only a part of faith. We are to show our faith by our works. Part of what this means to me is that the religious life, which is the living out of a relationship with God and one's fellow human beings, is the context in which religious beliefs have meaning, and it is the avenue through which those beliefs must be expressed in order for them to be of any value. Our beliefs have value insofar as they support a certain kind of life, a life of faith, love and joy. Thus, belief is a secondary part of faith, while the primary part is action. Further, some kinds of belief involved in faith may not be suited to inclusion in a theological system, for example, experiential knowledge, or knowledge of a personal being, or of how to live by faith.

Belief is only a part of faith, but still a part that deserves careful attention. A systematic approach to matters of belief in no way implies that belief is the whole of faith, or that all belief can be systematized, but merely aspires to completeness and cohesiveness in those matters of belief that can be brought into a system. Systematic theology may be associated with a rejection of continuing revelation, or an overly intellectualized notion of faith, but these problems are not a result of the systematic approach to theology; rather they are the result of misunderstanding the scriptures, or of a prideful attitude taken toward one's theology.

III. Neglecting the Polyphony of Scripture

Another concern is that a systematic method may ignore or conceal the fact that the scriptures have layers, or a chorus, of meanings, and Christ's parables are an excellent example. On one level, Christ is telling a simple story about a farmer or a shepherd; yet at the same time, for those who have ears to hear, he is teaching about the Kingdom of Heaven. In incorporating the messages of scripture into a systematic account, with its precisely defined and univocal terminology, it seems inevitable that the multiple meanings of scripture will be lost. To draw on many accounts and construct one, in this view, is not a gain but an impoverishment. Again, this concern is supported by the history of theology: from an LDS perspective, every system so far has reflected much less than the full truth we find in revelation.

I agree that the scriptures are polyphonic, and that our theology should reflect this fact. It is true that any given theological system is unlikely to reflect the multiple meanings of scripture. However, as I mention above, it is important to distinguish particular theologies from the larger activity of theology. I believe that a plurality of systematic accounts should be involved in our practice of theology, and that employing multiple accounts is a reasonable response to the polyphony of the scriptures. Having acknowledged how systematic theology should not be used, I will now turn to my positive view of how it should be used. I'll explain a context of presuppositions and expectations in which systematic theology makes sense for LDS.

Unity, Diversity, and Progression: An LDS Context for Theology

I compare life in the Church of Jesus Christ of Latter-day Saints to life in a one-room schoolhouse. A one-room schoolhouse gathers students at a variety of levels. The eleven-year-olds already know what the six-year-olds are supposed to be learning, while the six-year-olds can't possibly follow many of the eleven-year-olds' lessons. Yet somehow they are all expected to learn in the same room. This calls for a creative approach to teaching.

This is what the Church is like. People of all kinds come to the Church to learn together about God and his plan of happiness: old and young, new converts and great-grandchildren of pioneers. Children and youth are divided by age for some activities. Gospel Essentials helps investigators and new members start with the fundamentals. Dividing people up by their level of knowledge makes it simpler to plan an effective curriculum. Yet Gospel Doctrine class includes members spanning a wide range of stages of spiritual development. Sacrament meetings and conferences, especially general conference, address the full range of church members. As important as the other meetings are, I suggest these largest meetings, Gospel Doctrine, sacrament meeting, and conferences, set the primary standards for the content and form of gospel teaching in the Church.

On the one hand, the Church has the goal that all its members learn, and continue to learn throughout their lives, line upon line, and precept upon precept. On the other hand there is the goal that the members be unified, that they be of one faith and one doctrine. These goals call for a distinctive pattern of growth for individual members.

We are unified by core doctrines, and by a common set of scriptures. We believe that Jesus is the Christ, the Son of God, that he was born, lived and died to save us from our sins, that we take part in the redemption he has prepared for us by exercising faith, repenting of our sins, being baptized in his name, and receiving the Holy Spirit. The scriptures we share include both the standard works and the teachings of modern prophets. The scriptures are the basis of our common learning process. They define its scope and give us the terms with which to express spiritual truths. As they establish both the scope and primary basis of our learning, we may picture the scriptures as a planar space over which we rove as we learn. The core doctrines of the gospel are the starting point of this process and remain constant throughout. We may figure them as a vertical axis defining the center of the revelatory plane. Our understanding of the scriptures may expand, develop and change, but must remain anchored to the core doctrines.

If the scriptures meant just one thing, like an encyclopedia or a textbook, then we might think of spiritual learning as a process of simple expansion from the core doctrines, progressively covering more and more of the plane of revealed knowledge. However, the scriptures do not just mean one thing; they have layers of meaning. Accordingly, I suggest we think of individual spiritual knowledge as growing in a spiral pattern, revolving continually around the same axis and passing over the same ground again and again, but in a new way from time to time, reflecting higher levels of scriptural meaning as it rises. In some cases, a higher understanding will replace a lower one, superseding and overwriting it in our minds. In other cases, multiple meanings of the same scriptural texts will persist in our understandings, in parallel. The allegory of the olive tree in Jacob 5, for example, may be understood as describing God's cultivation of the nation of Israel as a whole, but it may also illuminate how he works with each of us individually. The structure of the core doctrines and shared scriptures keep the members of the Church unified, with a core of shared knowledge, and all learning together by studying the same scriptures and other revelations. Yet within this unifying structure, each of us is free to progress upward in our knowledge without limit.

For those of us who approach theology systematically, each turn of the spiral might represent a new, systematic understanding of the gospel, reflecting a new set of meanings found in the scriptures. In some ways theological progress might resemble progress in the scientific study of the natural world: we may build one system, finding it explains some things well and others badly, adjust this system, extend it where possible, and at some point replace it with another that explains more, but still doesn't capture it all. This movement from one system to the next may go on *ad infinitem.*

There is valuable progress in going from one ordered understanding to the next, even if there is no last or best or complete system in such a progression. Indeed, perhaps sometimes we must progress by developing several systems in parallel, none of which can capture the truths of the others. We may think of the atonement as Christ's paying a debt we owe, or suffering a punishment in our place, or learning how to empathize with us in our temptation and sin. Yet these quite different theories may each reflect portions of the truth. Parallel theological systems may be developed by different individuals within a spiritual community, or even by a single individual. Perhaps in God's mind all knowledge is tidily unified, perhaps not; either way this comprehensive tidiness is a long way off for us mortals.

While our understanding of the revelation we've received may shift and change as it grows, we can and should hold firmly all the while to our belief that it is the word of God, and our belief in the first principles of the gospel. We can constantly affirm that Christ is our Savior; that he came to earth, lived among us and died for us, to allow us to return to live with him and with our heavenly parents. We can hold to our belief that Christ is our Savior, even if our understanding of just what he saves us from, and how, and to what end, evolves.

We learn line upon line, precept upon precept, and sometimes we receive a line that requires deep revision of the understanding we may have based on a sincere study and faith in the earlier precepts. As Paul says, "For we know in part, and we prophesy in part. But when that which is perfect is come, then that which is in part shall be done away."[8] Perhaps there is no piece of revealed knowledge that will not eventually be transformed by future revelation, as we progress through the eternities, though Paul's language suggests there is a perfect knowledge to be had eventually.

All of our imperfect knowledge may pass away some day, but I suggest that if we don't work to systematize revelation, whether formally or informally at least in part, then we fail to respond to it as a body, and hence we forfeit vital opportunities to progress in our knowledge. Reading the revelations together, in light of each other, systematically, allows us to build an understanding that is more complete than the collection of things the individual revelations teach. As Jacob wrestled with the angel for a blessing, we should wrestle with the scriptures. The scriptures are stronger than we are, and if we pay attention they will always show us our knowledge is incomplete, but incomplete knowledge is better than ignorance.

The scriptures are messy, or to use a more positive word, they are polyphonic. Certainly the messiness of the scriptures is part of the divine pedagogy, and we should not try to replace them with a tidy system. There are many reasons I can think of why this should be so, and probably many that God only knows. For one thing, we are all at different levels of understanding, and for another, some of us need to learn things in a different order from others. Even if the scriptures ultimately lead to one tidy system of knowledge, presumably we are not able to leap there all at once. We must rely on the scriptures because they speak to us according to our own language, in our weakness. We must rely on the scriptures, though those who receive them and earnestly heed them will have still greater things revealed. We certainly should not expect everyone within the Church to subscribe to one authoritative theological system. Neither should there be one series of systems for all to move through as we grow. Only the scriptures and the words of the prophets are authoritative for us as a church, and their message is intentionally manifold. There are many systems of understanding, each with its own strengths and inadequacies, that are all compatible with a sincere, faithful reading of the scriptures, and with the first principles of the Gospel.

Paul says that we must build on the foundation Christ offers. We must build our character, our habits and desires. We must build our relationships with our brothers and sisters. We must build our knowledge of God. We must also build an understanding of God's plans for humanity, and I have argued that a systematic approach to this understanding can be fruitful. Not all of what we build will survive the fire at the last day, but if we build on Christ's foundation, then we will be saved, even if our work is not.[9] If we build nothing, for fear it will not survive the fire, then we are like the servant who hid his talent in a napkin rather than risk it in trade, and hence are not worthy of the greater gifts God would like to give us. Some of what we build will turn out to be straw; some may turn out to be gold. We may not know the value of what we are building until it is tried in the fire at the last day. Still, Paul tells us that part of how we accept Christ as our foundation is to build on that foundation, each in the best way we can.

BENJAMIN HUFF is currently Assistant Professor of Philosophy at Randolph-Macon College (Ashland, Virginia). He completed his Ph.D. at the University of Notre Dame in 2006, with a dissertation entitled, "Friendship and the Shared Life of Virtue." His research and teaching interests include ethical theory, especially virtue ethics, ancient Greek philosophy, social/political philosophy, and philosophy of religion. Interests within Mormon thought include ecclesiology, justice and atonement, and the unity of God.

Notes

1. This paper is based on a presentation given at the first annual meeting of the Society for Mormon Philosophy and Theology, March 19–20, 2004, as part of a panel entitled, "Perspectives on Theological Method." In developing the ideas expressed in this paper, I have benefited greatly from ongoing conversations with many people, particularly Richard Bushman, Jim Faulconer, David Paulsen, Dan Peterson, and Dennis Potter. I also received many helpful suggestions on the paper from Melissa Proctor.
2. Others have used the terms *theology* and *systematic theology* differently than I do. Certainly the way I do theology has been influenced by theological works I have read, for example by Aristotle, Al-Ghazali, Aquinas, and Alvin Plantinga. However, my intent is to work out an understanding of theology that harmonizes with Latter-day Saint faith, however much that may differ from other, pre-existing notions of theology.
3. Brigham Young, "Government of God," *Journal of Discourses* 7:148. He also said, "it is the business of the Elders of this Church . . . to gather up all the truths in the world . . . wherever it may be found in every nation, kindred, tongue, and people, and bring it to Zion" ("Intelligence, etc.," *Journal of Discourses* 7:283–4.
4. D&C 88:40.
5. 2 Nephi 29:8.

6. Clearly this example only begins to indicate the character of a systematic approach to theology. I have intentionally given an example whose appropriateness is relatively uncontroversial, to illustrate the attractions of a systematic method. I am also limited by the fact that at present there are not many well-known examples of systematic theology done by Latter-day Saints.
7. One would hope that this case would be the exception, as well, since a desire for completeness is a natural corollary to the desire for the truth. If one desires the truth, one naturally desires all of it.
8. 1 Corinthians 13:9–10.
9. 1 Corinthians 3:10–15.

Themes of Liberation

Liberation Theology in the Book of Mormon

R. Dennis Potter
Utah Valley State College

Introduction

I attended Dartmouth Elementary School in Richardson, Texas. Two of my friends were Shelton and Brent. Shelton was black and Brent was white. In the fourth grade we talked about the history of slavery and segregation. The teacher attempted to explain to us why these institutions were wrong. Brent raised his hand and said that it would have been good if we still had slavery because then Shelton (the only black in the whole school) would be our servant. Most of the class laughed. I saw that Shelton tried to force a laugh as well. It wasn't that Brent hated Shelton: they were friends and played together at recess. Brent was a child, and his comment was the comment of a child: hurtful and yet an immature reflection of the institutional and cultural racism in American society in 1977. As an adult, Brent's moral conscience would probably eventually awaken an indignation at the thought of our racist past.

Twenty-five years ago, the LDS Church extended the blessing of the priesthood to all worthy males, including those of African descent. With that act, the LDS Church began the process of coming out of its moral childhood. In its adulthood the Church must let its moral conscience guide its increasing activity in the socio-political realm. The moral conscience of the Church is God's revelation in the Book of Mormon, a text uniquely connected to this continent and its promise. That revelation is also reflected in

American ideals of freedom, equality, justice, opportunity, etc. Just as with the Nephites, these ideals are trampled on by the culture, social institutions, and political administrations of the United States.

The message of the Book of Mormon is a message of an atonement that involves the sacrifice of power and privilege. The atonement is not merely an act in which Jesus, despite his power and divine prestige, gives up his life for the lives of others. It is an atonement that is meant to be present in the community of God. It is uniquely crafted for a people of power and economic privilege, and it demands their emptying themselves, with Christ, into the oppressed. It is a message about the condescension of Christ and the condescension of the wealthiest and most powerful nation in human history. If taken seriously, the Book of Mormon would be the moral conscience of the United States and would unravel its economic and political pride. It would take the United States from the playground-like "biggest-kid-on-the-block" foreign policy to the adult morality that, with King Benjamin, answers the beggar's call with no judgment about the beggar's worthiness (contra the policies associated with institutions such as the International Monetary Fund).

The message of this book is a theology of liberation, not unlike the theology of liberation that was revealed to Latin American priests and bishops in the face of U.S.-backed human rights violations and economic exploitation. The difference is that Latin American liberation theology is a theology for the poor. The poor are "the people of God." In the Book of Mormon, the people of God become wealthy and proud. The people of God turn out to be the greater sinners. Liberation, in the Book of Mormon, is in the hands of the most powerful, just as atonement is in the hand of the almighty Son of God. And just as the almighty Son must give up that power and, in a very real sense, empty himself of his divinity, the powerful and "righteous" in the Americas must empty themselves of their pride.

But instead of being a story of salvation in which the ideal of liberation is fulfilled, the Book of Mormon is a story of damnation in which the people of God are condemned and destroyed by the "wicked". It is a warning to the "righteous" in today's promised land. Those who believe that God is on their side, that they are more than the dust of the earth, and that the poor of the world deserve their destitute state, will find themselves condemned to a similar fate, unless they yield their wills to God, and like his Son, empty themselves of their pride, power, and wealth.

Material and Spiritual Salvation

The first and most obvious obstacle to a socio-political reading of the Book of Mormon, or any religious text for that matter, is that religious salvation is spiritual, not material. It may be a good thing to help the poor, but it is an even better thing to help them obtain salvation. This is a common objection to liberation theology and it is a point that is also not uncommon in Mormon circles when someone suggests that we do something radical about poverty. However, this objection is fundamentally flawed in its presupposition about the metaphysical dichotomy between the spiritual and the temporal.

The liberation of the Israelites from Egyptian captivity was a socio-political liberation. And yet, it is one of the most important stories of salvation in the Bible. Central to Jesus's ministry is his healing the sick. This act not only has immediate material implications for the person healed (she gets better), but it has socio-political consequences for Jesus' ministry. Indeed, one does not touch a leper, one does not heal on the Sabbath, and one does not interact with women who are menstruating. Jesus breaks the social codes in his acts of healing. He not only heals the corporeal disease but he heals the societal diseases of self-righteousness and legalism. One of the central symbolic acts of his ministry is the last supper. Jesus breaks bread and drinks wine with his disciples. They eat. This sacrament, while most spiritual, is based on one of the most fundamental acts of an animal's material life: eating. That which is most mundane is infused with the most sacred.

So, in the Christian tradition there is adequate material to subvert the dominant view that radicalizes the separation of the spiritual from the temporal. In Mormonism, the material for this subversion is even more abundant. Indeed, it is given a metaphysical twist in the guise of the claims that all spirit is matter[1] and that God is embodied. If the spiritual is fundamentally material, how can we claim to separate spiritual from material salvation? They are inextricably intertwined.

In Mormon theology, God and the spirit are material beings. This materialism in Mormonism is not just theoretical. It undercuts the ontological basis for a religious praxis whose *telos* is "other-worldly." In a materialist view, spiritual change would imply material change and vice versa. It would have implications for this life. Liberation will not wait for the next life.

In making this claim about Mormonism's materialism I am not equivocating on the term "material." Being embodied cannot be understood independently of human history and interaction. Being embodied not only means that one is a collocation of physical particles; it also means that one is a body in a family, community, society, and world. This body plays societal roles. It has a history. It eats, drinks, passes waste, has sex, etc. These concrete historical circumstances that are the location of our embodiment are both material circumstances *and* spiritual circumstances. Spirituality is a way of being in the material/historical world.

Religion and Political Neutrality

There is another objection to a socio-political reading of the Book of Mormon. One may argue that a religion, and religious organization, must be politically neutral. Religion, in this view, has only to do with personal salvation and morality. Religious organizations should encourage its members to be politically active but should not take stances on issues that don't directly affect individual morality. However, when a political decision begins to affect an issue of "personal morality," then the organization may take a stand. This happened in the case of the Knight Amendment in California.

The view that the political can be separated from issues of personal morality is flawed. Politics deals with the way we should organize ourselves in our community. We cannot completely separate individual action from societal implications. What we do affects our community. It follows that anything that would have implications for individual morality would also have implications for social morality. Religion has implications for individual morality (at least). So, religion has implications for social morality, and this involves political decisions about how to organize society.

Another argument against the separation of the social and the individual is based on the principle that failure to act is action itself. A church that fails to denounce slavery or the holocaust tacitly enables it. There is no space to be neutral about grave societal injustices. Failure to act/prevent can be just as bad as causing something.

Once we have established that a religion and religious organization cannot avoid playing a socio-political role in the community, whether passively or actively, the question is "*what* role should religion play?" For Christians, the answer is that the church should unequivocally side with those who defend the poor, oppressed, disenfranchised, etc.

The Book of Mormon entails that Christian politics is necessarily progressive and radical in an American context. The Christian emphasizes the community and current American politics emphasizes the individual. The Christian favors the poor and current American politics favors the rich. The Christian pushes egalitarianism as far as possible and current American politics favors merit-based inequality. The Christian sees material substance as a communal good and current American economic orthodoxy sees it as potential private property. The Christian explains societal woes as coming from structures, institutions, and other forms of "communal sins" while the "Christian Right" explains societal woes on the basis of a breakdown of individual morality.

Themes in Traditional Liberation Theology

Liberation theology is the intellectual extension of Christianity's obligation to side with the oppressed. In liberation theology, the poor see themselves in the scriptural text. The text speaks of their liberation from oppression by God's incarnation in the Son. The text is the expression of the hope for salvation. Recognizing that the poor are "the people of God," liberation theology embraces them. This is called "the preferential option for the poor."

In liberation theology, there cannot be a strong distinction between the church and the world. The church is *in* the world but not *of* the world. But this means that the message of the church has implications for the world. One cannot separate Jesus's "good news" from the socio-political reality. Therefore, the church *is* political, either tacitly supporting the oppressive institutional structures of society or subverting them. The message of the gospel demands subversion of oppressive institutional structures. There is no such thing as apolitical religion.

In liberation theology, political action is not just an attempt to reform society but is radical in the etymological sense of the word. It attempts to get to the root cause of oppression. And this cause is not limited to bad individuals in power, but is based in the institutional structures that produce the hegemony of the powerful. Liberation theology involves a critique of wealth, private property, an individualistic conception of society, and structural forces of coercion that go beyond mere state violence. To say that liberation theology's critique of the current world order is radical is not to say that it is wedded to a Marxist ideology, or any other ideology of the left. Liberation theology takes its ideological cues from scripture and not from the Communist Manifesto. However, Marxism, Social Democracy, Syndicalism, and Anarchism all give concrete analyses of the root cause of societal oppression. Liberation theology pays attention to these analyses and incorporates their insights.

Liberation theology is not theological in the traditional systematic sense of the word. Orthodoxy (correct belief) matters less than orthopraxis (correct practice). And the latter is determined by the actual historical/material circumstances of one's local community. Theologies are ideologies and play functional roles in the religious community. They serve to uphold *or* subvert current structures.

The Unique Quality of Liberation Theology in the Book of Mormon

For most Christians in North America, the problem with traditional liberation theology is that it cannot speak to them. Not being poor, they are not the people of God. However, the Book of Mormon's theology of liberation speaks to the powerful, prideful, and privileged. It warns of their damnation. For it is clear that in the Book of Mormon, the people of God (i.e. the Nephites, the righteous, the Church, etc.) continually become evil and wicked due to their pride and wealth.[2]

The turn of the righteous to pride inevitably leads to a socioeconomic division, which is inherently sinful.[3] The wealthy of contemporary society should see their reflection in the text. The text is a warning to the people of God, describing how they will fall (have fallen) from grace.

4 Nephi as interpretative standard

In order to defend my claim that the Book of Mormon supports a unique theology of liberation in which the powerful and rich are the people of God and must divest themselves of their power and wealth, I will look at two texts: 4 Nephi and Mosiah 3–4. 4 Nephi will provide us with a standard with which we can begin our interpretation of the rest of the Book of Mormon. And King Benjamin's address in Mosiah will provide us with an example of putting this theology to work within the text.

A text must be read in terms of its purpose. The Book of Mormon is supposed to tell us how to live our lives.[4] If so, then we should look at the part of the book in which the people successfully build a Christian community as a guide to an interpretation of the rest of the book: 4 Nephi. Not only is this section the paradigm of righteousness, it is a microcosm of the whole Book of Mormon. It is a story that parallels the entire history of the Nephites and Lamanites condensed into several dozen pages.

At the very beginning of the book, we are reminded that Jesus has formed the Church and the people have repented and become "members." The first thing this leads to is that

> . . . there were no disputations among them, and every man did deal justly one with another. And they had all things in common among them; therefore there were not rich nor poor, bond and free, but they were all made free, and partakers of the heavenly gift. (4 Ne. 1:2–3)

The lack of disputations signals the extent to which this is now a *community* and not just a bunch of people living together. Society is necessarily social but not necessarily communal. Community involves a social *cohesion* that is largely destroyed by the individualist ethic in modern society. It is a state of *communion*, such as that found in the most ideal familial relationships. It is based on the pure love of Christ.

Sometimes it is argued that the lack of disputations indicates only the lack of any theological disputations. It is not at all clear that this phrase refers to theological disputations. There is no mention of doctrinal disputes. Moreover, this claim is put in an explicitly political and economic context, being framed by the questions of justice and economic distribution. It is more likely that the disputations being discussed are of a social nature and not a doctrinal one.

This people also have "all things in common among them." At the very least, this is the claim that there is an economic egalitarianism in the community. It may also involve the stronger claim that all property is communal. It is clear that "substance" includes *mate-*

rial substance, since in verses 24 and 25 it is the accumulation of unnecessary wealth that leads to them not having "their goods and their substance" in common any longer. This also leads to the society being divided into classes—i.e., where there are poor and rich among them. Clearly, this is a communitarian economy.

Additionally, there are no bond and free. Everyone is free. No one is enslaved or imprisoned. Indeed, later when the economic class division begins to occur again, among the first events is that the powerful create prisons and imprison the people of Christ (4 Ne. 1:30).

Conspicuously absent is the lack of any mention of a government or hierarchy of any other kind. To be sure, a church is formed with disciples. But no organizational structure is mentioned. No kings, prophets, or judges are mentioned. It would be an argument from ignorance to suggest that this fact alone is reason to think that there was no government or institutional hierarchy. But we may suggest that the economic communism and political freedom seem to be more important to the author than any element of church or governmental organization. It is also important that the terms "power" and "authority" are mentioned as something taken by the unrighteous to dominate the righteous (4 Nephi 1:30). These terms are not used to describe the position of the disciples in the society of Christ's church.

It is significant that this chapter starts off with a description of the political and economic conditions of the people of Christ's church. Where is the discussion of personal and/or individual morality? The morality that matters here is a communal morality. Here there is a focus on the moral issues that affect the community. In fact, the drama of righteousness and unrighteousness is played out on the communal stage. It is *not* an individual matter. There is no discussion of individuals' stories, only the initially wonderful but eventually tragic story of a community of Christ. To be sure, there are evils perpetrated by individuals, but what matters are the institutional evils that are the result of a radically evil *form of life*.

I appeal to a difference between individual morality and community morality, individual sin and communal sin. It seems clear to me that these are distinct and that one cannot reduce communal morality to individual morality. For example, in the philosophy department at Utah Valley State College we know that some of our faculty should show up to commencement. However, it is not necessary that all of our faculty should do so. No one in particular is required to attend. As a department, we have an obligation that no one particular individual has.

Mormonism's soteriology is clearly committed to a notion of communal morality. The argument for this is based on the premise that exaltation is the state of being in the presence of one's family and God. However, if one's other family members choose not to be exalted then this is not possible. Obviously, one cannot fulfill this obligation alone. So, it follows that it is a communal obligation. One cannot be exalted on one's own.

It is true that personal sin is intimately connected with communal sin, and hence is present in proportional degrees with the latter in society. This explains why 4 Nephi mentions the lack of sexual sin in this communal society (4 Ne. 1:16), but does so thirteen verses after mentioning the economic morality of this community of Christ. Indeed, there are sociological reasons to believe that personally destructive behavior in the form of sexual promiscuity, drug or alcohol abuse, theft, domestic violence, and the like is directly linked to economics.[5] Capitalism is a system in which one is urged to look out for one's own needs and ignore, if not neglect, others' needs. If this attitude is taken from the economic realm to other areas of behavior, then we should not be surprised if our society has an abundance of personal moral sin.

As I argued above, liberation theology emphasizes the communal or societal aspect of the sin that leads to oppression. Right-wing Christians argue that all problems in society can be traced back to individual or personal sins. Such a view is incomplete in its understanding of the nature of the human fall. In his seminal work of liberation theology, Gustavo Gutiérrez says,

> In the liberation approach sin is not considered as an individual, private, or merely interior reality—asserted just enough to necessitate "spiritual" redemption which does not challenge the order in which we live. Sin is regarded as a social, historical fact, the absence of fellowship and love in relationships among persons, the breach of friendship with God and with other persons, and, therefore, an interior, personal fracture. When it is considered in this way, the collective dimensions of sin are rediscovered.[6]

The communitarian approach to interpreting 4 Nephi is confirmed by the fact that when the people fall, the first thing they do is abandon economic communism. Indeed, one could go so far as to identify the fall *with* the change in the economic form of life. As Hugh Nibley puts it,

> The beginning of the end for the Nephites came when they changed their pattern of life: "And from that time forth they did have their substance no more common among them" (4 Ne. 1:25). Now the interesting thing about this change was that it was economically wise, leading immediately into a long period of unparalleled prosperity, a business civilization in which "they lay up in store in abundance, and did traffic in all manner of traffic" (4 Ne. 1:46). The unfortunate thing was that the Gadianton outfit got complete control of the economic life again. *And the economic life was all that counted.* The whole society was divided into economic classes (4 Ne. 1:26). . . .
>
> Such an economic order in which everyone was busy trafficking and getting rich was not, according to 4 Nephi, a free society. It was only under the old system, he tells us, that [they were] . . . "partakers of the heavenly gift."[7]

This fallen society is clearly very similar to Western European and American society. It is this economic inequality and competitiveness that is *the* fundamental social sin, and it is the downfall of the Nephite community. Similarly it will be our downfall unless we undergo a change in the form of our life.

The politics of King Benjamin's address

4 Nephi gives us a starting point for reading other texts in the Book of Mormon. It shows us that the salvation brought by Jesus is socio-political: it has direct implications for our way of life. 4 Nephi also tells us what this way of life is like. This way of life is grounded in our *economy*. It is our "economy" in the broad sense of that term—i.e., how we rule our "house." For King Benjamin, the fundamental sin is also economic. It is the failure to take care of the poor. King Benjamin develops a theology of salvation that subverts the *meritocratic theologies* that support economic inequality. To argue for this, we will look at two aspects of his address.

The first aspect of King Benjamin's address that is important for our purposes is his condemnation of those who reject the beggar's request. He says,

> And also, ye yourselves will succor those that stand in need of your succor; ye will administer of your substance unto him that standeth in need; and ye will not suffer that the beggar putteth up his petition to you in vain, and turn him out to perish.
>
> Perhaps thou shalt say: The man has brought upon himself his misery; therefore I will stay my hand, and will not give unto him of my hand, and will not give unto him of my food, nor impart unto him of my substance that he may not suffer, for his punishments are just--But I say unto you, O man, whosoever doeth this the same hath great cause to repent; and except he repenteth of that which he hath done he perisheth forever, and hath no interest in the kingdom of God.
>
> For behold, are we not all beggars? Do we not all depend upon the same Being, even God, for all the substance which we have, for both food and raiment, and for gold, and for silver, and for all the riches which we have of every kind? (Mosiah 4:16–19)

In this passage, Benjamin argues that we cannot justifiably fail to help those who petition us for material help. The reason that we cannot do this is that we depend upon God for anything we have.

It seems clear that he is responding to an assertion of this form: *I deserve the wealth I have because I alone earned it. Those who are poor deserve their poverty because they have failed to earn wealth.* An argument of this form assumes that individuals of their own accord earn or fail to earn material wealth. I will call this doctrine "economic meritocracy."

Many modern attempts to justify a capitalist economic system rely on economic meritocracy. We are all familiar with such justifications so I won't repeat them. The problems with economic meritocracy usually come down to the point that our economic status is mostly not in our power. Circumstances of our lives that are out of our control largely determine our economic class, with very few exceptions. Being raised in a white upper-middle class family, I was able to get a college education without much effort. If I had been born in south Chicago and were black I would not be where I am. Benjamin's critique is similar. If we assume that whatever is outside our control is in God's control, then it implies that we owe where we are at to God and not to any merit of our own.

Associated with the anti-meritocratic economic message of Benjamin's address is his anti-meritocratic soteriology. We cannot earn salvation on our own. We depend on God for salvation. Without God, we are "dust of the earth." But this anti-meritocratic message seems in tension with Benjamin's imperative to help the poor. He states the latter imperative over and over again. Moreover, he links our salvation with our ability to obey this command (Mosiah 4:26). This tension is not unique to Benjamin's address; it appears in the New Testament and leads to debates about the relationships between grace and works. These debates have led to Calvinist, Arminian, and Pelagian interpretations of their relationship.

However, what each of these latter positions assumes is that salvation is distributed individually. In the last section, we have argued that salvation is not distributed individually but at a communal level instead. Benjamin's address gives us another argument for this view. Indeed, Benjamin is speaking to the community that he governs. If we take the imperative to apply communally and not individually, then we can argue for both individual dependence and community merit. Individually, we are nothing without God or the community of God. We cannot be saved on our own and we cannot be liberated on our own. But as a community, we can liberate the poor. As community, we can become righteous and merit the salvation that is distributed to us communally. As a community, we *can* be "judged by our works."

Given this interpretation of Benjamin's injunction to help the beggar, we can better understand the theology presented in Mosiah 3. According to Benjamin, "Natural man is an enemy to God" (Mosiah 3:19). Usually, this is given a metaphysical reading. Arminianism is the current tendency in LDS interpretation. Arminianism asserts that we are naturally, intrinsically, and necessarily evil, although God can intervene and change us. Some LDS authors get close to this understanding insofar as they read Mosiah 3:19 as a comment about our individual *propensity* to do evil. It is not always clear whether they accept the notion that we can do no good without God doing it through us. But such a view assumes that salvation is meted out individually to those who are willing to accept it. Thus, the implication is that any salvation that happens is undeserved (it depends only on our willingness to accept it) and comes only at God's mercy. We, as individuals, merely have to accept God's transformation of our souls in order to be saved. Thus, we must submit our wills to the will of God.

This quasi-Arminian reading of Mosiah 3:19 has a social dimension. We must submit our will to God. However, we are epistemically distant from God. We don't, as individuals, know his will. Only the church knows the will of God. So, this entails that the choice of eternal life requires choosing submission to the church. It implies that we become conduits for the action of the church, whether this is the will of God or not. It implies a *de facto* infallibilism of the church. It disallows the anarchy and chaos that comes from individuals believing that they themselves know the will of God. In this way, the Arminian reading of Benjamin's address serves to support institutional orthopraxy and conservativism.

Moreover, the tension noticed in Mosiah 4 between human depravity and the injunction to take care of the poor is present in the Arminian reading of Mosiah 3:19 as well. If humans are naturally evil, then how can they choose to accept God's will?

An additional tension is located in the fact that we are supposed to shed our natural dispositions and become like a child. This is problematic since the child should be more naturally human than the adult. The Arminian and Calvinist readings of this passage would require that children are corrupt. So, why should we become as children? Similarly, how could this view of human nature be reconciled with the Article of Faith claim that human beings should be punished for their own sins and not for the sins of another (Cf. Alma 34:11)?

Finally, the move in the direction of a theology of individual depravity is a move away from the traditional "liberal" Mormon anthropology (captured beautifully in Truman Madsen's *Eternal Man*[8]), which allows that human beings are essentially good and must become bad by their own individual fall. This traditional liberal Mormon view has a difficulty explaining Mosiah 3:19, however.

A liberation theological reading of Mosiah 3 preserves the optimism of traditional liberal Mormon anthropology while making sense of humanity's natural opposition to God. A liberation theological reading denies that we are either good or evil in isolation from the community. Before the fall, Adam and Eve are in perfect *communion* with God. The fall takes them out of this *communion*; the fall is their falling out of communion with God. Instead of being in a *community* with God, they are "thrown out" on their own. They are made responsible for themselves. The material substance that they need is no longer provided. They have to *struggle* just to survive. They are like the animals. They are "natural."

This struggle comes from the breakdown of community. And conversely, true community eliminates the need for the struggle as it does in 4 Nephi. Being a natural enemy to God is being an enemy to community. On this reading, the "natural man" is not a metaphysical state of an individual. Instead, it has a social character. It is the state of rejecting communion with God and neighbor. It is the state of rejecting our radical dependence on our community. In this way, it is a form of self-deception and will always fail. Children recognize their radical dependence on their parents. Their lives are essentially communal.

This also explains how we can take part in the fall without individually doing it. We are complicit in the institutional structures of our society. Our failure to act against them is an action in their favor. And these institutional structures, in part, cause the breakdown of the community. Capitalism essentially rejects the utter dependence of the individual on the community and thus is the (current) economic form of the fall of humanity.

Nevertheless, humanity is in the image of God. We are *naturally* (in a metaphysical sense) communal. The institutional structures that tear apart community corrupt us and undermine our natural propensity to love each other. Traditional liberal Mormon theology is right to affirm the positive nature of humanity, but wrong to ignore the structural depravity of society. Arminian and Calvinist theologies are wrong to assert that individuals are naturally depraved. Pelagian theology is wrong to assert that the lack of individual depravity means that salvation is in the hands of the individual. Salvation is essentially communal and requires the grace of God. As I have argued elsewhere,[9] Christ's atonement is the most fundamental act of communion insofar as it is Christ's sharing of our experiences. Community life is primarily one in which we share our experiences with others. And Christ's atonement enables this shared life.

This socio-political reading of the meaning of "natural man" places Benjamin's discourse in the context of the social criticism throughout the Book of Mormon. It gives Benjamin's talk practical implications rather than merely abstract philosophical content. We act as a community with God to rectify socio-economic injustice. God judges us by these communal works. Throughout the Book of Mormon "righteous" society repeats the cycle of the fall as their pride and wealth lead them to become enemies to each other (and thereby to God), destroying community and salvation.

Conclusion

This short essay is only intended to offer some prolegomena to a liberation theological reading of the Book of Mormon. Most of what we should say about the Book of Mormon's message remains to be said. More importantly, most of what should be done about it remains to be done. Some of what remains to be said deals with how liberation theology would understand warfare in the Book of Mormon. Moreover, liberation theology has implications for social matters other than economics. What should we say about the role of women in the Church? What should we say about the past denial of the priesthood to blacks? Additionally, liberation theology has something to say about the institutional church. What are the ways in which it subverts oppressive structures? What are the ways in which it supports them? The Book of Mormon is a critique of the people of God in the times of Nephi, Alma, and Moroni; it would be very surprising if it weren't a critique of the people of God today.

For Latter-day Saints, the Book of Mormon should not be a mere historical record that could be confirmed or disconfirmed by archeological, linguistic, or genetic evidence. Nor is it an inspired fictional story. It should be a sacrament that points beyond itself to the divine. That is, God reveals himself in the book. To test it as a historical document, to treat it as mere fiction, or to read it as a proof text for a dogmatic theology is profane. We shouldn't read the book. We must live and breathe it. Only in this way will the text transform a fallen world and not merely describe its condemnation.

DENNIS POTTER is Associate Professor of Philosophy at Utah Valley State College, where he was also, formerly, the Mormon Studies Coordinator. His research interests are in philosophy of religion and history of analytic philosophy. His book, *Partakers of the Heavenly Gift: A Radical Reading of Mormon Theology*, is forthcoming from Kofford Books.

Notes

1. Doctrine and Covenants 131:4
2. See Hugh Nibley, *Since Cumorah* (Salt Lake City, UT: Deseret Book Co., 1967), 342ff.
3. Some, like Nibley, argue that wealth is not inherently sinful (Ibid., 355). It is certainly not necessarily the case that being wealthy is sinful. But when it is coupled with inequality it is always sinful in the Book of Mormon. See also D&C 104.
4. Indeed, the title page says that it was written so that the Gentile (among others) would not be destroyed.
5. See, for example, C. Wright Mills, *The Power Elite* (London: Oxford University Press, 2000).
6. Gustavo Gutiérrez, *A Theology of Liberation* (Maryknoll, NY: Orbis Books, 1988), 102–3.
7. Hugh Nibley, *An Approach to the Book of Mormon* (Salt Lake City, UT: Deseret Book Co., 1988), 397–8.
8. Truman Madsen, "The Eternal Man," in *Five Classics by Truman G. Madsen* (Salt Lake City, UT: Deseret Book Co., 2001).
9. R. Dennis Potter, "Did Christ Pay for Our Sins?" *Dialogue: A Journal of Mormon Thought*, Vol. 32 No. 4 (Winter 1999): 73–86.

Is There a Place for Heavenly Mother in Mormon Theology?

An Investigation into Discourses of Power

Margaret Merrill Toscano
University of Utah

Why are most Mormon theologians white males? And what does this question have to do with the nature of Mormon theology and how it is done?

Mormon theology is most often seen in either descriptive, prescriptive, or speculative terms; that is, it is either an explanation of Mormon doctrine (descriptive), an explication of what Mormons should believe and accept as doctrine (prescriptive), or an exploration of the implications of Mormon doctrine and its meaning (speculative). Of course these approaches overlap: describing means selecting what a scholar deems to be mainstream, which means marking something as important to be complied with as well as scrutinized, which leads to more description. All three approaches can be employed by orthodox and liberal Mormons alike. Although the groups may argue about what texts, doctrines, and approaches are most legitimate, they share the premise that theology involves a search for truth—whether it be the truth of historical context or ultimate divine truth—and that truth is always knowable.

While I value all three types of theologizing and recognize their importance in helping us understand both historical and metaphysical truths, neither the approaches themselves nor the truths they seek to discover are value free. That is, they are conditioned by authority structures (whether ecclesiastic, academic, or cultural) that pre-determine what gets included in Mormon theological discourse and who is allowed to do it. Too seldom do we consider how power structures influence not only what we are allowed to express, but the nature of knowledge itself and how we perceive and talk about it. Seldom do we ask what ideas we have failed to consider because society's organization, cultural frameworks, and language systems create blinders that close off a variety of perspectives from our view. For example, information in a text can be overlooked when it falls outside the experience or concern of a scholar. No one would have supposed fifty years ago that we could glean as much about women and gender from biblical texts as we have.

Power structures set up frameworks for how we think about things and whether or not we can even conceptualize, let alone promulgate, certain possibilities. Knowledge is not separate from human relationships, and all relationships are defined at least in part by power. This means that knowledge is not simply a list of objective propositions; it is intertwined with the way people relate to each other and how they create hierarchies, both social and intellectual. This also means that knowledge cannot be separated from ethics; knowledge always has moral implications for how individuals are treated. Emmanuel Levinas's famous idea that ethics are prior to epistemology succinctly states my point. How we set up the relationships among God and the members of a religious community determines the nature of theology and vice versa. An example may help clarify my point.

In a recent *Ensign* article,[1] President Hinckley outlines the four theological foundations of Mormonism—the "Four Cornerstones of Faith": The first is the "testimony of Jesus Christ as the Son of God"; the second is the "First Vision of the Prophet Joseph Smith"; the "third cornerstone is the Book of Mormon"; and the fourth is "the restoration to earth of priesthood power and authority." While these four propositions may appear fairly neutral, they all have implications for how women and ethnic minorities are positioned in the Church organization, since all four cornerstones center on male figures that are represented as white. It is true that the cornerstones could be restated as abstract principles that bless all: testimony of Christian salvation, restoration of the gospel, divine revelation, and priesthood ordinances. But because all of these gifts come through men who act in the place of God as conduits for his power, in each case the male mediator himself becomes a holy figure who is an essential part of God's work. The non-neutrality of these principles becomes more obvious when we look at the four pictures used by the *Ensign* to illustrate each one. The first and largest is a picture of a loving Christ holding a staff (*The Lord Is My Shepherd* by Simon Dewey); the second focuses on a young Joseph Smith on his knees with the light of God upon him (*Joseph Smith's First Vision* by Greg Olsen); the third portrays the Prophet Mormon writing God's word (*Mormon Abridging the Plates* by Tom Lovell); and the fourth depicts a transfigured John the Baptist bestowing the priesthood on Joseph Smith and Oliver Cowdery (*The Restoration of the Priesthood* by Del Parson). Note, too, that all four portraits are drawn by male artists and that President Hinckley's photograph begins the article as the authorization for this message from the First Presidency. The absence of female figures underscores their exclusion from serving as God's instruments to bring salvation to his children, and it even raises the question of how these basic gospel principles apply to women because as recipients only, through a male intermediary, their relationship to the divine is less direct than that of men.[2]

In asserting the interrelationship between knowledge and power, I am drawing on work that has colored academic discourse for the past thirty years, influenced by theorists such as Michel Foucault, for whom knowledge is always a form of power and the search for knowledge is indicative of the will to power. For Foucault, the question is always: How do power relationships set up conditions for the production of knowledge? How do such relationships open and close spaces for participation in discourse and the construction of cultural identity?[3] In other words, knowledge is not a set of mere abstractions but the way material reality and signifying systems shape both a person's identity within a community and the person's position and ability to speak.

I believe Foucault's insights have great potential for illuminating how authority structures predetermine who and what gets included in Mormon theological discourse.[4] Throughout this essay, I use the concept of a Heavenly Mother as a metaphor for what commonly gets marginalized and excluded in such discussions. In doing so, my purpose is not to develop a Heavenly Mother theology, but rather to use the Heavenly Mother doctrine as a test case for how theological legitimacy is established in Mormon discourse, and to explore why certain ideas and people get excluded in the process. Though I focus here on gender, this metaphor also contains clear implications for issues of legitimization and exclusion with regard to race and class. Moreover, by linking Mother in Heaven with larger issues of theological methodology and authorization, I want to suggest that gender relationships do not merely affect how women function within the LDS community, but they also fashion the way men interact with each other and whose ideas get validated. The question then is not simply what is true, but what people get valued more when certain truths are labeled orthodox and take center stage.

In Mormonism, the relationship between power and knowledge is crucial. In fact, the main problem any scholar faces in addressing Mormon theology is that of authorization. Since legitimate authority is central both to LDS Church structure and self-definition, any Mormon theologian must establish both the personal authority to speak and the authority of the texts upon which his or her theology is based. Typically, Mormon theology is established in two ways: first, by statements of Church priesthood authorities, and second, by unofficial statements of independent Church scholars (a broad category ranging from work found in conservative publications, such as *BYU Studies* or Deseret Book's fare, to what appears in more liberal presses or magazines).[5] I also suggest that the membership as a whole has an important role in what assumes importance in Mormon discourse, creating a third type of authorization.

Revelation from the prophet signifies ultimate authorization. But official or semi-official pronouncements by General Authorities or other Church leaders also carry enormous authoritative weight; this second category would include signed and unsigned statements found in Church publications (official manuals, magazines, and so forth). While official authorization may appear to be fairly straightforward—either a doctrine is accepted or not—the validity of the concept of the Heavenly Mother provides an illustration of the complexity of such authorization. Joseph Smith himself likely introduced the doctrine of Heavenly Mother; subsequent Church priesthood authorities (including President Hinckley) have reiterated her existence; and the *Encyclopedia of Mormonism* includes an entry on the subject, asserting that "the belief in a living Mother in Heaven is implicit in Latter-day Saint thought."[6] All of these factors solidly establish the Heavenly Mother doctrine as mainstream. However, a recent informal internet survey reveals that most Latter-day Saints believe that discourse about the Heavenly Mother is forbidden, which puts the doctrine in a contested, or at least problematic, position. In describing her findings, Doe Daughtrey, the survey's author, confirms what many of us have observed in our own interactions in LDS meetings and discussions:

> After posting a list of questions as to the relevance of Heavenly Mother to Mormons today on Beliefnet.com, I was not surprised to be repeatedly warned by faithful Mormons that I had chosen an inappropriate topic and to hear almost verbatim statements regarding her sacrality and the necessity of her protection. Several of them warned me away from discussion about Heavenly Mother after seeking advice from their local church leaders.[7]

While no General Authority has made an official statement denying belief in a Heavenly Mother nor stating that her existence is too sacred to discuss, several factors may influence the current trend that sees even a mention of Heavenly Mother as treading on forbidden ground. Members take their cues about what is acceptable doctrine from talks of General Authorities and official Church manuals and magazines. A word search on the Church's website, lds.org, yields only twenty-six direct references to either "Heavenly Mother" or "Mother in Heaven" in the past thirty years of Church publications.[8] Such sparse referencing to the Mother in Heaven implies that she should not be a topic of major concern for members of the Church.

The most recent reference to her was made by President Gordon B. Hinckley in a talk given at the general women's meeting in October of 1991 and printed in that year's November *Ensign*.[9] President Hinckley there responds to a letter addressed to then-Church President Ezra Taft Benson from a fourteen-year old girl, "Virginia" (a pseudonym), who asks, "Are men more important than women?" As part of his response, President Hinckley legitimizes the doctrine of the Heavenly Mother by attributing it to Joseph Smith and adding his own belief: "Logic and reason would certainly suggest that if we have a Father in Heaven, we have a Mother in Heaven. That doctrine rests well with me." But he then limits the influence of the Heavenly Mother by explaining that "in light of the instruction we have received from the Lord Himself, I regard it as inappropriate for anyone in the Church to pray to our Mother in Heaven."

President Hinckley says this prohibition in no way "belittles or denigrates her," but it surely makes her subordinate in some way to Heavenly Father and less important to the Church since her children have no access to her. President Hinckley's assertion that men have a "governing responsibility" over women (though he does say men are not supposed to rule despotically) has a similar effect on her role since it implies this governing pattern is eternal. While he does not forbid discussion about Heavenly Mother, he does mark her place as troubling and perhaps dangerous, given the way he contextualizes his comments about her. After assuring Virginia that women are of equal worth with men to their Heavenly Father, who loves them, and after advising her that she should talk to her Father in prayer, President Hinckley uses the mention of prayer as his segue to the inappropriateness of praying to the Heavenly Mother, privately or in public. He then remarks that those who have done so "are well-meaning, but they are misguided."[10]

For Church members eager to follow their leaders down to the letter of the law, President Hinckley's prohibition can easily be read to mean that any who pursue the topic of the Heavenly Mother are also "misguided." Add to this a grassroots feeling that Heavenly Mother is too sacred to talk about because her husband does not want her name "taken in vain" like his is (a rationale that itself endorses male control), and the result is the disappearance of references to the Heavenly Mother altogether in Church publications since 1991.[11] No doubt the publicly discussed excommunications of feminists like Janice Allred, Lynne Knavel Whitesides (disfellowshipped), Maxine Hanks, and me, all of whom were disciplined in part simply for talking about the Heavenly Mother, adds to the general sense that discourse about her is strictly forbidden.

While I have never seen any study that documents when or how the idea developed in the Church that Heavenly Mother cannot be talked about because she is too sacred, my sense is that it began in the 1960s and 1970s, at about the same time that there was a resurgence of interest in feminist questions in the Church, accompanied by the renewed interest of some women and men to search for the divine feminine.[12] Since sacred taboos often connect the holy with what a society sees as dangerous, the language of sacredness that surrounds the LDS silence about the Heavenly Mother is likely an expression of fear on the part of leaders and members that feminism might creep into the Church and disrupt current structures, as implied by President Hinckley's remarks about the "misguided" who pray to a female deity.[13] While some regard the need for silence about the Heavenly Mother as reverence, absolute silence about her does not protect her; it erases her. Temples may be considered too sacred to reveal much of what goes on inside, but still we constantly talk about them, put up pictures of them, attend them, and devote resources to them—all of which reinforce their importance and sacredness. But we accord no such treatment to the Mother in Heaven, which convinces me that all arguments about her sacredness are a cover-up for something else.[14] Whatever that something is, insisting on silence about Heavenly Mother is iconoclastic—the smashing of an image that takes away its sacrality. It does not matter whether the doctrine of the Heavenly Mother remains part of official LDS theology or not; if there are no private or public occasions on which we can invoke her name and image, Mother in Heaven will surely fade from our memory and eventually from our doctrine as well.

This willingness by members to expand the taboo about the Heavenly Mother indicates that they themselves have a say in authorizing theology. Not every statement of a prophet gets promoted or even obeyed, in spite of the almost obsessive desire many Latter-day Saints have "to follow the leaders." For example, President Kimball's 1978 speech against hunting,[15] while causing a stir initially, was quickly forgotten. Mormon hunters as a group have never been subject to church discipline, at least to my knowledge, while Mormon feminists have. Ironically, though the principle of common consent is nearly void in official Church meetings since members are expected simply to sustain the decisions of their Church leaders without question, if the members do not emphasize and promulgate their leaders' teachings, the authority of those teachings eventually fades away. Therefore, in a subtle way, the membership as a whole plays a role in authorizing Mormon theology—more as a matter of practice than of verbal agreement or dissent. But practice in due course reshapes stated belief. While most LDS people may acknowledge the soundness of President Benson's 1987 directive about women staying home with children rather than joining the workforce, economic realities justify disobedience when two incomes are needed to meet basic family needs or single mothers are faced with being the sole support.[16] In fact, many women in the workforce do not perceive themselves as disobeying prophetic injunction as long as they agree with the principle of the primacy of motherhood. Thus, faithful LDS women rationalize, "I would rather stay home, but my particular circumstances don't allow me that luxury." While the desire of the heart may indeed be more important spiritually, actual practice is more crucial for defining religion sociologically. A career woman who advocates conservative values will be seen as less of a threat to the Church than a full-time homemaker who questions women's roles. Nonetheless, the conservative career woman is still reshaping the image of what a Mormon woman is and can be.[17]

The recent LDS interest in the theme of the divine feminine in Dan Brown's *The Da Vinci Code*, as manifest by the highly popular lecture series at BYU attended by more than a thousand people, may also show the power of members "voting with their feet" about certain ideas, in this case a countermovement to the silencing about the Heavenly Mother.[18] Why so much enthusiasm about Dan Brown's book?[19] I believe it reveals the hunger that develops when a psychologically important element of religion—such as the divine feminine—is suppressed. Jewish scholar Raphael Patai, in his book *The Hebrew Goddess*, suggests that the human craving for a divine mother may be one reason for the ongoing reemergence of feminine images to depict God in the highly masculine and monotheistic faith of Judaism.[20] While LDS people may not express their interest in the divine feminine by speaking directly about the Mormon Mother God, they can redirect their interest in an acceptable manner through participating in discussions about the way other traditions treat the feminine divine, and perhaps even subtly challenge the prevailing taboo at the same time.

Mormon scholars also play a vital role in unofficially authorizing theology because the community at large inevitably adopts some ideas that enter the membership's consciousness indirectly through scholarly discourse.[21] Typically scholars have taken two approaches: first, exegesis of past authoritative statements and, second, Mormon philosophical theology. A good example of the exegesis of authoritative statements is Linda Wilcox's important essay "The Mormon Concept of a Mother in Heaven," in which she reviews the inception and reception of the doctrine, outlining references by Church leaders, as well as responses from the membership, particularly women. Although such exegetical efforts are vital as intellectual history and as groundwork for clarifying theological possibilities, they generally do not uncover or examine legitimacy or power issues directly because they are descriptive rather than analytic. However, such historical descriptions carry a good deal of weight for what gets validated in Mormon culture, which usually prizes history above theology because it seems more concrete and factual. Moreover, for many members truth is connected only with what we already know. A number of people have told me that the reason we cannot talk about the Heavenly Mother is that we do not know anything about her (which of course is not true on several levels, as well as being a tautology). On the other hand, our lack of knowledge about God the Father does not stop discussion.

Mormon philosophical theology is better able to question assumptions about power and knowledge but has not often done so, most likely because of its historical dependency upon the Enlightenment paradigm that assumes that reason is the primary tool for unlocking the truths of the universe and establishing legitimacy. Therefore, this kind of typology typically has been able to validate only certain ideas and methodologies, in particular a systematic approach that favors logic and objectivity. Even though this group has included both believers and non-believers, their objective stance has often covered over the effects of their underlying positions on the way they have described Mormon theology. I do not wish to devalue a systematic approach in any way but mean only to point out that some perspective is lost when one view monopolizes.[22] Here the loss may be the suppression of other approaches to knowing, such as the poetic, narrative, mythic, and bodily.[23] Ironically, while Mormon philosophical theology has argued, for example, against an absolutist, disembodied God, it has retreated back to this concept when dealing with gender. The God of Mormon philosophical writing is usually male but sexless and thus, in a curious way, both instantiated in gender while simultaneously beyond gender.

Blake Ostler's recent book, *Exploring Mormon Thought: The Attributes of God*, provides a striking illustration of this point.[24] In 485 pages of text, Ostler provides no discussion whatsoever of the question of God's gender although he refers to God with the male pronoun throughout, thereby underscoring not only God's anthropomorphism but also his maleness. In fairness to Ostler's very fine book, his purpose is to contrast Mormon notions of God with traditional Christian notions, especially in relation to such thorny issues as God's foreknowledge, human free will, the problem of timelessness and immutability, and the relation of these concerns to Christology. However, his failure to engage with recent Christian discussions of God's gender is significant. While Ostler claims he is discussing the ways in which the Mormon concept of God differs from traditional Christianity, he does not present Mormonism's unique view of an embodied God whose gender is more than a metaphor or long-standing narrative tradition, as held by other Christian sects.

According to Mormon scripture, God has "a body of flesh and bones as tangible as man's" (D&C 130:22). This assertion, it seems to me, has both positive and negative significance. On the one hand, it valorizes human embodiment. Because it posits the incarnation not only of the earthly Christ but of the Heavenly Father himself, Mormon theology does not share with orthodox Christianity the penchant for denigrating the body or human experience.[25] Of course, as Ostler states, God's body must have qualities that transcend those of a mortal body; in other words, it must be a "spiritualized" body subject neither to time or death; and I agree with Ostler that Christ fully reflects the nature of God in all respects. However, the question Ostler's book raises, though unstated and unexplored, is whether or not the valorization in God of the body is meant also as a preference for the male body over the female body. Where does the Mormon notion of an embodied God put women? Can women reflect God? Ostler's book presents us with a chart that shows how the "Sons of God" go through the same process as the "Son of God" in order to return to God's presence and be glorified. But what about women? Ostler's chart makes no reference to them.

Traditional Christians can argue that gender is merely an ephemeral expression of mortal embodiment and that God and salvation are beyond gender; therefore, women need not worry about the potential for eternal subordination (though historically the transcendent God has not validated women in this way).[26] Mormon doctrine is otherwise. It asserts, according to the official "Proclamation on the Family," that gender "is an essential characteristic of individual pre-mortal, mortal, and eternal identity and purpose."[27] This Proclamation also states that each human being is "created in the image of God" as "a beloved spirit son or daughter of heavenly parents." But the Proclamation further states that it is the male God alone, the Eternal Father, who is worshiped and whose plan governs and guides his children along the path toward immortality. What then of the Heavenly Mother? Is she involved at all in the salvation of her children? Is she an "equal partner" with her divine spouse as the Proclamation says earthly men and women are to be? How can she be an equal partner if she is absent from or invisible in the work of the Godhead? More important for our discussion here, does her absence impinge upon the authority that women may assume in Mormon theological discourse? Does gender matter when it comes to how theology is done? Why the dearth of women theologians? Since it certainly cannot be because of their lack of intelligence, it is more likely due to the authority structure of the LDS community itself that discourages women from taking interest or fully participating in theological and philosophical discourse. In a world where Heavenly Mother is cut off from communicating with her children, how can women communicate authoritatively about God? The ethical implications of women's absence in matters of theology are profoundly disturbing. Such an absence creates a class system where at least half of the Church is denied the benefits of full citizenship. This situation certainly impacts women's individual sense of their own worth; and for the community as a whole, the absence of women's voices limits Mormon theology, both in its methodology and its fruits.

Because LDS texts focus on males, both as figures of authority and as depictions of the normative person, women can find it difficult to see how they participate in God's work. Let me give you a pertinent example, of which there are countless others. The Doctrine and Covenants sets forth the following characteristics of the inheritors of celestial glory:

> They are they who are the church of the Firstborn. They are they into whose hands the Father has given all things— They are they who are priests and kings, who have received of his fulness, and of his glory; And are priests of the Most High, after the order of Melchizedek, which was after the order of Enoch, which was after the order of the Only Begotten Son. Wherefore, as it is written, they are gods, even the sons of God— Wherefore, all things are theirs, whether life or death, or things present, or things to come, all are theirs and they are Christ's, and Christ is God's. (D&C 76: 54–59)

The language in this passage is not merely male-centered; it is priesthood-conditioned. Inheritors of the celestial glory are identified as priests, a status that raises the question whether or not women, barred as they are from priesthood, are included in this group of exalted beings. You may answer, "yes," that certainly a passage like this must include women because it is describing entrance into the celestial kingdom, which we know by tradition is open to men and women alike.

But this interpretation is not obvious from the text. For a woman to understand and be edified by this text, she must first read herself into it. She must shoulder the extra burden that male priesthood holders do not carry of imagining herself in a description of heaven which does not in fact include her in a literal sense. This is why gender is not merely a secondary question; it is about core epistemology that establishes knowledge about the world and self. It is about the way a woman (or a person of color or anyone on the margins of a white male church) establishes personhood. Every act of reading a canonical text demands the re-construction of female subjectivity. In such a power structure, a woman's status as a full person is always in question, always unstable, always tenuous. Women must always cope with the nagging questions: Do I have the right to insert myself into this textual space? Can I assume that these promises apply to me? Or are these promises reserved for men only—for priesthood holders, as this instance in D&C 76 could imply? Again the Heavenly Mother is illustrative. Women who need a model for connecting themselves to the divine and celestial glory are forbidden to create a picture of God that includes their femaleness. Men are not under this same prohibition and are in fact encouraged to see themselves in the image of God (as illustrated by Ostler's chart).

Interestingly, fourteen-year-old "Virginia," to whom President Hinckley directed his talk discussed above, refers to this same male language in D&C 76. Virginia perceives the issue clearly when she expresses her worry that in "the scriptures I could not seem to find anywhere whether women may enter into the celestial kingdom if they are worthy. Also, when someone such as Joseph Smith had a vision of the celestial kingdom, he only seemed to see men there."[28] President Hinckley assures Virginia that women are included and tells her not to "be disturbed, my dear young friend, by the fact that the word *man* and the word *men* are used in scripture without also mentioning the words *woman* and *women*. I emphasize that these terms are generic, including both sexes."[29] He then goes on to explain that this type of generic use of "man" was common historically, and he cites the phrase "all men are created equal" from the Declaration of Independence to show that such usage must include "men, women, and children."

President Hinckley could not have chosen a worse example of historical equality and a better example for showing how exclusive language reflects and promotes discrimination.[30] Surely he must remember that it took almost two hundred years, a civil war, several constitutional amendments and major Supreme Court decisions to demonstrate legally that the "self-evident" equality of "all men" under the law in America includes all races and genders. What seems to me to be President Hinckley's genuine and openhearted concern for this young woman's sense of her own worth (he did not have to address the question at all) is undermined by the over-powering evidence of male privilege and value in the talk itself, as demonstrated by the scriptures quoted, the subordination of Heavenly Mother to Heavenly Father throughout, and the overall structure of male authority that circumscribes every level of text and subtext. How can women believe President Hinckley that they "occupy a high and sacred place in the eternal plan of God, our Father in Heaven" when his plan seems to leave out the Heavenly Mother? Can they expect a better place than she is given? The very fact that men do not need to be assured of their inclusion, worth, and equal position evidences the imbalance.

If every act of reading a religious text for a Mormon woman involves the reestablishment of her personhood in order to occupy the space of a good Mormon, then what extra burdens must she carry in order to occupy the space of a good Mormon theologian? This problem is further complicated because the models available to LDS women are almost all male. The Book of Mormon is a powerful text that presents us with prophetic figures who do not simply proclaim the word of God but seek to explain it in rational terms. Nephi, Alma, and Mormon are all examples of profound theologians. But once again, does this male pattern imply that women are excluded from this role? "Virginia" can write only to a male prophet to get an authoritative answer to her concerns about women's place in the LDS religion. Only two females speak at each general conference amid a sea of male authorities who outrank them in authority as well as number. The BYU Religion Department has only five full-time female faculty members among seventy-two males (of whom, only one is non-white); and the BYU Philosophy Department includes no women faculty.[31] Clearly the absence of women in authoritative positions and authoritative discourse makes it difficult for younger women to imagine themselves as theologians.[32] But even worse, the lack of women theologians reinforces the idea that to men alone belongs the power to teach, define, and explore what the LDS religion is. In addition, the lack of women's perspectives limits the pool from which creative answers to religious problems can be drawn.

A basic assumption of feminist theory is that power resides in the ability to name; authority is related to authorship, etymologically and culturally. For this reason, feminist theologians of other traditions have emphasized the importance of women speaking for and about God if equality is ever to be achieved in the religious realm. Ada Maria Isasi-Diaz, a leading Latina *mujerista* (womanist) theologian, asserts:

> What has guided *mujerista* theology from the beginning are those wonderful words of Miriam in the book of Numbers, "Has Yahweh indeed spoken only through Moses?" (Num. 12:2). Well aware of the fact that she suffered severe penalties for daring to scold Moses, for daring to claim that Yahweh also spoke to her and through her, our sister Miriam invites *mujerista* theologians to throw our lot with the people of God and to hope that, just as in her case, the authorities will catch up with us, that they will eventually also see that we have no leprosy, that we are clean.[33]

As the words of Isasi-Diaz imply, one of the primary functions of feminist theologians is to develop hermeneutical techniques for reading women into sacred texts and sacred spaces. What may not be evident from Isasi-Diaz's statement is her desire to do this from a believing perspective. Many mainstream LDS people assume that feminism is at odds with religion in general and Mormonism in particular. However, my reading in feminist theologies and my conversations with feminists of other religious persuasions has convinced me that most women who try to reinterpret religion as favorable to women do so because they have found many positive aspects in their traditions and therefore do not want to reject the whole, in spite of the manifestations of gender inequality.[34] Elisabeth Schussler Fiorenza explains the irony that religious traditions, and the biblical tradition in particular, have empowered women as well as oppressed them:

> Reclaiming the Bible as a feminist heritage and resource is only possible because it has not functioned only to legitimate the oppression of *all* women: freeborn, slave, black and white, native American, European and Asian, immigrant, poor, working-class and middle-class, Third World and First World women. It has also provided authorization and legitimization for women who have rejected slavery, racism, anti-Semitism, colonial exploitation, and misogynism as unbiblical and against God's will. The Bible has inspired and continues to inspire countless women to speak out and to struggle against injustice, exploitation, and stereotyping.[35]

Such women claim that the edification and love they experience through God and their religious community are what compels them to stay and work for gender change from within.

Women have used three main techniques to reclaim a role in defining religion for themselves and other marginalized groups. The first is what is sometimes called "reconstructive theology," or what Schussler Fiorenza also calls a "hermeneutics of remembrance."[36] This approach uses historical-critical methodology to uncover the social-political layers that underlie the biblical text and other church traditions to reveal which elements are products of the patriarchal cultures out of which church traditions emerge and which elements are central to the on-going universal Christian,

Jewish, or Muslim message. Proponents of this approach also use literary and rhetorical techniques to remember and recover texts and patterns favorable to women, such as the important role of women in the ministry of Jesus or other historical instances of women's theological and revelatory presence (e.g., the role of mystics like Hildegard of Bingen or Teresa of Avila).

The second hermeneutical approach borrows from philosophical feminism, such as that of Sandra Harding, to question the very foundations of western metaphysics, with its use of objective, rational modes of discourse that have traditionally privileged males.[37] The best voices in this approach do not suggest abandoning reason and systematic thought, nor do they assert that women are irrational. Rather, they insist on an ongoing questioning of the way reality is defined and a deconstruction of the methods we use to discover and construct it. In theological terms, this means looking at the underlying assumptions behind privileged doctrines. It means always asking how certain ideas reach center stage and remain prominent. It means examining how language and cultural values shape theory.

The third approach is represented by two major groups in America: Black, African-American Womanist theologians and Latina/Chicana feminists, sometimes called *mujerista* theologians, who connect with the liberationist theology movement.[38] Both groups of women assert their right to construct theories of religion on an equal footing with white women and men of color who often overlook the concerns of their sisters. These women add gender to the class and race issues raised by male liberationist theologians, arguing that their focus on equality arises out of biblical texts of redemption and justice. Jesus' treatment of the outcast and poor in the New Testament forms the center of this gospel message. Maria Pilar Aquino explains:

> The core content and ultimate finality of God's revelation is resumed in the term *salvation*. As the most precious gift of God to humans and to the

> world around us, salvation is understood by Latina feminist theology as liberation from every oppression. Thus the historical process of liberation from poverty, social injustice, and exclusion becomes the most effective and credible manifestation of God's salvation.[39]

Unfortunately, as womanist theologian Delores Williams argues, black women's experience is more often one of survival than liberation. By speaking of both "a God who liberates (the God of the enslaved Hebrews) and a God who does not liberate (the God of the non-Hebrew female slave Hagar),"[40] Williams hopes to point out hidden oppressions as well as to develop a hermeneutics that sees the personal encounter with God in the wilderness of faith as the center of empowerment.[41]

A central belief of all three approaches—the reconstructive, the philosophical, and the liberationist/womanist—is that theology begins with the lived experiences of the people of God or, in other words, that practice and theory are not separate. Certainly theoretical principles should inform the behavior of a believer ("whatsoever ye would that men should do to you, do ye even so to them"—Matt. 7:12). In the same way, if the experience of the believer is at odds with principle ("Let your women keep silence in the churches, for it is not permitted unto them to speak"—1 Cor. 14:34), then the believer should question and seek further enlightenment. What this interaction encourages is an ongoing dialogue between tradition and experience, which assumes that God is always speaking in the lives of the whole body of Christ.

But can these three approaches appropriately apply to Mormon theology, which is so thoroughly embedded in hierarchical structures that assume the rightness of the received tradition as perceived by the mainstream Church? In other words, is feminist theology at odds with LDS doctrine? I do not think so for three reasons. First, Mormonism asserts an open canon and acknowledges that even scriptural texts can contain the "mistakes of men"—human "weakness," as the prophet Moroni calls it (Ether 12). The importance of pairing these two beliefs—the need for ongoing revelation and the possibility of error—cannot be overstated. Continuing revelation then is not merely the addition of new doctrine, but also the clarification, correction, recontextualization, and perhaps even the rejection of existing doctrine. Under this theory, the 1978 revelation on priesthood and blacks does not have to be asserted as God suddenly changing his mind. Rather, we should be able to admit that the prohibitive policy itself was the result of our own human prejudice. Taking responsibility for our mistakes, institutionally as well as individually, opens the door for new revelation.[42]

The second reason for seeing compatibility between feminist concerns and LDS doctrine is that Mormon scriptural texts reinforce the most important biblical texts of equality. For example, the famous Pauline statement that in Christ Jesus there is "neither Jew nor Greek, there is neither bond nor free, there is neither male nor female" (Galations 3:28) is expanded by the prophet Nephi, who teaches: "For none of these iniquities come of the Lord . . . he inviteth them all to come unto him and partake of his goodness; and he denieth none that come unto him, black and white, bond and free, male and female; and he remembereth the heathen; and all are alike unto God, both Jew and Gentile" (2 Nephi 26:33). In fact, the Book of Mormon can easily be read as a text of liberation because of its ongoing motif of connecting spiritual liberation with political and class liberation (which is an ironic example of Delores Williams' God who both does and does not liberate, considering the fact that women are less visible in the Book of Mormon than in the Bible). The first section of the Doctrine and Covenants continues the theme of liberation by declaring that God "is no respecter of persons" and that the purpose of the Restoration is that the "weak things" might "break down the mighty and strong" and that every person "might speak in the name of God" (D&C 1:19, 20, 35).

My third reason for believing that feminist theology is not inimical to Mormonism is that current prophets have reasserted women's dignity and equal worth with men. As the Proclamation on the Family states, they are to be "equal partners," which is a goal of feminist theologies as well. The scripture which states that the "worth of souls is great in the sight of God" (D&C 18:10) is central to an LDS theology of personhood, central to the thesis of this paper, and the foundation for moral behavior in Mormon thought.

Although I sincerely believe that in theory feminist theology is compatible with Mormon doctrine, in practice I also believe that no such compatibility now exists. Though in theory Mormonism asserts that all are alike unto God and that women are equal partners with men, in current practice Mormonism is, at best, a religion of "separate but equal" genders, as illustrated by the Proclamation on the Family that divides the roles of men and women into the traditional public and private realms and puts men in a proprietary position over women. Men are to "preside," "provide," and "protect," while women are "primarily responsible" for nurturing children. And the Heavenly Mother has even fewer privileges than her daughters because she is the silent and invisible parent in the proclamation and the heavenly home. Further, by making Heavenly Mother a taboo topic, questions about the meaning of gender and of women's theological role are also rendered taboo. Today, all discussions of Heavenly Mother are seen by Church members and authorities as the dangerous concerns only of radical feminists. There is no space within the Church where one can argue that "separate but equal" inevitably creates a hierarchy privileging the powerful and disenfranchising the weak; there is no space to argue that "separate but equal" is no more an ethical policy when applied among the genders of a church than when applied to the races of a nation.

To my initial question—"Is there a place for Mother in Heaven in Mormon theology?"—I conclude that the weight of current Church practice and authority says no. When I began this project, my purpose was to develop a methodological model that balances the Mormon demand for official authorization with the theological need for rigorous philosophical analysis. I had hoped that in doing so I could create a model that is cognizant of LDS sensibilities about authority but that could also suggest ways in which theologizing could be more open to and inclusive of women, people of color, or others who are disenfranchised. Sadly, my efforts have failed and I must admit defeat for now because no amount of theorizing can change the dominant pattern in a church that accepts the present status quo as God's will and those who question it as heretics. Further, if the majority of LDS women do not feel that they are in a subordinate position and are content with their present role in Mormon culture and discourse, then it would be unethical for me to try to define them otherwise. Nevertheless, my own ethical sense also compels me to explain what I see as the ways in which the present structure is at odds with the demands of Christ's gospel, which is to say that balancing authority with inclusion is theoretically possible in my mind. My work in Mormon feminism for the past twenty years has attempted to show how core LDS texts and doctrines give a greater justification for women's equality than perhaps any other Christian tradition.[43] In spite of my present discouragement, I continue to write because a small part of me still hopes that others will see the gap between the Savior's injunctions for love and inclusion and the stratified hierarchy of the LDS Church. Much of my discouragement comes from my awareness of the allure of power. Why should men give up their power and share it with women? The LDS Church currently has one of the highest rates of male activity of any American religious organization. If women had priesthood, would men see it as less desirable? Would their activity rate drop if they didn't preside?[44] And what is at stake for failing to ask such questions?

This brings us back to my initial concern about the relationship between knowledge and power. In this paper I have tried to raise fundamental questions about the way we do Mormon theology, which for me is absolutely crucial for a scholarly organization like the Society of Mormon Philosophical Theology (SMPT) to consider, especially at its inception when precedents are being set for how we set up our organization. Who should control the forums and set up systems of evaluation, publication, distribution, and validation? Who decides and on what basis? Will some withdraw if others are in charge? Are we willing to give time to those with whom we disagree? What makes someone an authority, scholarly or religious? Are there any ideas and texts that should be privileged, and why? Is there any person or idea that should be excluded in our conversations about Mormon theology? SMPT's stated policy is that general academic standards apply, namely that the only criterion for inclusion or exclusion is scholarly excellence. But surely there is some conflict with SMPT being an open, academic forum when most of its members owe allegiance to the LDS Church that is uncomfortable with certain topics even being discussed. I do not mean this observation in a caustic or polemical way but more as a plea for all of us (liberal and conservative alike) to make an honest evaluation of the ways we inevitably bring our own biases and epistemological assumptions into play when we consider what makes something scholarly or not.[45] Are any of us really objective? From a larger philosophical perspective, poststructural theory has allowed us to see that complete objectivity is impossible, which is one of the factors that has mainstreamed feminism in the American academy in the last thirty years. Just consider the historical difficulty feminist theologians had in being taken seriously in the 1960s/1970s and that now some knowledge of feminism is mandatory in all major theological and religious studies programs across the country.[46] The changing status of various disciplines and approaches in American universities over the past fifty years shows the way in which ideology and politics shape systems of knowledge. If you think power is not an issue, it is because you have had it.

By framing the sexism question in this paper within the larger question of how power structures determine theological legitimacy in a Mormon setting, I have hoped to show the danger of letting authority hold sway over truth or beauty or love, not just for women, but for all. Though I have used the Heavenly Mother as a metaphor for whatever is currently marginalized and for whoever is disenfranchised, beaten, and left by the side of the road to die, men as well as women can occupy this spot. Men often think that gender issues do not apply to them, but they are as much the products of gender construction as are women. "Gender" is not simply about the relationship between "male" and "female" but about the way dichotomies create stratified systems of power (such as light and dark or black and white). In a hierarchical structure such as the Church's, every man is a "girl" to the men above him in the priesthood pipeline. Every doctrine is capable of becoming taboo like the Heavenly Mother, not on the basis of truth or logic or even popular disregard, but if it is pronounced such by those with the power to make it unspeakable. And every person can be labeled apostate when disagreement with any authority is made a sign of sin. Once the weight of authority is against a doctrine or a person, the only compelling argument for inclusion is an ethical one, based on principles of justice and love.[47] But can love ever prevail over power?

If we relegate the Heavenly Mother, her daughters, people of color, the poor, the outcast, the ignorant, the despised—the least of us—to the trash bin of theology and culture, then we have visited the same treatment upon Jesus Christ and the Heavenly Father, whom we claim to honor above all. Christ said, "As ye have done it unto the least of these, ye have done it unto me." This is both a cursing and a blessing, depending on where we stand. We worship not by prayer alone but through our answer to the Lord's call to "succor the weak, lift up the hands that hang down, and strengthen the feeble knees" (D&C 81:5). We are Christ's so long as we do the work of Christ, which is to empower the powerless and to relieve the pain of any who suffer. To fall short of this ideal is not only to fail to live Christ's gospel but to create bad theology as well.

MARGARET TOSCANO is an Assistant Professor of Classics at the University of Utah, where she received her Ph.D. in Comparative Literature; she received her M.A. in Classical Languages from Brigham Young University. She has spoken and written extensively on Mormon theology and feminism, including a book co-authored with Paul Toscano, *Strangers in Paradox: Explorations in Mormon Theology*, and a chapter in *Transforming the Faiths of Our Fathers: Women Who Changed American Religion*. She is currently organizing an international conference on "Hell and Its Afterlife: Comparative and Historical Perspectives," to take place in October 2006 at the University of Utah.

Notes

1. Gordon B. Hinckley, "Four Cornerstones of Faith," *Ensign*, February 2004, 3.
2. President Hinckley says that the fourth cornerstone, priesthood, "is the power and authority to govern in the affairs of the kingdom of God" and that the "qualification for eligibility is obedience to the commandments of God." He emphasizes all men may receive it, regardless of their "station in life," the "color of their skin," or "the nation in which they live." Gender, then, is the one difference that disqualifies half of the Church.
3. I am simplifying Michel Foucault's complex theory, represented by such books as *The Archaeology of Knowledge and the Discourse on Language*; trans. A. M. Sheridan Smith (New York: Pantheon Books, 1972) and *Power/Knowledge: Selected Interviews and Other Writings, 1972–1977*; trans. Colin Gordon (Sussex, England: Harvester Press, 1980).
4. This does not mean that I find his theories fully sufficient. Feminists have critiqued Foucault for failing to engage enough with the way gender relates to the question of discourse and power. See, for example, Ramazanoglu, Caroline, ed. *Up Against Foucault: Explorations of Some Tensions between Foucault and Feminism.* (London; New York: Routledge, 1993). Also, from

an LDS perspective, Foucault's theories are fairly deterministic since they downplay human agency.

5. While the term "independent publication" often implies a more liberal press, such as *Sunstone*, *Dialogue* or Signature Books, in one sense anything not published by the Church itself is "independent" of direct Church control. However, the use of the term to designate "liberal" is telling because it implies that such publications are not *dependent enough* on Church strictures. Thus, there are layers of perceived legitimacy in non-official publications, perceptions based simply on what seems to look to the Church and priesthood approval for its theological guidelines.
6. *Encyclopedia of Mormonism*. ed. Daniel H. Ludlow. 5 vols. (New York: Macmillan, 1992), s.v. "Mother in Heaven." Linda Wilcox gives the best history of the Heavenly Mother doctrine and explains the problems with attributing it to Joseph Smith. Elaine Cannon is the author of the entry in the *Encyclopedia of Mormonism*. It is significant that the Church's official website has no reference to the Heavenly Mother, which has a wider audience and more influence than the *Encyclopedia*.
7. Doe Daughtrey. "Bodies, Parts, and Passions," paper delivered at the 2002 Salt Lake Sunstone Symposium. Tape #SL02-254. Daughtrey's query generated a total of about forty posts on beliefnet.com.
8. The result here is misleading, in reality representing an even smaller number. Two references in talks by Mark E. Petersen describe the belief in a Mother God as a characteristic of early Christian dissenting groups. And most of the others are quoting or referencing two authoritative statements, one by Orson F. Whitney and one by Spencer W. Kimball.
9. Gordon B. Hinckley, "Daughters of God," Ensign, November 1991, 97.
10. Ibid.
11. President Hinckley could be interpreted as contradicting the idea that Heavenly Father is protecting the Heavenly Mother by forbidding reference to her when President Hinckley says that "none of us can add to or diminish the glory of her of whom we have no revealed knowledge." See ibid.
12. Linda Wilcox quotes a 1960 statement from an LDS seminary teacher who speculates that "the name of our Mother in Heaven has been withheld" because of the way God the Father and Jesus Christ's names have been pro-

faned. See Linda Wilcox, "The Mormon Concept of a Mother in Heaven," in *Women and Authority: Re-emerging Mormon Feminism*, ed. Maxine Hanks (Salt Lake City: Signature Books, 1992), 7. Whether he is the source of the idea or is reflecting a prevalent belief is hard to say. See also Melvin R. Brooks, *LDS Reference Encyclopedia*, (Salt Lake City: Deseret Book Co., 1960), 142.

13. In Daughtrey's work on the "disappearing discourse" about the Heavenly Mother (cited above), she asserts that the LDS Church's interest in covering up the Heavenly Mother doctrine is related to its desire to be seen as Christian by Protestants, which means erasing anything that may seem "weird" to Protestant sensibilities, such as a plurality of gods. While I agree wholeheartedly with Daughtrey that this is a central concern, I still believe that the fear of feminism's demands may be an even stronger reason to eliminate discourse about Heavenly Mother. Consider the fact that many mainstream Protestant denominations allow feminine references to God.
14. Mary Douglas' classic *Purity and Danger: An Analysis of Concepts of Pollution and Taboo*, (New York: Routledge, 1966) still offers insight. She says that taboos result from a desire for order as much as from fear and that the object or person under taboo may be considered holy as well as dangerous and polluted.
15. Spencer W. Kimball, "Fundamental Principles to Ponder and Live," *Ensign*, November 1978, 43–46.
16. First given as an address at a televised, Church-wide fireside, 22 February 1987, Ezra Taft Benson's remarks were later reprinted in his *Come Listen to a Prophet's Voice*. (Salt Lake City: Deseret Book Co., 1990), 25–37.
17. Divorce and birth control practices among LDS people are other examples of how practice subtly reshapes belief. Where Joseph Fielding Smith advised my generation not to practice birth control at all, most LDS people today see birth control as a perfectly acceptable element of prayerful family planning.
18. Articles in *BYU Today* and *Salt Lake Tribune* both dealt with this phenomenon. Another factor may be the human fascination with secrets.
19. The marriage of Jesus to Mary Magdalene is obviously a topic of interest as well. But the fact that this idea makes women more visible and central to Christianity is relevant here.

20. Raphael Patai, *The Hebrew Goddess*, 3rd ed. (Detroit: Wayne State UP, 1990).
21. Most likely, Mormon scholars in the mainstream have a more direct influence over the views of the membership, especially those who speak and publish in popular forums.
22. A panel on postmodernism at the March 2004 Mormon Theology Conference, which is included in this volume, did suggest that there are other valid approaches for Mormon theology. But these have not dominated in Mormon theological discourse, which instead has tended to follow the pattern set by philosophical thinkers such as Sterling McMurrin, who exemplifies the tendency to position Mormon theology within the Enlightenment framework. Typical of his generation, McMurrin also uses exclusively male language to describe the norm—a pattern that few have broken away from since. It should be obvious that I am more influenced by postmodern thought, which has some exciting implications for Mormon theology.
23. The result is also that important theological contributions can be overlooked. In the work I have done on medieval women mystics, I found that their often poetic approach seems to put them in a secondary category of theologians, or they are not seen as theologians at all. The fact that poetic male mystics, like John of the Cross, are nevertheless considered theological may indicate that gender and power issues are at work here too.
24. Blake Ostler, *Exploring Mormon Thought: The Attributes of God.* (Salt Lake City: Greg Kofford Books, 2001).
25. Paul Toscano and I treat the importance of Mormonism's contribution in our book *Strangers in Paradox: Explorations in Mormon Theology*, (Salt Lake City: Signature Books, 1990), 29–48.
26. While some scholars have argued that female deities are not linked with political or social power for women, I believe this is a misleading interpretation of historical evidence. Since all cultures we know about are patriarchal, female deities have obviously not changed this pattern in the cultures where they exist. However, to use the example of ancient Athens where male power was supreme, the following was still true: religion was the *one* area of life where women had public visibility, leadership roles as priestesses over men,

and the right to move freely and act for the benefit of the whole community. The power of goddesses in Athenian religion was no doubt an influence.

27. Church of Jesus Christ of Latter-day Saints, "Family: A Proclamation to the World"; available from http://www.lds.org/library/display/0,4945,161-1-11-1,00.html ; Internet; accessed 22 November 2005.
28. Gordon B. Hinckley, "Daughters of God," 97.
29. If this is true, we could ask why the terms "God" or "Heavenly Father" do not include the feminine. If they do, then praying to Heavenly Father includes the Heavenly Mother too.
30. Lynne Whitesides, Martha Esplin, and I interacted with President Hinckley's talk in a panel discussion, "Finding Our Bodies, Hearts, Voices: A Three-Part Invention," *The Mormon Women's Forum: A Feminist Quarterly* 4.2 (September 1993): 18–22.
31. I have taken these numbers from BYU's web page, July 2005.
32. As explained in the Introduction to this volume, this is an expansion of the paper I gave at the Mormon Theology Conference, held 19–20 March 2004 and co-sponsored by the Utah Valley State College Religious Studies Program and the Society for Mormon Philosophy and Theology (SMPT). Not only was I the only woman participant on the program, but I was also apparently the only woman who submitted a proposal (happily there were two women on the program in 2005). Moreover, the audience itself was predominantly male, with about twelve men for every woman. Thus the conference itself was an enactment of my premise that there is something about the power and authority structure of the LDS community that discourages women from full participation in theological and philosophical discourse, not only in Church settings but in academic ones too. I owe my inclusion mostly to the strong support of Brian Birch and Dennis Potter, UVSC faculty members and two of SMPT's founders.
33. Ada Maria Isasi-Diaz, "Mujerista Theology," *Oxford Readings in Feminism: Feminism & Theology*, ed. Janet Martin Soskice and Diana Lipton (Oxford; New York: Oxford UP, 2003), 95
34. In the new book, *Transforming the Faiths of Our Fathers: Women Who Changed American Religion*, ed. Ann Braude, (New York: Palgrave, 2004), leading women theologians of various faiths describe their feminist journeys. This book emerged from a 2002 Harvard Conference in which I was privi-

leged to participate. I was profoundly moved by the spirituality and commitment of all these women.

35. Elizabeth Schussler Fiorenza, *Bread Not Stone: The Challenge of Feminist Biblical Interpretation*, (Boston: Beacon Press, 1984), viii.
36. Ibid., xx.
37. Sandra Harding and Merrill B. Hintikka, eds., *Discovering Reality: Feminist Perspectives on Epistemology, Metaphysics, Metholdology, and Philosophy of Science*. 2nd ed. (Boston: Kluwer Academic Publishers, 2003).
38. Linda Moody's *Women Encounter God: Theology Across the Boundaries of Difference*, (Maryknoll, NY: Orbis Books, 1996), not only gives an excellent summary of both of these types of feminist theology but also gives a good overview of white feminist theology as she explains similarities and differences among the various groups.
39. Maria Pilar Aquino, "Latina Feminist Theology: Central Features," in *A Reader in Latina Feminist Theology: Religion and Justice*, ed. Maria Pilar Aquino, Daisy L. Machado, and Jeanette Rodriguez (Austin, TX: U of Texas P, 2002) 151.
40. Delores S. Williams, *Sisters in the Wilderness: The Challenge of Womanist God-talk* (Maryknoll, NY: Orbis Books, 1993), 148.
41. Ibid., 120.
42. Of course, the Church has never admitted a mistake in its past policy on blacks and the priesthood. This adds, in my opinion, to our ongoing race problems. See roundtable discussion, "Speak the Truth and Shame the Devil," *Sunstone* (May 2003): 28–39, for experiences of black LDS members on race problems. And see Newell Bringhurst, *Saints, Slaves, and Blacks: The Changing Place of Black People within Mormonism* (Westport, CN: Greenwood Press, 1981) and Lester E. Bush Jr. and Armand L. Mauss, eds. *Neither White nor Black: Mormon Scholars Confront the Race Issue in a Universal Church* (Salt Lake City: Signature Books, 1984) for discussions on the complex historical and textual problems of sorting out the Church's doctrine before and after the 1978 revelation.
43. *Strangers in Paradox* contains most of my work up to 1990. Since then, my essays have appeared either in *Dialogue* or the *Mormon Women's Forum: A Feminist Publication.*

44. Inevitably the question of equality brings us back to questions about priesthood and Heavenly Mother. See my "Put on Your Strength, O Daughters of Zion: Claiming the Priesthood and Knowing the Mother," in *Women and Authority: Re-emerging Mormon Feminism*, ed. Maxine Hanks (Salt Lake City: Signature Books, 1992), 411–437.
45. This means that liberal Mormons and liberal publications are as guilty as conservative ones in limiting both the free expression of ideas and the type of knowledge that is circulated. It seems to me, that ethics, as well as intellectual openness, demand that Mormon scholars of all persuasions must be willing to critique their own systems of authorization.
46. For first-hand accounts of how this happened, see the essays by Rosemary Radford Ruether, Carol P. Christ, Elisabeth Schussler Fiorenza, and Judith Plaskow in Ann Braude's collection *Transforming the Faiths of Our Fathers.*
47. I am profoundly moved by Emmanuel Levinas' assertion that a "face to face" interaction with the Other demands an "I-Thou" exchange. This kind of relationship provides the only immunity against the objectification of others as commodities to be eliminated when they do not readily fit into a privileged power system, theological or otherwise. To read about this theme in Levinas, see especially *Otherwise than Being or Beyond Essence*, trans. Alphonso Lingis (The Hague, Netherlands: Martinus Nijhoff, 1981) and *Totality and Infinity: An Essay on Exteriority*, trans. Alphonso Lingis (Pittsburgh: Duquesne UP, 1969).

Scripture and Doctrine

Messianic History

Walter Benjamin and the Book of Mormon

Adam S. Miller
Collin College

Mormon history is haunted throughout by anachrony. Historical incongruities are abundant in the Book of Mormon and in accounts dealing with both the First Vision and the restoration of the priesthood. In this respect, however, the Book of Mormon is exemplary. Page after page its pre-advent Christian message illustrates clearly the kind of anachronisms here at stake. Its anachrony is manifest both in terms of the details it gives of future events in the life of Christ and in terms of the highly developed Christian vocabulary that it employs. What are we to make of this? The thesis to be explored here may be simply stated as follows: this anachrony is neither accidental, nor debilitating. Rather, that which is messianic is necessarily anachronic. To state our thesis as precisely as possible right from the start we should say: the messianic, as messianic, is that which retroactively reconfigures history itself.

This paper will proceed through a series of overlapping reformulations of the above thesis. Each unit in this series will consist of the following three parts: (1) a concise, single sentence re-formulation of the initial thesis, (2) an elaboration of the thesis in connection with the work of Walter Benjamin, and (3) an exploration of the ways in which the thesis finds expression in the Book of Mormon.

Reformulation 1: The messianic, as messianic, involves the rediscovery of that which was lost

1a. According to Isaiah it is necessary, at least for a time, that the Messiah go unrecognized. It is crucial, at least for a certain while, that he remain hidden, that he *not* shine forth, that he have "no form, nor comeliness" and that he possess "no beauty that we should desire him" (Isa. 53:2). In other words, his coming must be delayed. This is necessarily so, at least in part, because the very act of recognition bears in itself a revolutionary or messianic force. The inception of revolution, the advent of the messianic, is: to see what was previously unseen and to stand exposed in the face of that which was concealed but now appears. It follows that it should come as no surprise to us when that which is messianic is hidden under a rock, given in a grove, or stowed in a stable.

1b. Angels began appearing to Joseph Smith in 1823 in upstate New York. He was seventeen. On the twenty-first of September 1823 an angel came to Joseph three times in one night and once more in the morning. Four times the messenger from eternity repeated the same message: four times he quoted verses from the Bible and four times he told Joseph of a book long hidden and long lost and long forgotten. Go, the angel told him, to a big hill just south of your house; look under a rock and you will find it.

Reformulation 2: The messianic, as messianic, occurs within history without belonging to history

2a. In relation to the messianic, time is the crucial factor. The messianic must, as we said, "at least for a time" go unrecognized. It is this delay, this beat between repetitions, between arrival and appearance, between being buried and unearthed, that allows the messianic to gather light before bursting forth. This space, the gap of the "for a time," is the space of history. Whether or not we are in a position to recognize the messianic depends on the way in which we do history; that is to say, it is a question of how we live time. If time is lived homogeneously, as simply temporal, then the messianic will never appear. But if time remains open to interruption by the eternal, then its heterogeneity preserves the possibility of the messianic. The heterogeneity of time is crucial and it is manifest, precisely, in anachronism. That is to say, that which is eternal, that which is time-*less* shows up in history as the *un*-timely, as anachrony.

2b. After the angel's initial appearances, Joseph went, as instructed, to the location shown to him. There he found the rock, unearthed the book, and saw that which had remained hidden for hundreds of years. Joseph attempted to remove the book, but with a shock the angel appeared again, interrupting him. Wait, the angel told him. Come back every year for four years, then it will be time. So, for the space of four years Joseph waited, the visits were repeated and the book remained in the ground. For another four years history remained exactly that: history.

Reformulation 3: The messianic, as messianic, interrupts the tyranny of homogeneous time

3a. Walter Benjamin distinguishes two ways of doing history: one is messianic, the other is not. The kind of history that is not messianic—"universal history"—is merely additive. It simply "musters a mass of data to fill the homogeneous, empty time."[1] This type of history is homogenous because it is content to string events together strictly according to "causal" connections. But, as Benjamin is quick to point out, "no fact that is a cause is for that very reason historical."[2] Rather, causes become "historical posthumously, as it were."[3] On what basis are causes retroactively selected as historical? The criterion is straightforward: universal history selects and relates those events that are most obviously momentous and epoch forming. In other words, universal history is elaborated from the victor's point of view. It is a history articulated by the powerful about their uses of power. From them accounts are handed down of great men and celebrated events that shape and inform our entire sense of history. Indeed, the very weight and magnitude of these epochal events imprint on us a distinct notion of time: in light of them history appears as both inevitable and progressive. In light of them time becomes flattened, is rendered empty and homogeneous, and incongruities are effaced in favor of a temporality that appears only as a streamlined linearity, rocketing of its own power towards an appropriate climax. This kind of temporal linearity is familiar. It characterizes the kind of inexorable temporality that naturally belongs to any kind of history that is ordered strictly according to causal connections: determinism.

3b. When addressing the Book of Mormon, it is important to remember that the angel initially appeared to Joseph in response to a very specific prayer. Joseph relates that prayer as follows: "on the evening of the above mentioned twenty-first of September, after I had retired to my bed for the night, I betook myself to prayer and supplication to Almighty God for forgiveness of all my sins and follies" (Joseph Smith—History 1:29). In other words, late at night, in his bed clothes, Joseph was pleading for a fresh start. He was asking to be freed from the inevitable consequences of his sins and follies. That is to say: Joseph was looking to interrupt the homogeneous chain of cause and effect. It is possible to name with precision this plea for messianic intervention in a single word: repentance. Repentance is the one word summation of all that we mean to say by the messianic anachrony characteristic of heterogeneous time. In response to Joseph's prayer the angel appears and says to him: if that is what you want, there is a lost book hidden under a rock not far from your home; go and see.

Reformulation 4: The messianic, as messianic, marks the intervention of the eternal in time via a pure repetition

4a. It is clear to Benjamin that "calendars do not measure time as clocks do."[4] Instead of incessantly ticking forward like clocks, calendars repeat the same days of the same months every year. They rotate on an axis that moves them ahead only as they are turning back around. For Benjamin, calendars exemplify the double movement of messianic time: they are a pure repetition that succeeds in going beyond only by circling back. When Benjamin wishes to describe the kind of history proper to this notion of time, he uses a particular word: constellation. A historian who takes messianic time "as his point of departure stops telling the sequence of events like the beads of a rosary. Instead, he grasps the constellation which his own era has formed with a definite earlier one."[5] This image of stars aligning, of constellations forming, is precisely in sync with Benjamin's description of messianic time as calendrical. The messianic historian is able to gather both the past and present in a single glance because for her time moves only by means of novel repetition. She watches the stars run their course as they turn through the seasons and waits for the moment in which the events of her own era will repeat, correspond with and thus be illuminated by events from an earlier time. For her, events correspond and form distinct constellations in accordance with criteria that are not causal; rather, constellations form on the basis of affinities and resemblances. Here, the homogeneous diachrony of history is interrupted by the synchrony of resemblance, and time is interrupted by the eternal thus, history itself becomes novel. These synchronic constellations are messianic when they involve events or images from the past that have gone unrecognized or remained hidden, images that have been lost, discounted or repressed, but remain nonetheless. When recognized, the revelatory shock produced by such surprising constellations fractures the hegemony of the present, touches eternity, opens new horizons and ushers in a revolutionary moment. This revolutionary potential borne by that which has been lost or discarded indicates precisely the reason why Benjamin refers to this kind of history as messianic.

4b. The Book of Mormon defines a seer as one who is able to recover and "translate all records that are of an ancient date; and it is a gift from God" (Mosiah 8:13). As a result, a seer is even greater than a prophet and is able, in a single glance, to hold all of time together. Quote: "But a seer can know of things which are past, and also of things which are to come, and by them shall all things be revealed, or, rather, shall secret things be made manifest, and hidden things shall come to light, and things which are not known shall be made known by them" (Mosiah 8:17). Thus it is that by means of a seer, "God has provided a means that man, through faith, might work mighty miracles; therefore he" the seer becomes, because of his messianic testimony, "a great benefit unto his fellow beings" (Mosiah 8:18).

Reformulation 5: The messianic, as messianic, exposes homogeneous "progress" as vain

5a. This much must become clear: it is necessary that our faith in "progress" be broken. All is not well, nor are things proceeding along smoothly from cause to effect to effect. We must learn to see history from a new perspective. When we learn to view history as does Benjamin's own remarkable "angel of history," then we will find ourselves incapable of continued belief in the paralyzing promise of progress. Instead of viewing the past as a wave of momentous events whose crest has successfully carried us thus far and will continue to carry us as far as we need ever go, we will learn to see the past and present as they genuinely stand: in need of salvation. This is the revelation borne by Benjamin's angel of history: "where we perceive a chain of events," each improving upon and adding to those that preceded it, Benjamin says, the angel sees only

> one single catastrophe which keeps piling wreckage upon wreckage and hurls it in front of his feet. The angel would like to stay, awaken the dead, and make whole what has been smashed. But a storm is blowing from Paradise; it has got caught in his wings with such violence that the angel can no longer close them. This storm irresistibly propels him into the future to which his back is turned, while the pile of debris grows skyward. This storm is what we call progress.[6]

The angel's traumatic vision of the past and present is both unnerving and necessary. Without it we fail to recognize both the need for the messianic ("things will turn out!") and the moments in which its inception may be possible.

5b. The history recounted by the Book of Mormon is, in its consummation, bleak: a virtually universal rejection of the Messiah sets in motion a devastating ethnic conflict that results in the nearly complete annihilation of the people and civilization to which Mormon had belonged. The desolation is augmented by the fact that a catastrophically oriented vision of the past and present tangibly shapes Mormon's own editorial efforts. Mormon not only watched his world self-destruct as thousands of bodies literally piled up at his feet, but he also found himself, as an angel of history, incapable of making things whole again.

Reformulation 6: The messianic, as messianic, carefully collects the heterogeneous debris of history

6a. Benjamin's messianic historian is the consummate collector whose methods often bear a closer resemblance to those "of the nineteenth century ragpicker, than to those of the modern historian."[7] While quaint, this description is essential. We must be careful to not underestimate the gravity of the difference between the methods of the "ragpicker" and the modern historian. While it is true that the modern historian commendably attempts to trade in measured objectivity, it is also true that only the collector possesses both the affection and attention needed in order to breathe new life into old anonymous things. Only the collector lovingly gathers and cares for that which others have cast off as outmoded, unusable or unimportant. Only the collector attends to what is materially inassimilable for homogeneous history. Only the collector possesses the passion for anomalous detail capable of allowing peculiar affinities and resemblances to gather weight and unity until they stand forth together with striking and illuminating clarity. Unlike the historians of the powerful, the collector is interested not only in objects, but in their history. She is interested not only in use, but in memory. Like the disparaged ragpicker or the foolish star-gazer, only the collector has the leisure time needed to attend to remnants and contingencies with the kind of concerned patience and long-suffering that allows surprising constellations to align, appear, and transform us.

6b. In the destructive wake of those vying for power there remained for Mormon only one thing to do. He turned to the task of collecting and examining the debris. He poured over the stacks of records at his disposal chronicling the events of the last thousand years and asked as he read: What has been rejected? What shards remained of that which once was valued? What was on the verge of being forgotten? He was looking for the messianic and as he found a piece here and a fragment there he strung them all together into a single volume that no one would read for fourteen centuries more.

Reformulation 7: The messianic, as messianic, speaks from the dust

7a. What is it that collects around the lost objects desired by the collector? The dust of history—a dust that is not to be brushed off, but treasured in itself. One name for this dust that the collector treasures is aura. Benjamin's use of the term "aura" is slippery, but we can at the very least indicate a general sense: aura is the history that congeals around objects. Benjamin says, "If we designate as aura the associations which . . . tend to cluster around the object of a perception, then its analogue in the case of the utilitarian object is the experience which has left traces of the practiced hand."[8] It is important to see that an object's aura is not something banally subjective or purely personal; rather, aura is tied to the autonomy of the signifier. It is a "matter of tradition" that involves "collective existence as well as private life," and "it is less the product of facts firmly anchored in memory than of a convergence in memory of accumulated and frequently unconscious data" (157). These accumulated and convergent associations which constitute an aura are, according to Benjamin, based on the kind of non-sensuous, but non-arbitrary similarities that he takes as constitutive of language itself. Auras, like the traces left behind on a well-worn tool by a practiced hand, are in some sense both collective and personal, both conscious and unconscious. They are actually there—one need only learn to look in order to see them.

7b. The Book of Mormon predicts its own messianic advent. Drawing on Isaiah 29 it explicitly describes its own recovery in terms of dust. "For those who shall be destroyed shall speak unto them out of the ground, and their speech shall be low out of the dust, and their voice shall be one that hath a familiar spirit; for the Lord God will give unto him power, that he may whisper concerning them, even as it were out of the ground; and their speech will whisper out of the dust" (2 Ne. 26:16). The voice of the Book of Mormon is a voice that is both hauntingly familiar and disconcertingly other. It is a repetition of that which was lost, but remains. It is the whisper out of the ground, unearthed, of those who had been lost, forgotten, destroyed. It is, according to its own description, the voice from the dust—or, better, the voice *of* the dust. Of us it says:

> The Lord hath poured out upon you the spirit of deep sleep. For behold, ye have closed your eyes, and ye have rejected the prophets; and your rulers, and the seers hath he covered because of your iniquity. And it shall come to pass that the Lord God will bring forth unto you the words of a book, and they shall be the words of them which have slumbered. And behold the book shall be sealed; and in the book shall be a revelation from God, from the beginning of the world to the ending thereof. Wherefore, because of the things which are sealed up, the things which are sealed shall not be delivered in the day of wickedness and abominations of the people. Wherefore the book shall be kept from them. But the book shall be delivered unto a man, and he shall deliver the words of the book, which are the words of those who have slumbered in the dust. (2 Ne. 27:5–9)

Reformulation 8: The messianic, as messianic, is both monadological and universal

8a. Messianic history is monadological. That is to say, the discarded materials from which it draws its strength are each meant to be, as Benjamin describes it, "a magic encyclopedia" that is at once both esoteric and comprehensive.[9] It is esoteric in that its revelatory capacity is neither obvious nor immediately accessible. It is comprehensive in that by means of it, the whole world is offered to our view. By means of its aura, of its convergence of associations, each separate article in the collection offers an image of the entire epoch to which it belongs. For Benjamin, that which can be divined from the hem of a dress, the heft of a lighter, or the binding of a book is limitless. Hence, Benjamin describes messianic history as monadological: each article in the collection opens the whole world to our gaze from that monad's particular and singular point of view. It is from this magically encyclopedic capacity of the aura that messianic history derives its revolutionary capacity and its universal import. We unavoidably and continuously view the entire world from our own particular, homogeneous, well-worn perspective. Here the historical monad intervenes. It offers us just what we need: a new point of view. It does not, however, offer just any novel point of view. Rather, it offers us the whole world from the point of view of that which has been systematically excluded from history—the very exclusion necessary in order for homogeneous history to be constituted as such. In short, the monad is messianic because it shows us the world, the whole world, from the dust-filled perspective of the forgotten and oppressed.

8b. The Book of Mormon is a monad. It is intentionally microcosmic. Spanning nearly a thousand years it narrates the messianic journey of a family from the old world to the new, their expansion into a people, their fracture into parties vying for power, their rejection of the Messiah and the nearly genocidal catastrophe that ensues. It gives us, despite all its concrete particularities and idiosyncrasies, the world as a whole in "the words of them which have slumbered" in the dust. It is, as we have noted, a book that is "sealed" and made unavailable, but also a book that is conjointly a "revelation from God, from the beginning of the world to the ending thereof" (2 Ne. 27:6–7). It is meant to be revelatory in a universal way, revealing the world from beginning to end, and revealing it in such a way as to usher in the coming of the Messiah.

Reformulation 9: The messianic, as messianic, reveals "necessities" as contingent

9a. The historical monad allows that which has been present, but unrecognized to appear. In a well-known essay, "The Work of Art in the Age of Mechanical Reproduction," Benjamin offers a vivid description of the revolutionary punch potentially packed by the advent of the camera.

> By close-ups of things around us, by focusing on hidden details of familiar objects, by exploring commonplace milieus under the ingenious guidance of the camera, the film, on the one hand, extends our comprehension of the necessities which rule our lives; on the other hand, it manages to assure us of an immense and unexpected field of action. Our taverns and our metropolitan streets, our offices and our furnished rooms, our railroad stations and our factories appeared to have us locked up hopelessly. Then came the film and burst this prison-world asunder by the dynamite of the tenth of a second, so that now, in the midst of far-flung ruins and debris, we calmly and adventurously go traveling.[10]

The camera is the historical monad. It freezes the diachrony of history in a moment of synchronic exposure. It offers us the familiar world from an unfamiliar perspective. It extends our comprehension of the necessities that rule our lives even as it calls those very necessities into question. The very immutability of these necessities appeared much more immutable when they presented to us only the side they wished us to see. Hence, an immense field of action opens itself before us: not only does the world appear in new and unexpected ways, but we find ourselves capable of performing surprising and revolutionary deeds. A gap in time opens between *what must be* and *what is* and so, as Benjamin puts it, "every second" becomes "the strait gate through which the Messiah might enter."[11]

9b. When Joseph Smith unearthed the book for the first time in the fall of 1823, he found with it a number of objects in addition to the book itself. Joseph recounts that "on the west side of the hill, not far from the top, under a stone of considerable size, lay the plates" on which the lost record was written,

> deposited in a stone box. This stone was thick and rounding in the middle on the upper side, and thinner towards the edges, so that the middle part of it was visible above the ground, but the edge all around was covered with earth. Having removed the earth, I obtained a lever, which I got fixed under the edge of the stone, and with a little exertion raised it up. I looked in, and there indeed did I behold the plates, the Urim and Thummim, and the breastplate. (JS—H 1:51–52)

What is a Urim and Thummim? Joseph describes it simply as "two stones in silver bows" into which he could look in order to translate the Book of Mormon. They operated, apparently, as a set of lenses that unsealed the book, revealed its world and opened what was to be the dispensation of the fullness of times. And here "dispensation" acquires for us a very precise sense: a dispensation is an epoch forming retroactive reconfiguration of history.

Reformulation 10: The messianic, as messianic, persists out of its time, irremediably

10a. We catch wind of the vanity of "progress" in that it fails to assimilate what it ought to have assimilated. Discarded, lost, and forgotten objects have the power to arrest our gaze and command us simply on the basis of the fact that they are a genuine surprise. How could this thing still be around? It no longer has a place in this world. It no longer belongs to us. The sheer brute material incongruity of an object's continuing subsistence stares back at us in a way that calls into question the hegemony of the present moment. Rather, one is constrained to exclaim: that thing is still here?!? Benjamin cites Proust in relation to the importance of this materiality: though "the past is 'somewhere beyond the reach of the intellect, [it remains] unmistakably present in some material object.'"[12] Benjamin goes further in this regard when, addressing the nature of a collector, he asks, "And the non-reading of books, you will object, should be characteristic of collectors?"[13] It goes almost without saying for Benjamin that this is the case. The collector is not primarily interested in the contents of the book, in what is relatively accessible by the intellect on its own power, but in the book as a material object that is itself capable of bearing the necessary convergence of revelatory associations in the same way that it is capable of collecting dust. This is the power of the collector: while the universal historian, bent on progress and causally myopic, is only able to look *through* objects, the collector is able to look *at* them and *stay* with them.

10b. In his recent study, *By the Hand of Mormon: The American Scripture that Launched a New World Religion*, Terryl Givens is clear about what has always mattered most to Mormons about the Book of Mormon. Serious, widespread study of the actual text of the Book of Mormon is a relatively recent phenomenon. What has always mattered most is that *there is* such a book.[14] Joseph had visions and visits from angels, but his experiences also produced this brute material thing and its sheer material incongruity is, of itself, incontrovertible. This in itself provokes the need for a response and incites a messianic interruption of the status quo.

Reformulation 11: The messianic, as messianic, is anachronistic

11a. A messianic constellation is formed when present events align with and repeat that which is lost in such a way as to reveal revolutionary possibilities. Such a constellation is simply the synchronic actualization of an aura. That is to say, such a constellation is an experience of the convergence of associations that belong to any historical object and constitute it as an object with a life history. The crystallization of such a constellation produces a shock that arrests the inevitable forward march of progress and realigns past and present in a way that is not causal. It follows then that such a realignment of past and present opens a future that is no longer "predetermined" and is now "free" for revolution. When a lost or discarded object is actualized in this way it is reborn. "I am not exaggerating," Benjamin insists, "when I say that to a true collector the acquisition of an old book is its rebirth."[15] That which is reborn in this way both does and does not properly belong to the present moment. That is to say: an articulation of this "rebirth" forces again the question that concerns us most: the question of anachrony. This synchronic rebirth involves both a retroactive reconfiguration of the past in light of what had been forgotten, but is now re-born and an opening of the present to messianic intervention. Benjamin describes this process as follows:

> Thinking involves not only the flow of thoughts, but their arrest as well. Where thinking suddenly stops in a configuration pregnant with tensions, it gives that configuration a shock, by which it crystallizes into a monad. A historical materialist approaches a historical subject only where he encounters it as a monad. In this structure he recognizes the sign of a Messianic cessation of happening, or, put differently, a revolutionary chance in the fight for the oppressed past."[16]

It follows, then, that to such historical objects there is a certain kind of un/timeliness. Benjamin indicates this dimension of un/timeliness when he notes that

> If we are prepared to consider history as a text, we can say about it what some modern author said about a literary text: the past has deposed in it images which could be compared to those retained by a photographic plate. Only the future disposes of developers strong enough to make appear the picture with all its details. More than one page of Marivaux or

> of Rousseau attests to a meaning which their contemporary readers were unable to decipher completely.[17]

The past retains in it images that are incapable of appearing as contemporaneous with its milieu. Before they can appear they require the space of a "for a time." Only in light of the future can they appear as what they are. Only when the past is anachronistically and retroactively reconstituted can the lost and excluded elements of history be redeemed. And only if such an anachronically and retroactively reconfigured history is legitimate is repentance possible. Further, to return to the initial point, this event of retroactive reconfiguration is what makes the "actualization" of a historical monad possible. The thesis, remember, is this: Without anachrony the messianic would simply fail to appear.

11b. In regard to anachrony, the Book of Mormon is, as we have said, exemplary. This correlates fundamentally with its essential messianicity. It is certainly the case that any attempt to neatly peg the Book of Mormon as belonging clearly to one particular historical period (e.g., to nineteenth century rural American or to ancient Hebrew refugees living most likely somewhere in Central America) quickly becomes unwieldy. Further, nothing is more disconcerting to the historically attuned reader than to find Hebrew prophets predicting with great precision the details of Jesus's life and ministry. The ways in which the Book of Mormon so profoundly and unabashedly employs the theological vocabulary and addresses the religious aporias of nineteenth-century rural America are also astonishing. This is to say, the Book of Mormon accomplishes the task of retroactively reconfiguring all of history with surprising alacrity: In light of it, *all* of history becomes explicitly and undeniably Christ-centered. The wager of this paper is that this anachrony is the very condition necessary for the Book of Mormon to operate in an explicitly Messianic fashion. Were the book otherwise, it would fail to accomplish its own explicit purpose of testifying universally, to both Jew and Gentile, "that Jesus is the Christ," the

Messiah, "manifesting himself unto all nations."

We have, then, offered twelve complementary formulations of our thesis. Gathering them all together they include the following:

1. The messianic is that which retroactively reconfigures history itself.
2. The messianic involves the rediscovery of that which was lost.
3. The messianic occurs within history without belonging to history.
4. The messianic interrupts the tyranny of homogeneous time.
5. The messianic marks the intervention of the eternal in time via a pure repetition.
6. The messianic exposes homogeneous "progress" as vain.
7. The messianic carefully collects the heterogeneous debris of history.
8. The messianic speaks from the dust.
9. The messianic is both monadological and universal.
10. The messianic reveals "necessities" as contingent.
11. The messianic persists out of its time, irremediably.
12. The messianic is anachronistic.

In light of these theses a final reformulation can be offered.

Final Reformulation: The messianic, as messianic, is that which, with the smallest synchronic displacement, anachronically and retroactively reconfigures history itself.

Conclusion. Walter Benjamin conceives of eternity, of synchronic repetition, as impinging on time in the form of anachrony. This surprising interruption, however slight, is capable of ushering in the Messiah. Giorgio Agamben relates:

> There is a well-known parable about the Kingdom of the Messiah that Walter Benjamin (who heard it from Gershom Scholem) recounted one evening to Ernst Bloch, who in turn transcribed it in *Spuren*: "A rabbi, a real cabalist, once said that in order to establish the reign of peace it is not necessary to destroy everything nor to begin a completely new world. It is sufficient to displace this cup or this bush or this stone just a little, and thus everything. But this small displacement is so difficult to achieve and

> its measure so difficult to find that, with regard to the world, humans are incapable of it and it is necessary that the Messiah come."[18]

This infinitely small displacement that changes both everything and nothing, that reveals the whole of the world and its history as meaning something radically different from what had been supposed while retaining everything that had hitherto been acknowledged, is the displacement of anachrony. And it is *this* anachrony that is manifest in the Book of Mormon, even as the Book of Mormon works to make manifest this anachrony in the world itself.

ADAM S. MILLER is currently a Professor of Philosophy at Collin County Community College (McKinney, TX). He received his M.A. and Ph.D. in Philosophy from Villanova University. His areas of specialization include contemporary French philosophy and the philosophy of religion. He is the founder of the *Journal of Philosophy and Scripture* (www.philosophyandscripture.org) and the author of a number of articles on both contemporary continental philosophy and Mormonism.

Notes

1. Walter Benjamin, "Theses on the Philosophy of History." *Illuminations*, ed. Hannah Arendt (New York: Schocken, 1969).
2. Ibid., 263.
3. Ibid.
4. Ibid., 262.
5. Ibid., 263.
6. Ibid., 257.
7. Howard Eiland and Kevin McLaughlin, "Translators' Foreword," *Arcades Project* (Cambridge: Belknap Press, 1999), ix.
8. Walter Benjamin, "On Some Motifs in Baudelaire," *Illuminations*, ed. Hannah Arendt (New York: Schocken, 1969), 186.
9. Walter Benjamin, "Unpacking My Liberty," *Illuminations*, ed. Hannah Arendt (New York: Schocken, 1969), 60.
10. Walter Benjamin, "The Work of Art in the Age of Mechanical Reproduction," *Illuminations*, ed. Hannah Arendt (New York: Schocken, 1969), 236.
11. Benjamin, "Theses," 264.
12. Benjamin, "On Some Motifs," 158.
13. Benjamin, "Unpacking," 62.

14. Terryl Givens, *By the Hand of Mormon: The American Scripture that Launched a New World Religion* (New York: Oxford University Press, 2002).
15. Benjamin, "Unpacking," 61.
16. Benjamin, "Thesis," 263.
17. Slavoj éiûek, *The Sublime Object of Ideology* (New York: Verso, 1989), 141.
18. Giorgio Agamben, *The Coming Community*, trans. Michael Hardt (Minneapolis: University of Minnesota Press, 1993), 53.

On Scripture

or

Idolatry versus True Religion

James E. Faulconer
Brigham Young University

Ancient Israel was often called away from idolatry. Perhaps no theme is more common in the Old Testament than that Israel must give up idolatry. Michael Fishbane has argued that Judaism's essence is to be found in its rejection of idolatry and the world view of idolatry, "idolatrous metaphysics" ("Mothers").[1] We hear that theme much less in modern Israel. Usually when we hear someone speak of idolatry, he or she does so primarily in terms of materialism or some such; we think our idolatry is primarily metaphorical. However, the question of what idolatry is and how we avoid it remains. Those are as much questions for us as they were for ancient Israel.

If we look closely, I think we see that at least three things mark the difference between pure religion—in LDS terms, Zion—and idolatry. First, pure religion is founding but not founded. It is originary in that those "within" it are constantly reborn, constantly re-originated. But pure religion has no *theos*, no foundation. If it did, it would have an idol rather than a God. The word *theos* is the Greek word for "god," and it is the word that Aristotle uses for the ultimate being in his metaphysics, a usage determinative for the rest of the Western intellectual tradition. Traditional metaphysical systems each have something like the Aristotelean *theos* as their foundation or goal. Each assumes a *theos*, in Aristotle's terms, as the basis for what-is, whether that *theos* is God or something else. In the terms of the twentieth-century German philosophy, Martin Heidegger, each is onto-theological. Given that traditional usage, I will use the word *theos* here to designate any such metaphysical being or any being that performs the same structural function as Aristotle's *theos*.

In contrast, rather than a *theos* that acts as a foundation or goal, pure religion finds its origin in our relation to a beneficent, living Person rather than a metaphysical origin. Thus, the religions that have their origin in the Bible, which of course includes the Latter-day Saints, are strictly speaking a-theistic: their scriptures deny the unmoved and unmoving god (whether it is called *theos*, Law, or Reason), whatever their theologies might assert. LDS doctrine, by asserting not only that God is a beneficent, living Person, but also an embodied one insists on that denial. It implicitly denies any foundation, at least as that word is used in the tradition. There may be some sense in which God remains a foundation in LDS thinking. If so, however, it is in a sense quite different from the sense of *foundation* in the philosophical tradition, a sense that has infiltrated most of our everyday thinking and talk about foundations and about divine things. The God of Abraham, Isaac, and Jacob is a person—not a foundation, except to the degree that a person can be said to be a foundation. (See 1 Corinthians 3:11.) He is not a metaphysical foundation.

For more than 2,500 years, however, when they have reflected on religion philosophically or theologically, Western thinkers have almost always assumed that to speak of God is to speak in terms of a metaphysical foundation, in terms of a *theos*. The language of foundations and the *theos* are virtually everywhere in our culture, even in our discussions of our particular religious experiences, and Latter-day Saints have not been immune to that way of talking. In spite of what we intend, that language and its assumptions infiltrates our discussions because it comes to us naturally. It is the common sense of our culture and, so, something about which we give little thought, and we do not yet have another language to use. The question is, if we reject the assumption that we must speak of God as a *theos*, what can we say of our relation to the person who is God? In other words, how can we make sense of the world and its Creator if we reject the traditional philosophical-theological understanding of the world and its Creator as metaphysical foundation? What is the alternative to idolatry, given that our reflective religious language is permeated by traditional understanding?

Among others, the work of the contemporary French/Lithuanian philosopher, Emmanuel Levinas, provides us some outlines of part of a philosophical answer. Levinas shows us much about our relations to one another, focusing for example, on the family as the model for human being.[2] Levinas's work is too complicated to *précis* here,[3] but among other things, in it we see how the other person gives the self itself, its ego. Levinas shows, convincingly I believe, that I am not, fundamentally, an entity, beholden to no one. Rather, my very existence as an autonomous entity is a response to my relation to another person. And my continuation as a person, as a self, is based on my continuing relation to an other. The result is that the self and the growth of the self—its repentance—have their origins in the other.

But though the self and its repentance originate in the other, the other is no foundation in any usual sense of that term. And in the philosophical and theological sense of the term, the other is no founder. Instead, the other is a person, a Creator, not a thing, and the founding occurs in ethical demand, in the face-to-face of Joseph Smith before God, not in ontology or in its bastard child, theology. Persons, specifically other persons, rather than metaphysical or some other kind of principles are fundamental. Persons can found us, but they are not themselves a foundation. They are living, continuing persons, not static, impersonal, dead foundations. As a consquence we could go so far as to say, shockingly, that in a strict sense, pure and true religion is nihilistic, but that is only to say that it is not idolatrous, having no onto-theological foundation. True religion posits no ultimate thing; instead it responds to an Ultimate Person.

Second, because pure religion is not founded, because it has no *theos*, it recognizes no power before which it must bow, though it bows. True religion bows before ethical demand—the relation of one person to another rather than rules for moral conduct—not superior and potentially threatening power.[4] (Though true religion sometimes uses the word *power*, I think that use refers not to the power found and feared in idolatrous religion, but to the power of the ethical command.) True religion is a-theistic in refusing to bow before the supposed power of the idolatrous god, the *theos* of traditional philosophy and theology, with its implicit threats.[5] Instead it bows before the God it loves and respects.

A third difference between true and idolatrous religion—between Zion and "the world"—is that because the obedience of true religion is a matter of service rather than appeasement, true religion is, at one and the same time, both obedient and beyond any law. It is obedient to the ethical demand that occurs when the Other disrupts my totalizing, comprehending, dominating relation to the world. In other words, true religion occurs when I respond to the obligation I have to the Other rather than to my reasoned and coherent understanding of the Other.

If I respond to my understanding of the world and of the Other's place in that world, I do not respond to the Other. I respond only to myself: I have come to an understanding of things and I respond to that understanding, *my* understanding rather than the other person whose life impinges on me. In contrast, ethical obligation requires that I respond to something that is other than myself, something I am unlikely fully to understand intellectually. I must respond to what is outside of myself, to what is beyond my ability to grasp, comprehend, and dominate (even intellectually) or thematize. Law is always at least a thematization of the ethical obligation I experience: to universalize what I learn in my relation to others is to make of theme of that relation. Therefore, as universalization, in principle law always occurs within my comprehension and even under my domination. As the product of human understanding, thematizing is in principle something that human beings can dominate.[6]

We cannot escape the thematizing of law if we continue to speak to one another, for example when we admonish another or apologize for our behavior. We *should* not escape it. Not only is it not wrong to thematize, it is essential that we do. Nevertheless, ultimately pure religion goes beyond any thematizing of the demands made upon me by the Other. Pure religion is beyond any mere law: "Therefore, my brothers, you too are dead to the law" (Romans 7:4). That is inconceivable within idolatry, and will seem nihilistic to those insist that there must be a *theos*.

Of course, the nihilism of being without foundation and beyond the law has nothing at all to do with the anarchic nihilism that rejects all law and opts for chaos. As mentioned, an ethical demand can occur only where there is also a thematizing of that demand. It may be impossible for me to experience the ethical obligation and, at the same time, not to thematize that obligation in consciousness. Consequently, ethical demand may never be separable from law—so much so that the law is essential to the demand; the law is a blessing, an appearance of the command of God. But the ethical demand, God's continuing command—its appear*ing* rather than its appear*ance*—always exceeds any thematizing in which it occurs. No law captures the ethical demand that it thematizes. In true religion the moral law is not that by which humans become calculable. Instead, it is that in which we fulfill the ethical obligation that confronts us, an ethical obligation that always exceeds and makes possible any moral law in which it is necessarily embodied.

But if no law is sufficient, if true religion cannot be reduced to a law, what remains for us to do? To quote someone now defunct, "What will become of us?" How do we speak of this description of our being, of fundamental ethics, of Zion, of the fact that we are *already* in Zion? How do we speak of non-idolatrous, in other words, true, religion? And where do we find such a speaking?

At first glance, it seems that the failure of philosophy and its issuance in the nihilism of onto-theology—its reliance on the idol of the *theos*, which turns out to be nothing and nothingness—means that we cannot expect philosophy to take account of its failure and to remedy itself. As traditionally conceived, philosophy is incapable of saying what needs to be said. In fact, as traditionally conceived, philosophy is *essentially* totalizing. As *traditionally conceived*, I find it difficult to doubt that philosophy is bankrupt.

But that is not to say that all philosophers or philosophies have been totalizers. In general, great philosophers are great precisely because their work did not and, for the most part, still does not fit within the traditional, totalizing conception of philosophy.[7] The tradition tames the great philosophers for its own use, but the tamed philosopher is not the great philosopher. There may be other possiblities for philosophy than those of the tradition. Perhaps Heidegger or Ludwig Wittgenstein provides the beginnings of an alternative. Perhaps some of the experimental work of Edmund Jabes, Jacques Derrida, François Lyotard, Levinas, or others points in the direction of an alternative. Or perhaps a careful return to our tradition will do the job. Perhaps a fresh reading of Plato or Aristotle or Augustine will teach us much.

Thus, though it is not clear what we are to do philosophically in face of the totalitarian character of traditional philosophy, it is clear that, in some sense, philosophy will probably remain. In his discussion of this point Levinas insists that a role for philosophy remains, a role that does not rely on the merely deconstructive or rhetorical (cf. *Otherwise than Being*, 1981). In spite of his criticisms of philosophy, Levinas consciously remains a philosopher. The bankruptcy of philosophy is not a given, however common it may be.

But whatever we eventually decide about philosophy, Levinas shows us that when we see the priority of ethics to ontology, when we see that persons are prior to principles, then from the beginning, our question is not "What is it?" (as philosophy has traditionally asked), but "What must be done?" There are ostensibly any number of ways one could take up this question. Perhaps, as Levinas, Derrida, Luce Irigaray, and others indicate, some of these ways are philosophical. But, however other many ways there might be, I believe that sacred scripture is such a speaking. In fact, I think it is the most important of such ways because it is the "most ethical," asking us to listen not only to others, but to *the* Other. And scripture is a speaking that has the virtue of being considerably more accessible to most of us than the work of writers like Heidegger, Derrida, and Levinas. And it is always better written.

As much as I am enamored of contemporary philosophy, as much as I find contemporary Continental philosophy not only useful but morally compelling, I nonetheless find scripture more appealing and more accessible than contemporary philosophy, and more morally compelling. But more than that, I find scripture more genuinely revelatory. Paul Ricoeur notes that the philosopher can be no preacher ("Religious Significance," 1969), and Heidegger has made a similar point.[8] The philosopher must wait for the prophet. Heidegger and Derrida may help us wait for the prophets.[9] Levinas may announce the necessity of the prophet. I believe these thinkers have helped me hear the prophets' voices. But they can do no more than that. They cannot even be John the Baptist for us, announcing the prophet. Only in the living prophets and in scripture can I find the announcement, the call, of what philosophy has helped me wait for. In spite of the possibility that, turned against itself, philosophy may be able to say something about Zion, I believe that only in the prophets will we be returned to what is beyond philosophy, namely to Zion.

But though many, if not most, Latter-day Saints are committed to the idea that scripture is more important and more revelatory than philosophy, it is also true that our mental commitment runs aground on our everyday practices. We know what it means to take philosophy seriously. We do not usually know what it means to take the scriptures seriously.

We usually read scripture as if it were naive philosophy and ontology, looking for the principle of principles, for the *theos* that stands behind what we are reading, asking constantly the question, "What is it?"—even when we want to ask the question, "What must be done?" We are taught to read scripture that way from our births, both inside and outside the Church. That way of reading scripture is something we share with many, especially the majority of those in the evangelical, charismatic, and other Christian fundamentalist traditions. Like the image of good traditional philosophers, those who read the scriptures in this way take the gospel to be a set of doctrinal propositions that one is to know, and they take the scriptures to be a speaking of those principles and propositions behind which the "theological" gospel hides. When we read scripture this way, it is as if we assume that God is simply a poor writer—or that he chooses poor mouthpieces—and finds himself unable to lay out clearly and distinctly, in an ordered fashion, the principles he wants to teach us. And, with amazing hubris, we assume it is our job to do the work he was unable to do, the work of making everything clear, distinct, and orderly.

But scripture need not be read that way. In the New Testament, the word *gospel* refers much more to the proclamation of the gospel than to the content of that proclamation, though the content is certainly not irrelevant. Levinas has distinguished between the Saying and the said: the Saying is the event, the said is the objectification of the event of Saying, its transcription, whether in writing, memory, or a recording. There can be no Saying without a resultant said, but it is a mistake to think that the two are the same. That is a mistake we make when we idolize a text. The Saying is in the said only as a trace, as something we can hear, but never see because when we try to look directly at it, we see only its after-image. Similarly, there could be no proclamation of the gospel if there were not a content of the gospel. But as used in the New Testament and, therefore, as it also informs our later uses, the word *gospel* puts its emphasis on the Saying, not the said. What is most important is the preaching, the call to repentance.

Like the gospel, the scriptures are a proclamation more than they are a content. They are a proclamation that, if we hear what is proclaimed, disrupts what we are, what we have made ourselves. It invites our response, our repentance. Scripture speaks the ethical rupture of my constant though implicit claim to autonomy. Scripture ruptures the interiority I prize so much, my consciousness and self-consciousness. Scripture disrupts the natural and necessary movement of consciousness into itself and its principles, into its understanding, and it does so by calling me outside of myself. Scripture calls me out of the solipsistic universe I create with reason and in doing so it calls me to my ethical obligation to the Divine. It disrupts my focus on principle by pointing out that my field of vision, as *my* field, excludes the Other, what is not mine in that field. And speaking of scripture opens me to that rupture of my solipsism.

It follows that scripture can and should be read ethically rather than philosophically. Scripture reading can be the responsive Saying of the ethical rupture, rather than the thematizing said of principle and ontology. To use Levinas's language because I find it useful, scripture reading and study can be an encounter with the unsaying Saying of the Other, rather than the Said of the Same.

Unlike most of what is done in philosophy, scripture does not demand violence in response to violence, though it often reveals violence. Scripture does not take up philosophy against itself, so unlike the current criticisms of philosophy, including my own, scripture is not guilty of parricide. When not taken up as a defective or naive form of philosophy, scripture engenders. It replaces murder and scapegoating (the desire that everything be totalized in some One and static thing) with the call for fecundity: "be fruitful, and multiply, and replenish the earth" (Genesis 1:28). When read as ethical demand, scripture disrupts my interiority with exteriority. It disrupts the universal and the merely moral (using Nietzsche's sense of that word), the desire for the *theos*. In doing so, scripture opens the ethical demand and makes generation and continued life possible as well as necessary.

In scripture and with the prophets, I stand before the Other, exposed and "put upon," prior to being anything at all. In fact, whatever I am is a consequence of my position before the Other. The ethical response to the ethical demand is the desire for the Other rather than for the *theos* which dissimulates and displaces the Other, as in idolatry. Desire for the Other and the concomitant rupture of interiority by the Other are what philosophy has called community. They are what the scriptures call Zion. Zion is always already here; it is already here, within us though not our creation:

> And when he was questioned by the Pharisees concerning when the kingdom of God is to come, he answered them and said, "The kingdom of God does not come with careful watching, neither will they say 'Look here!' or 'There!' For behold, the kingdom of God is within you." (Luke 17:20–21)

For the most part, philosophy demands that we watch carefully. Sometimes it demands nothing else. Usually it *can* demand nothing else. Philosophy is primarily, but perhaps not necessarily, oriented toward vision and the unifying and individualistic perspective of vision, toward seeing as staring, as the gaze. Scripture, on the other hand, speaks the a priori character of Zion and its demand for our ethical response. It speaks and asks us to listen, though not necessarily to see. Scripture calls us back to the Zion in which we are constituted; it calls us to a continuation of that Zion.

It is possible to end this discussion here, with an abstract, philosophical appeal to the non-philosophical. But surely that self-deconstructing appeal is insufficient. So as a gesture, but no more than a gesture, in the direction of allowing scripture to speak the ethical demand, let me outline "disruptive" readings of two scriptural stories, attempting to show some of the ways in which the Other exceeds principle and mere being in these stories. I have fuller expositions of these stories in another place awaiting completion.[10] But these outlines should serve to show some of what I find in an ethical rather than philosophical reading of scripture. Because they are outlines, these readings will ignore the attention to textual details that scripture calls for. They will remain philosophical in spite of themselves. But I think they will be enough to show that an ethical reading of scripture is possible. I hope they will at least indicate that such a reading can be fruitful.

The first story is that of the creation, a story that focuses explicitly on ethical relation rather than ontology. First notice Genesis 1:1, 1:26, and 3:22 (Moses 2:1, 2:26, 3:28; Abr. 4–5):

> In the beginning God created the heaven and the earth. (Gen. 1:1)
>
> And God said, Let us make man in our image, after our likeness. (Gen. 1:26)
>
> And the LORD God said, Behold, the man is become as one of us, to know good and evil. (Gen. 3:22)

God's oneness is the unity of Zion, a unity of multiple individuals who remain individual in their unity. God's unity is not the unity of an overarching, metaphysical *theos*, for, as Latter-day Saints have pointed out for years, God is spoken of in the multiple, not the singular. He is not alone in any sense.

Latter-day Saints often use the language of the tradition to speak of God, as well as the assumptions of the philosophical/theological tradition to understand the scriptures. Therefore, they often assume, although usually only implicitly and unconsciously, either that God is the principle of principles or that he exists in virtue of his compliance with such a principle or set of principles. But because this assumption is a postulation of the *theos*, in making it, we implicitly deny God's multiplicity and the possibility of divine togetherness. In other words, the assumption denies Zion because it takes God to be ultimately alone. However, in spite of that, the Latter-day Saint God is everywhere implicated in multiplicity. As so implicated, the one God cannot be the principle of principles. As those who accuse the Latter-day Saints of heresy recognize quickly, a God who cannot avoid multiplicity breaks the bond between unity and being, destroying recourse to God as *theos*. If traditional belief is the standard, we are heretics and should be happy to be heretics. But that heresy is not only a revealed truth and, so a better standard, it is also a philosophical advantage.

As both one and multiple, God can be the Other of ethical relation, for every ethical relation implies not the I and Thou of Martin Buber, but the Thou and *we* (Levinas, *Totality and Infinity*, 1969).[11] Truth is reason—measure, account—and "I've a Mother there"—and a Brother, and brothers and sisters. The creation story, beginning in Genesis 1 and ending with Genesis 4:1, is the story of multiplicity and the Other, the story of a living and loving parent who creates, not a philosophical story of how a Parmenidean One generated the many.

The multiplicity of the Other is recapitulated in the story of Adam and Eve. Genesis 2:18 (Moses 3:18; Abr. 5:14) speaks of Woman as "the one who stands over against Adam," though our translation of the Hebrew is "help meet," in other words the appropriate helper. But Woman is an appropriate help to Man, not by being another hand, or an extra arm, or an additional set of eyes; Woman is not an addition to Man, not an ordinary supplement, if a supplement at all. She is neither his subordinate nor his alter ego. She cannot be reduced either to him or to some third term that encapsulates them both. Woman is an Other of Man, one who stands opposite him, helping by making ethical relation possible and by giving Man his identity. It turns out, in fact, that Woman is not simply an extension of Man, but "the mother of *all* living" (Gen. 3:20; Moses 4:26). In fact, in the Genesis version of the story, as long as Woman can be thought of as an extension of Man, she remains uncreated; she has no name. She is named only when she has ceased to be such an extension. As the mother of all living, presumably including Man, she creates Man. As named by Man, she is created by him. Adam and Eve are mutually created in God.

Fecundity, sexuality, fraternity and sorority—Zion—are functions of alterity, not functions of identity and sameness.

Note too that the knowledge gained in the creation story is explicitly ethical knowledge, not comprehending, encapsulating, totalizing knowledge. Man does not know of his need for an Other because God tells him; his knowledge of Woman's necessity is not propositional knowledge. Man knows that need, a need beyond simple want or lack, only through his relation to the Divine and through the experience engendered in that disruptive experience. Man learns of the need for Woman by assisting in the creation of animals and discovering that there is nothing that is opposite him (Gen. 2:18–23; Moses 3:18–23; Abr. 5:14–21): "And Adam gave names to all cattle, and to the fowl of the air, and to every beast of the field; but for Adam there was not found an help meet for him" (Gen. 2:20).

Likewise, having eaten of the Tree of the Knowledge of Good and Evil, having the knowledge of the Gods (explicitly ethical knowledge), Adam and Eve are like the Gods at the same time that they are set over against them: "Behold the man is become as of us, to know good and evil" (Gen. 3:22). Divine knowledge makes Adam and Eve in the image of the Gods at the same time that it makes the Gods truly Other. The story of Adam and Eve is the story of the necessity of the Other—a sexed Other—with whom one can stand before God, as a god, in ethical labor and ethical knowledge. It is a story that undoes philosophical knowledge in favor of personal and even sexual knowledge. (See Gen. 4:1 and Moses 5:2, where *know* is not a euphemism.) It is a story that demands ethical response. The story of Adam and Eve disrupts our totalizing knowledge of each other and of God and demands, instead, that we hear the ethical demand.

The question of the story is not, "*What* art thou?" (as much philosophy and all psychology supposes), but "*Where* art thou?" (Gen. 3:9, Moses 4:15). And the "where" of this question supposes neither a geographic position nor a Heideggerian site in being. It asks about the ethical where: standing before me, face-to-face, God asks "Where are you?" The question of the story of Adam and Eve is explicitly the question of ethics, not ontology.

The second story I would like briefly to consider is also the story of ethical response and the welcoming of the Other. It is the story of Abraham and Isaac. That story begins when Abram is set apart from his country, his kindred, and his father's house—in an order the reverse of geographic order (Gen. 12:1). Chronologically and geographically, one must leave one's father's house first, then one's kindred, and finally one's country. Abram's leave-taking is not merely a chronological and geographic leave-taking. He takes his leave spiritually. Given that he is defined by country, kindred, and father, Abram becomes other than himself and other than his family. Why? In order to make family and Zion possible. Abraham's blessing has it origin in his alterity.

But having been cut off from his family, having become other, as I read the story, Abraham searches for a *theos*. He seeks to create Zion himself, to force it. He thinks of the promised seed as something he can bring about, so he agrees to create that promised posterity with Hagar. In doing so, he implicitly assumes that the Other is not Other: one son is as good as another; for the purposes of the blessing that has become abstract, one wife is as good as another. The otherness of Abraham's promise is totalizable by his will; he believes that the future promised in the original disruption is to be brought about by totalizing, by taking control, by his will.

In spite of Abraham's attempts to control, his search for the community founded on a *theos* is interrupted. First it is interrupted by his forced dismissal of Ishmael and Hagar. Then it is interrupted by a call that implicitly asks, as Adam was asked, where he is, a call that erupts in the command to sacrifice Isaac (Gen. 22:1). However, unlike Adam, Abraham responds to this interruptive call with "Here I am"—"Behold me here" or "Ready."

Within the space opened by God's call, Abraham is finally able to be separated from his son, and his son is finally able to be separated from him. The totality that Abraham has willed is finally broken. The binding of the sacrifice, the binding that separates father and son at the altar on Moriah, separates Isaac from Abraham. Isaac is no longer the product of Abraham's endeavor, the product of Abraham's totalizing. Isaac is now an other to him, given by God in the disruption of Abraham's totality. Isaac is an other whose existence before Abraham makes an ethical demand on Abraham. Isaac is one to whom Abraham must respond, one whom, in his confrontation with the Divine Other, Abraham is called to serve. In separating father and son, the sacrificial binding binds father to son in Zion.

Now the promise of posterity can be fulfilled; now it *is* fulfilled. Thus, as soon as the sacrifice is over, the text tells of the birth of Isaac's wife (Gen. 22:20–24), the Other who marks the beginning of Abraham's posterity. Though Abraham's trial begins with him alone, speaking not even to his wife, this second separation from his family at Moriah—separation from both wife and son—a separation that marks the disruption of the totalized community, results in the biding forth and the binding of Zion.

The binding of the sacrificial victim at Moriah results in the binding of Zion, but this binding is not the application of a universal principle. As Søren Kierkegaard argues in *Fear and Trembling*,[12] Abraham's response defies all universal principles. Instead, it is the ethical response to the Other that makes possible the continuation of the other, of otherness and response. In the beginning, Abram's response is the welcome of the power of the Divine Other. In the end, Abraham's response is the welcome of the filial other and the Divine Other himself.

Though both these stories are stories of unity, they both warn us against looking for the unity of Zion in unity of being, in a totality. In a certain sense, both tell the same story, the story of our fruitful separation (difference), from each other and from God, in Zion. Both are stories of welcoming the other. Both call us to our lives before each other, both make the ethical demand. Both deconstruct totality in favor of Zion.

Both these stories do what I believe all scripture does. They do not *describe* the life that is required nor do they give us its principles. Scripture is not guilty of idolatry, though as readers of scripture we often are. Rather than doing philosophy, these stories call to us and disrupt the lazy and unethical comfort of our being-at-home with ourselves and our situation. In them we hear that Zion is not to be found by looking because it is already here. As I assume do also other scriptural stories, the stories of Adam and Eve and of Abraham and Isaac call us back to where we already are so we can be there for the first time and so we can continue to be there, constantly reborn into Zion.

JAMES E. FAULCONER is a professor of Philosophy at Brigham Young University. He obtained his Ph.D. in philosophy from Pennsylvania State University. His areas of specialization include contemporary European philosophy (especially Heidegger, hermeneutics, and contemporary French philosophy) and the philosophy of religion. He is the author and editor of several books and essays in philosophy, religion, and Mormon thought.

Notes

1. Michael Fishbane, *The Garments of Torah: Essays in Biblical Hermeneutics* (Bloomington: Indiana UP, 1989).
2. Emmanuel Levinas *Totality and Infinity: An Essay on Exteriority.* Trans. A. Lingis. (Pittsburgh: Duquesne UP, 1969) discusses the relevant points most directly—the section on fecundity comes immediately to mind—but *Otherwise than Being or Beyond Essence.* Trans. A. Lingis. (The Hague: Martinus Nijhoff, 1981) also has a number of important discussions of these points.
3. For an overview, see my "Levinas," in *Dictionary of Literary Biography* (Bloomfield Hills, Michigan: Bruccoli Clark Layman/Manley, 2004) 285–295.
4. This is the way that Levinas uses the term, and understanding him requires that we not forget that his use is not what we usually expect.
5. See Paul Ricoeur, "Religion, Atheism, and Faith," in A. MacIntyre and P. Ricoeur, *The Religious Significance of Atheism* (New York: Columbia UP, 1969), 58–98.
6. Of course, the irony with which the atonement deals is that we do not dominate the law and, in fact, find ourselves incapable fo doing so: "what I would, that I do not" (Rom. 7:15).
7. Though I've used Aristotle as a bogeyman earlier, I think what I say here applies at least as much to him as to any other philosopher.

8. See, for example, Martin Heidegger, "Phenomenology and Theology," trans. by James G. Hart and John C. Maraldo, in Pathmarks, edited by William McNeil (Cambridge: Cambridge University Press, 1998), 39-62.
9. Marlène Zarader, *La Dette Impensée: Heidegger et l'Héritage Hébraïque*, (Paris, France: Seuil, 1990) does an excellent job of showing how Heidegger's work depends, probably without him being conscious of it, on his understanding of the Bible and of prophecy.
10. For more complete, but still incomplete reading of the first of these stories, see my "Adam and Eve—Community: Reading Genesis 2–3," *Journal of Philosophy and Scripture* 1.1 (Fall 2003), http://www.philosophyandscripture.org/Archives/Issue1-1/James_Faulconer/james_faulconer.html. A similar reading of a third story, that of Moses and Israel, can be found in "Philosophy and Transcendence: Religion and the Possibility of Justice," in *Transcendence in Religion and Philosophy*, ed. James E. Faulconer (Indianapolis: Indiana University Press, 2003), 70–84.
11. Levinas is deeply indebted to Buber, but nevertheless critical. He criticizes Buber in several essays. For an example, see Emmanuel Levinas, "Martin Buber and the Theory of Knowledge," in *Proper Names*, trans. Michael B. Smith (Stanford: Stanford UP, 1996), 17–35.
12. Søren Kierkegaard, *Fear and Trembling* (Penguin Classic, 1986).

What Do We Really Believe?

Identifying Doctrinal Parameters within Mormonism

Robert L. Millet
Brigham Young University

Doctrine is "the basic body of Christian teaching or understanding."[1] "Christian doctrine is composed of teachings which are to be handed on through instruction and proclamation. . . . Religious doctrine deals with the ultimate and most comprehensive questions."[2] The central, saving doctrine is that Jesus is the Christ, the Son of God, the Savior and Redeemer of humankind; that he lived, taught, healed, suffered and died for our sins; and that he rose from the dead the third day with an immortal, resurrected body.[3] It was Joseph Smith who spoke of these central truths as the "fundamental principles" of our religion to which all other doctrines are but appendages.[4]

There is power in doctrine, power in the word,[5] power to heal the wounded soul,[6] power to transform human behavior. "True doctrine, understood, changes attitudes and behavior," Elder Boyd K. Packer explained. "The study of the doctrines of the gospel will improve behavior quicker than a study of behavior will improve behavior. That is why we stress so forcefully the study of the doctrines of the gospel.[7] Elder Neal A. Maxwell also pointed out that, "Doctrines believed and practiced do change and improve us, while insuring our vital access to the Spirit. Both outcomes are crucial."[8]

Doctrinal Parameters

In recent years, I have tried to look beneath the surface and discern the nature of the objections that so many in the religious world have toward the Latter-day Saints. To be sure, the phenomenal growth of the Church poses a real threat to many; more specifically, the Christian groups resent the way we "steal their sheep." We are not in the line of historic Christianity and thus are neither Catholic nor Protestant. We believe in scripture beyond the Bible and in continuing revelation through apostles and prophets. We do not accept the concepts concerning God, Christ, and the Godhead that grew out of the post-New Testament church councils. All of these things constitute reasons why many Protestants and Catholics label us as non-Christian. There is another reason we are suspect, one in particular that underlies and buttresses large amounts of anti-Mormon propaganda is what they perceive to be some of our "unusual doctrines," many of which were presented by a few Church leaders of the past.

A minister friend was in my office one day. He said: "Bob, many of my fellow Christians have noted how hard it is to figure out what Mormons believe. They say it's like trying to nail green Jell-O to the wall! What *do* you people believe? How do you decide what *is* your doctrine and what is not?" I suggested that he consider the following ideas:

1. The teachings of the Church today have a rather narrow focus, range, and direction; central and saving doctrine is what we are called upon to teach and emphasize, not tangential and peripheral concepts.
2. Very often what is drawn from Church leaders of the past is misrepresented, improperly weighted, or taken out of context. Further, not everything that was ever spoken or written by a Church leader in the past is a part of what we teach today.
3. In determining whether something is a part of the doctrine of the Church, we might ask: is it found within the four standard works and/or within official declarations or proclamations? Is it taught or discussed in general conference or

> other official gatherings by general Church leaders today? Is it found in the general handbooks or approved curriculum of the Church today? If it meets at least one of these criteria, we can feel secure and appropriate about teaching it. We might also add that included within the category of "all that God does reveal" would be certain matters about which we maintain "sacred silence." For example, the content of the temple endowment today would certainly be considered a part of the doctrine of the Church.

A significant percentage of anti-Mormonism focuses on statements by Church leaders of the past that deal with peripheral or non-central issues. No one criticizes us for a belief in God; in the divinity of Jesus Christ or his atoning work; in the literal bodily resurrection of the Savior and the eventual resurrection of humankind; in baptism by immersion; in the gift of the Holy Ghost; the sacrament of the Lord's Supper, etc. We are challenged regularly for statements in our literature on such matters as the following:

- God's life before he was God.
- How Jesus was conceived.
- The specific fate of sons of perdition.
- Teachings about Adam as God.
- Details concerning what it means to become like God hereafter.
- That plural marriage is essential to one's exaltation.
- Why blacks were denied the priesthood prior to 1978, etc.

Loyalty to Imperfect Leaders

While we love the Bible and thank God regularly for it, we believe that one can have sufficient confidence and even reverence for holy writ without believing that every word between Genesis 1:1 and Revelation 22:21 is the word-for-word dictation of the Almighty or that the Bible now reads as it has always read.[9] But we still cherish the sacred volume, recognize and teach the doctrines of salvation within it, and seek to pattern our lives according to its timeless teachings.

In like manner, we can sustain with all our hearts the prophets and apostles without believing that they are perfect or that everything they say or do is exactly what God wants said and done. In short, we do not believe in apostolic or prophetic infallibility. Moses, Peter, and Paul made mistakes, but we love and sustain them and accept their writings nonetheless. James pointed out that Elijah "was a man subject to like passions as we are."[10] Lorenzo Snow stated:

> I can fellowship the President of the Church if he does not know everything I know. . . . I saw the . . . imperfections in [Joseph Smith]. . . . I thanked God that he would put upon a man who had those imperfections the power and authority he placed upon him . . . for I knew that I myself had weakness, and I thought there was a chance for me.[11]

Every member of the Church, including those called to guide its destiny, has the right to be wrong at one time or another or to say something that simply isn't true. They also have the right to improve their views, to change their minds and correct mistakes, to refine and clarify matters as new light and new truth become available. Joseph Smith once remarked: "I did not like the old man [a brother Pelatiah Brown] being called up for erring in doctrine. . . . It does not prove that a man is not a good man because he errs in doctrine."[12] Being called as an apostle or even as president of the Church does not remove the man from mortality or make him perfect. President David O. McKay explained that, "When God makes the prophet He does not unmake the man."[13]

"With all their inspiration and greatness," Elder Bruce R. McConkie declared, "prophets are yet mortal men with imperfections common to mankind in general. They have their opinions and prejudices and are left to work out their problems without inspiration in many instances."[14] "Thus the opinions and views, even of a prophet, may contain error, unless those opinions and views were inspired by the Spirit."[15]

President Gordon B. Hinckley stated: "I have worked with seven Presidents of this Church. I have recognized that all have been human. But I have never been concerned over this. They may have had some weaknesses. But this has never troubled me. I know that the God of heaven has used mortal men throughout history to accomplish His divine purposes."[16] On another occasion President Hinckley pleaded with the Saints:

> As we continue our search for truth . . . we look for strength and goodness rather than weakness and foibles in those who did so great a work in their time. We recognize that our forebears were human. They doubtless made mistakes. . . . There was only one perfect man who ever walked the earth. The Lord has used imperfect people in the process of building his perfect society. If some of them occasionally stumbled, or if their characters may have been slightly flawed in one way or another, the wonder is the greater that they accomplished so much.[17]

The work of the Restoration entails a gradual unfolding of divine truth. Some years ago my colleague Joseph McConkie remarked to a group of religious educators:

> We have the scholarship of the early brethren to build upon; we have the advantage of additional history; we have inched our way up the mountain of our destiny and now stand in a position to see things with greater clarity than did they. . . . We live in finer houses than did our pioneer forefathers, but this does not argue that we are better or that our rewards will be greater. In like manner our understanding of gospel principles should be better housed, and we should constantly be seeking to make it so. There is no honor in our reading by oil lamps when we have been granted better light.[18]

Thus it is important to note that ultimately the Lord will hold us responsible for the teachings and direction and focus provided by the living oracles of our own day, both in terms of their commentary upon canonized scripture, as well as the living scripture that is delivered through them by the power of the Holy Ghost.[19]

Facing Hard Issues

Most Latter-day Saints are eager to sustain and uphold their leaders. Consequently, we are especially hesitant to suggest that something taught by President Brigham Young or Elders Orson Pratt or Orson Hyde might not be in harmony with the truth as God has made it known to us "line upon line, precept upon precept."[20]

Some time ago a colleague and I were in southern California speaking to a group of about 500 people, both Latter-day Saint and Protestant. During the question and answer phase of the program, someone asked the inevitable: "Are you really Christian? Do you, as many claim, worship a different Jesus?" I explained that we worship the Christ of the New Testament; that we believe wholeheartedly in his virgin birth, his divine Sonship, his miracles, his transforming teachings, his atoning sacrifice, and his bodily resurrection from the dead. I added that we also believe in the teachings of and about Christ found in the Book of Mormon and modern revelation.

After the meeting an LDS woman came up to me and said: "You didn't tell the truth about what we believe!" Startled, I asked: "What do you mean?" She responded: "You said we believe in the virgin birth of Christ, and you know very well that we don't believe that." "Yes we do," I retorted. She then said with a great deal of emotion: "I want to believe you, but people have told me for years that we believe that God the Father had sexual relations with Mary and thereby Jesus was conceived." I looked her in the eyes and said: "I'm aware of that teaching, but that is not the doctrine of the Church; that is not what we teach in the Church today. Have you ever heard the Brethren teach it in conference? Is it in the standard works, the curricular materials, or the handbooks of the Church? Is it a part of an official declaration or proclamation?" I watched, as a 500-pound weight seemed to come off her shoulders, as tears came into her eyes, and she simply said: "Thank you, Brother Millet."

Not long ago, Pastor Greg Johnson and I met with the congregation of an Evangelical Christian church just outside Salt Lake City. After we had made a presentation on how to build relationships in spite of theological differences, we opened the meeting to questions. There were many hands in the air at this point. I called on a woman close to the front of the church. Her question was: "How do you deal with the Adam-God doctrine?" I responded: "Thank you for that question. It gives me an opportunity to explain a principle early in our exchange that will lay the foundation for other things to be said." I took a few moments to address the questions, "What is our doctrine? What do we teach today?" I indicated that if some teaching or idea was not in the standard works, not among official declarations or proclamations, was not taught currently by living apostles or prophets in general conference or other official gatherings, or was not in the general handbooks or approved curriculum of the Church, it is probably *not* a part of the doctrine or teachings of the Church.

I was surprised when my pastor friend then said to the group: "Are you listening to Bob? Do you hear what he is saying? This is important! It's time for us to stop criticizing Latter-day Saints on matters they don't even teach today." At this point in the meeting, two things happened: first, the number of hands of questioners went down, and second, the tone of the meeting changed quite dramatically. The questions were not baiting or challenging ones, but rather efforts to clarify.

I have no hesitation telling an individual or a group "I don't know" when I am asked why men are ordained to the priesthood and women are not; why blacks were denied the blessings of the priesthood for almost a century and a half; and several other matters that have neither been revealed nor clarified by those holding the proper keys. The difficulty comes when someone in the past *has* spoken on these matters, *has* put forward ideas that are out of harmony with what we know and teach today, and when those teachings are still available, either in print or among the everyday conversations of the members, and have never been corrected or clarified.

It's inevitable that some persons, either Latter-day Saints or those of other faiths, who are told that not everything stated by an LDS prophet or apostle is a part of the doctrine of the Church and of what we teach today, will be troubled and ask follow-up questions: "Well then, what *else* did this Church leader teach that is not considered doctrine today? How can we confidently accept anything else he taught? What other directions taken or procedures pursued by the Church in an earlier time do we not follow in our day?" The fact is, one need not take such an approach. This is like throwing the baby out with the bath water. We must never allow ourselves to overgeneralize and thus overreact. Nor must we be guilty of discounting all that is good and uplifting and divinely given because of an aberration. After all, because a prophet once expressed an opinion or perhaps even put forward a doctrinal view that needed further clarification or even correction, does not invalidate all else that he did or said. I would certainly hate to be judged that way and have no desire to be guilty of doing the same to the Lord's anointed. God calls his prophets, and God corrects them. He knows their strengths, and he knows their weakness.

Those of other faiths who leap to criticize the Church and question its truthfulness because of past teachings from Church leaders that are not accepted as doctrine today, would do well to ask themselves if they are prepared to apply the same standards of judgment to their own tradition, their own prominent speakers, or their own past. This is like asking someone, "Would you like to better understand Roman Catholicism today? Then study carefully the atrocities of the Crusades or the horrors of the Inquisition." Or: "Would you like a deeper glimpse into the hearts of Lutherans today? Then make it your business to study the anti-Semitic writings of Martin Luther." Or: "Would you care to better understand where Southern Baptists are coming from? Then simply read the many sermons of Baptist preachers during the time of the Civil War who utilized biblical passages to justify the practice of slavery."

True doctrine has what might be called "sticking power," i.e., it is taught and discussed and perpetuated over time, and with the passing of years seems to take on greater significance. Time, experience, careful and ponderous thought, and subsequent revelation through prophets all either reinforce and support, or bring into question and eventually discount a particular idea. For example, matters such as doctrines pertaining to the proper relationship between the grace of God and the good works of humans, the redemption of the dead, exaltation through eternal marriage, and the overall significance of temples have been discussed, clarified and/or reinforced by those holding the keys of the kingdom. This has been to such an extent that we not only accept them fully as true and from God, but we also grasp their profundity even more than when they were first made known. Falsehood and error will eventually be detected and dismissed by those charged to guide the destiny of the kingdom of God, but truth, as Joseph Smith observed, "will cut its own way."[21]

Other Illustrations

I was raised in the Church, just as many of you were, and was well aware of the priesthood restriction for black members of the Church. For as long as I can remember, the explanation for why our black brothers and sisters were denied the full blessings of the priesthood (including the temple) was some variation of the theme that they had been less valiant in the pre-mortal life and thus had come to earth under a curse, an explanation that has been perpetuated as doctrine for most of our Church's history. In June of 1978 everything changed; not just the matter of who could or could not be ordained to the priesthood, but also the nature of the explanation for why the restriction had been in place from the beginning. Elder Dallin H. Oaks, in a 1988 interview, was asked:

> As much as any doctrine the Church has espoused, or controversy the Church has been embroiled in, this one [the priesthood restriction] seems to stand out. Church members seemed to have less to go on to get a grasp of the issue. Can you address why this was the case, and what can be learned from it?

In response, Elder Oaks stated that:

> If you read the scriptures with this question in mind, "Why did the Lord command this or why did he command that," you find that in less than one in a hundred commands was any reason given. It's not the pattern of the Lord to give reasons. We can put reason to revelation. We can put reasons to commandments. When we do we're on our own. Some people put reasons to the one we're talking about here, and they turned out to be spectacularly wrong. There is a lesson in that. The lesson I've drawn . . . [is that] I decided a long time ago that I had faith in the command and I had no faith in the reasons that had been suggested for it.

Then came a follow-up question: "Are you referring to reasons given even by general authorities?" Elder Oaks answered:

> Sure. I'm referring to reasons given by general authorities and reasons elaborated upon that reason by others. The whole set of reasons seemed to me to be unnecessary risk-taking. . . . Let's don't make the mistake that's been made in the past, here and in other areas, trying to put reasons to revelation. The reasons turn out to be man-made to a great extent. The revelations are what we sustain as the will of the Lord and that's where safety lies.[22]

In other words, we really do not know why the restriction on the priesthood existed. The First Presidency stated in January 1970 that the priesthood was restricted "for reasons which we believe are known to God, but which he has not made fully known to man."

I have come to realize that this is what Elder McConkie meant in his August 1978 address to the Church Educational System when he counseled us to:

> Forget everything that I have said, or what President Brigham Young or President George Q. Cannon or whosoever has said in days past that is contrary to the present revelation. We spoke with a limited understanding and without the light and knowledge that now has come into the world. We get our truth and our light line upon line and precept upon precept. We have now had added a new flood of intelligence and light on this particular subject, and it erases all the darkness and all the views and all the thoughts of the past. They don't matter any more. . . . It is a new day and a new arrangement, and the Lord has now given the revelation that sheds light out into the world on this subject. As to any slivers of light or any particles of darkness of the past, we forget about them.

Consider a second illustration. I think that I have never opened myself to questions before a group of persons not of our faith that I have not been asked about our doctrine of God and the Godhead, particularly concerning the teachings of Joseph Smith and Lorenzo Snow. I generally do not have too much difficulty explaining our view of how through the Atonement humans can eventually become like God, and become more and more Christ-like. For that matter, Orthodox Christianity, a huge segment of the Christian world, still holds to a view of theosis or human deification. The Bible itself teaches that men and women may become "partakers of the divine nature,"[25] "joint heirs with Christ"[26] gain "the mind of Christ"[27] and become perfect, even as our Father in heaven is perfect.[28]

The Apostle John declared: "Beloved, now are we the [children] of God, and it doth not yet appear what we shall be: but we know that, when He shall appear, we shall be like Him; for we shall see Him as He is."[29] More important for Latter-day Saints, this doctrine is taught clearly in modern revelation.[30]

The tougher issue for many Christians to deal with is the accompanying doctrine set forth in the King Follett Sermon and the Lorenzo Snow couplet,[31] namely, that God was once a man. Latter-day scriptures state unequivocally that God is a man, a Man of Holiness,[32] who possesses a body of flesh and bones.[33] These concepts are a part of the doctrinal restoration. We teach that humans are not of a lower order or different species than God. This, of course, makes many of our Christian friends extremely nervous (if not angry), for it appears to them that we are lowering God in the scheme of things and thus attempting to bridge the Creator/creature chasm. I suppose all we can say in response is that we know what we know as a result of modern revelation, and that from our perspective the distance between God and humans is still tremendous; almost infinite.[34] Modern revelation attests that the Almighty sits enthroned "with glory, honor, power, majesty, might, dominion, truth, justice, judgment, mercy, and an infinity of fullness."[35]

What do we know beyond the fact that God is an exalted Man, of his mortal existence, and before he became God? Nothing. We really do not know any more than what was said by the Prophet Joseph Smith, and that is precious little. Insights concerning God's life before Godhood are not found in the standard works, in official declarations or proclamations, in current handbooks or curricular materials, nor are doctrinal expositions on the subject delivered in general conference today. This topic is not what we would call a central and saving doctrine, one that must be believed (or understood) in order to hold a temple recommend, or be in good standing in the Church.

Let's take another question: Was Jesus married? The scriptures do not provide an answer. "We do not know anything about Jesus Christ being married," President Charles W. Penrose stated in 1912. "The Church has no authoritative declaration on the subject."[36] So whether he was, or was not, is not part of the doctrine of the Church. It would be well for us to apply the following lesson from President Harold B. Lee:

> With respect to doctrines and meanings of scriptures, let me give you a safe counsel. It is usually not well to use a single passage of scripture [or, I would

> add, isolated sermons] in proof of a point of doctrine unless it is confirmed by modern revelation or by the Book of Mormon. . . . To single out a passage of scripture to prove a point, unless it is [so] confirmed . . . is always a hazardous thing.[37]

Conclusion

I state to my classes regularly that it is as important for us to know what we do not know as it is for us to know what we know. Far too many things are taught or discussed or even argued about that fit into the realm of the unrevealed and thus the unresolved. Such matters, particularly if they do not fall within that range of revealed truth we teach today, do not edify or inspire. Very often, they lead to confusion and sow discord. This does not, however, in any way suggest that we should not seek to study and grow and expand in our gospel understanding, to gain what Peter called a *reason* for the *hope* within us,[38] a personal witness that is as settling to the mind as it is soothing to the heart.

In that spirit, President Hugh B. Brown once wrote:

> I am impressed with the testimony of a man who can stand and say he knows the gospel is true. But what I would like to ask is 'But, sir, do you know the gospel?' . . . Mere testimony can be gained with but perfunctory knowledge of the Church and its teachings. . . . But to retain a testimony, to be of service in building the Lord's kingdom, requires a serious study of the gospel and knowing what it is.[39]

There is a valid reason why it is difficult to "tie down" Latter-day Saint doctrine, one that derives from the very nature of the Restoration. The fact that God continues to speak through his anointed servants; the fact that He, through those servants, continues to reveal, elucidate, and clarify what has already been given; and the fact that our canon of scripture is open, flexible, and expanding—all of this militates against what many in the Christian world would call a systematic theology.

It is the declaration of sound and solid doctrine, the doctrine found in scripture and taught regularly by Church leaders, which builds faith and strengthens testimony and commitment to the Lord and his kingdom. The teaching and application of sound doctrine are great safeguards to us in these last days, shields against the fiery darts of the adversary. Understanding true doctrine and being true to that doctrine can keep us from ignorance, from error, and from sin. The Apostle Paul counseled Timothy: "If thou put the brethren [and sisters] in remembrance of these things, thou shalt be a good minister of Jesus Christ, nourished up in the word of faith and of good doctrine whereunto thou hast attained. . . . Till I come, give attendance to reading, to exhortation, to doctrine."[40]

ROBERT L. MILLET is Professor of Religious Education at Brigham Young University, with specific interests and responsibilities in Outreach and Interfaith Relations. He received his bachelor's and master's degrees from BYU in Psychology and his Ph.D. from Florida State University in Religious Studies. Since being at BYU he has served as chairman of the department of Ancient Scripture, dean of Religious Education, director of the Religious Studies Center, and Richard L. Evans Professor of Religious Understanding.

Notes

1. 2 Timothy 3:16.
2. *Holman Bible Dictionary* (Nashville: Holman, 1991), 374.
3. 1 Corinthians 15: 1–3; D&C 76: 40–42.
4. Joseph Smith Jr., *Teachings of the Prophet Joseph Smith*, Comp. Joseph Fielding Smith, (Salt Lake City: Deseret, 1976), 121.
5. Alma 31:5.
6. Jacob 2:8.
7. Boyd K. Packer, "Little Children," in *Conference Report of the One Hundred Fifty-sixth Semiannual General Conference of The Church of Jesus Christ of Latter-day Saints* (Salt Lake City: The Church of Jesus Christ of Latter-day Saints, Oct. 1986), 20.
8. Neal A. Maxwell, *One More Strain of Praise* (Salt Lake City: Bookcraft, 1999), x.
9. 1 Nephi 13:20–29; Moses 1:40–41; Articles of Faith 1:8. Joseph Smith Jr., *Teachings of the Prophet Joseph Smith* Comp. Joseph Fielding Smith, (Salt Lake City: Deseret, 1976), 9–10, 61, 327.
10. Ibid., 268, 278; James 5:17.
11. Cited in Neal A. Maxwell, "Out of Obscurity," in *Conference Report of the One Hundred Fifty-sixth Semiannual General Conference of the Church of*

Jesus Christ of Latter-day Saints (Salt Lake City: The Church of Jesus Christ of Latter-day Saints, Oct. 1984), 10.

12. B. H. Roberts, ed., *History of the Church of Jesus Christ of Latter-day Saints* 7 vols. (Salt Lake City: Deseret Book Company, 1957), 340.
13. David O. McKay, in *Conference Report of the One Hundred Fifty-sixth Semiannual General Conference of The Church of Jesus Christ of Latter-day Saints* (Salt Lake City: The Church of Jesus Christ of Latter-day Saints, Apr. 1907), 11–12. See also October 1912, 121 and April 1962, 7.
14. Bruce R. McConkie, *Mormon Doctrine*, 2nd ed. (Salt Lake City: Bookcraft 1966), 608.
15. BruceMcConkie, "Are the General Authorities Human?" *Address, Institute of Religion Forum. University of Utah*, (28 Oct. 1966). Harold B. Lee, *The Teachings of Harold B. Lee* (Salt Lake City: Bookcraft, 1996), 542.
16. Gordon B. Hinckley, "Believe His Prophets," in *Conference Report of the One Hundred Fifty-sixth Semiannual General Conference of The Church of Jesus Christ of Latter-day Saints* (Salt Lake City: The Church of Jesus Christ of Latter-day Saints, Apr. 1992), 77.
17. Gordon B. Hinckley, "The Continuous Pursuit of Truth." *Ensign*, April 1986, 5.
18. Joseph F. McConkie, "The Gathering of Israel and the Return of Christ," in *The Sixth Annual Church Educational System Religious Educators' Symposium on the Book of Mormon held Aug. 1982*, Brigham Young University, Provo, Utah, 3, 5.
19. D&C 68:3–4.
20. Isaiah 28:10; 2 Nephi 28:30.
21. Joseph Smith Jr., *Teachings of the Prophet Joseph Smith* Comp. Joseph Fielding Smith, (Salt Lake City: Deseret, 1976), 313.
22. Dallin H. Oaks, *Daily Herald* (Provo), 5 June 1988: 21.
23. First Presidency Message, David O. McKay, Hugh B. Brown, N. Eldon Tanner. Jan. 1970.
24. Joseph F. McConkie, "The Gathering of Israel and the Return of Christ," in *The Sixth Annual Church Educational System Religious Educators' Symposium on the Book of Mormon held Aug. 1982*, Brigham Young University, Provo, Utah.

25. 2 Pet. 1:4.
26. Rom. 8:17.
27. 1 Cor. 2:16.
28. Matt. 5:48.
29. 1 Jn. 3:2.
30. D&C 76:58; 132:19–20.
31. Joseph Smith Jr., *Teachings of the Prophet Joseph Smith*, Comp. Joseph Fielding Smith, (Salt Lake City: Deseret, 1976), 345–46. Lorenzo Snow, *Teachings of Lorenzo Snow*, Ed. Clyde J. Williams (Salt Lake City: Bookcraft, 1996), 1.
32. Moses 6:57.
33. D&C 130:22.
34. Joseph Smith Jr., *Lectures on Faith* (Salt Lake City: Deseret, 1985), 2:2.
35. D&C 109:77.
36. Charles W. Penrose, "Editor's Table." *Improvement Era*. September 1912, 1042.
37. Harold B. Lee, *The Teachings of Harold B. Lee* (Salt Lake City: Bookcraft, 1996), 157.
38. 1 Pet. 3:15.
39. Robert J. Matthews, "Using the Scriptures," *Brigham Young University Fireside and Devotional Speeches, held in 1981*, Provo, Utah: BYU Publications. Personal correspondence to Robert J. Matthews, 28 Jan. 1969, 124. Neal A. Maxwell, *Men and Women of Christ* (Salt Lake City: Bookcraft, 1991), 2.
40. 1 Timothy 4:6,13.

Scripture Index

Subject Index

I

Also available from

GREG KOFFORD BOOKS

Perspectives on Mormon Theology Series

Brian D. Birch and Loyd Ericson, series editors

(forthcoming)

This series will feature multiple volumes published on particular theological topics of interest in Latter-day Saint thought. Volumes will be co-edited by leading scholars and graduate students whose interests and knowledge will ensure that the essays in each volume represent quality scholarship and acknowledge the diversity of thought found and expressed in Mormon theological studies. Topics for the first few volumes include: revelation, apostasy, atonement, scripture, and grace.

The *Perspectives on Mormon Theology* series will bring together the best of new and previously published essays on various theological subjects. Each volume will be both a valued resource for academics in Mormon Studies and an illuminating introduction to the broad and sophisticated approaches to Mormon theology.

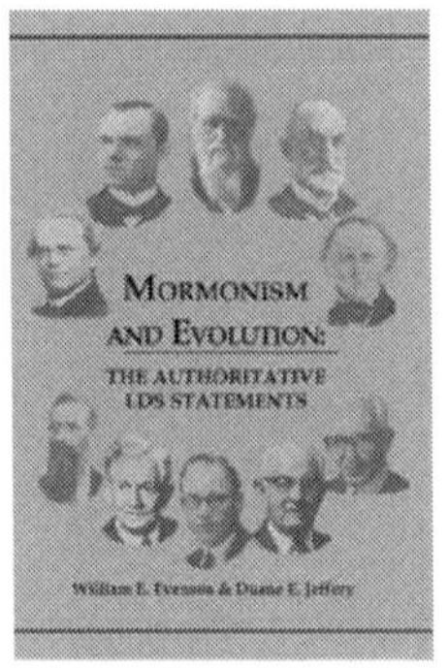

Mormonism and Evolution: The Authoritative LDS Statements

Edited by William E. Evenson
and Duane E. Jeffrey

Paperback, ISBN: 978-1-58958-093-0

The Church of Jesus Christ of Latter-day Saints (the Mormon Church) has generally been viewed by the public as anti-evolutionary in its doctrine and teachings. But official statements on the subject by the Church's highest governing quorum and/or president have been considerably more open and diverse than is popularly believed.

This book compiles in full all known authoritative statements (either authored or formally approved for publication) by the Church's highest leaders on the topics of evolution and the origin of human beings. The editors provide historical context for these statements that allows the reader to see what stimulated the issuing of each particular document and how they stand in relation to one another.

The Gift and Power: Translating the Book of Mormon

Brant A. Gardner

Hardcover, ISBN: 978-1-58958-131-9

From Brant A. Gardner, the author of the highly praised *Second Witness* commentaries on the Book of Mormon, comes *The Gift and Power: Translating the Book of Mormon*. In this first book-length treatment of the translation process, Gardner closely examines the accounts surrounding Joseph Smith's translation of the Book of Mormon to answer a wide spectrum of questions about the process, including: Did the Prophet use seerstones common to folk magicians of his time? How did he use them? And, what is the relationship to the golden plates and the printed text?

Approaching the topic in three sections, part 1 examines the stories told about Joseph, folk magic, and the translation. Part 2 examines the available evidence to determine how closely the English text replicates the original plate text. And part 3 seeks to explain how seer stones worked, why they no longer work, and how Joseph Smith could have produced a translation with them.

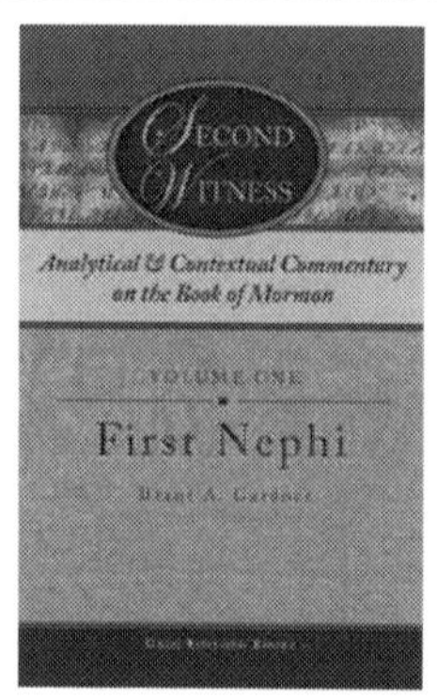

Second Witness:
Analytical and Contextual Commentatry on the Book of Mormon

Brant A. Gardner

Second Witness, a new six-volume series from Greg Kofford Books, takes a detailed, verse-by-verse look at the Book of Mormon. It marshals the best of modern scholarship and new insights into a consistent picture of the Book of Mormon as a historical document. Taking a faithful but scholarly approach to the text and reading it through the insights of linguistics, anthropology, and ethnohistory, the commentary approaches the text from a variety of perspectives: how it was created, how it relates to history and culture, and what religious insights it provides.

The commentary accepts the best modern scholarship, which focuses on a particular region of Mesoamerica as the most plausible location for the Book of Mormon's setting. For the first time, that location—its peoples, cultures, and historical trends—are used as the backdrop for reading the text. The historical background is not presented as proof, but rather as an explanatory context.

The commentary does not forget Mormon's purpose in writing. It discusses the doctrinal and theological aspects of the text and highlights the way in which Mormon created it to meet his goal of "convincing . . . the Jew and Gentile that Jesus is the Christ, the Eternal God."

Praise for the *Second Witness* series:

"Gardner not only provides a unique tool for understanding the Book of Mormon as an ancient document written by real, living prophets, but he sets a standard for Latter-day Saint thinking and writing about scripture, providing a model for all who follow. . . . No other reference source will prove as thorough and valuable for serious readers of the Book of Mormon."

-Neal A. Maxwell Institute, Brigham Young University

1. 1st Nephi: 978-1-58958-041-1
2. 2nd Nephi–Jacob: 978-1-58958-042-8
3. Enos–Mosiah: 978-1-58958-043-5
4. Alma: 978-1-58958-044-2
5. Helaman–3rd Nephi: 978-1-58958-045-9
6. 4th Nephi–Moroni: 978-1-58958-046-6

Complete set: 978-1-58958-047-3

"This is My Doctrine": The Development of Mormon Theology

Charles R. Harrell

Hardcover, ISBN: 978-1-58958-103-6

The principal doctrines defining Mormonism today often bear little resemblance to those it started out with in the early 1830s. This book shows that these doctrines did not originate in a vacuum but were rather prompted and informed by the religious culture from which Mormonism arose. Early Mormons, like their early Christian and even earlier Israelite predecessors, brought with them their own varied culturally conditioned theological presuppositions (a process of convergence) and only later acquired a more distinctive theological outlook (a process of differentiation).

In this first-of-its-kind comprehensive treatment of the development of Mormon theology, Charles Harrell traces the history of Latter-day Saint doctrines from the times of the Old Testament to the present. He describes how Mormonism has carried on the tradition of the biblical authors, early Christians, and later Protestants in reinterpreting scripture to accommodate new theological ideas while attempting to uphold the integrity and authority of the scriptures. In the process, he probes three questions: How did Mormon doctrines develop? What are the scriptural underpinnings of these doctrines? And what do critical scholars make of these same scriptures? In this enlightening study, Harrell systematically peels back the doctrinal accretions of time to provide a fresh new look at Mormon theology.

"This Is My Doctrine" will provide those already versed in Mormonism's theological tradition with a new and richer perspective of Mormon theology. Those unacquainted with Mormonism will gain an appreciation for how Mormon theology fits into the larger Jewish and Christian theological traditions.

Latter-Day Dissent: At the Crossroads of Intellectual Inquiry and Ecclesiastical Authority

Philip Lindholm

Paperback, ISBN: 978-1-58958-128-9

This volume collects, for the first time in book form, stories from the "September Six," a group of intellectuals officially excommunicated or disfellowshipped from the LDS Church in September of 1993 on charges of "apostasy" or "conduct unbecoming" Church members. Their experiences are significant and yet are largely unknown outside of scholarly or more liberal Mormon circles, which is surprising given that their story was immediately propelled onto screens and cover pages across the Western world.

Interviews by Dr. Philip Lindholm (Ph.D. Theology, University of Oxford) include those of the "September Six," Lynne Kanavel Whitesides, Paul James Toscano, Maxine Hanks, Lavina Fielding Anderson, and D. Michael Quinn; as well as Janice Merrill Allred, Margaret Merrill Toscano, Thomas W. Murphy , and former employee of the LDS Church's Public Affairs Department, Donald B. Jessee.

Each interview illustrates the tension that often exists between the Church and its intellectual critics, and highlights the difficulty of accommodating congregational diversity while maintaining doctrinal unity—a difficulty hearkening back to the very heart of ancient Christianity.

Who Are the Children of Lehi? DNA and the Book of Mormon

D. Jeffrey Meldrum
and Trent D. Stephens

Hardcover, ISBN: 978-1-58958-048-0
Paperback, ISBN: 978-1-58958-129-6

How does the Book of Mormon, keystone of the LDS faith, stand up to data about DNA sequencing that puts the ancestors of modern Native Americans in northeast Asia instead of Palestine?

In *Who Are the Children of Lehi?* Meldrum and Stephens examine the merits and the fallacies of DNA-based interpretations that challenge the Book of Mormon's historicity. They provide clear guides to the science, summarize the studies, illuminate technical points with easy-to-grasp examples, and spell out the data's implications.

The results? There is no straight-line conclusion between DNA evidence and "Lamanites." The Book of Mormon's validity lies beyond the purview of scientific empiricism—as it always has. And finally, inspiringly, they affirm Lehi's kinship as one of covenant, not genes.

Modern Mormonism: Myths and Realities

Robert L. Millet

Paperback, ISBN: 978-1-58958-127-2

What answer may a Latter-day Saint make to accusations from those of other faiths that "Mormons aren't Christians," or "You think God is a man," and "You worship a different Jesus"? Not only are these charges disconcerting, but the hostility with which they are frequently hurled is equally likely to catch Latter-day Saints off guard.

Now Robert L. Millet, veteran of hundreds of such verbal battles, cogently, helpfully, and scripturally provides important clarifications for Latter-day Saints about eleven of the most frequent myths used to discredit the Church. Along the way, he models how to conduct such a Bible based discussion respectfully, weaving in enlightenment from LDS scriptures and quotations from religious figures in other faiths, ranging from the early church fathers to the archbishop of Canterbury.

Millet enlivens this book with personal experiences as a boy growing up in an area where Mormons were a minuscule and not particularly welcome minority, in one-on-one conversations with men of faith who believed differently, and with his own BYU students who also had lessons to learn about interfaith dialogue. He pleads for greater cooperation in dealing with the genuine moral and social evils afflicting the world, and concludes with his own ardent and reverent testimony of the Savior.

Exploring Mormon Thought Series

Blake T. Ostler

In volume one, *The Attributes of God,* Blake T. Ostler explores Christian and Mormon notions about God. ISBN: 978-1-58958-003-9

In volume two, *The Problems of Theism and the Love of God,* Blake Ostler explores issues related to soteriology, or the theory of salvation. ISBN: 978-1-58958-095-4

In volume three, *Of God and Gods,* Ostler analyzes and responds to the arguments of contemporary international theologians, reconstructs and interprets Joseph Smith's important King Follett Discourse and Sermon in the Grove, and argues persuasively for the Mormon doctrine of "robust deification." ISBN: 978-1-58958-107-4

Praise for the *Exploring Mormon Thought* series:

"These books are the most important works on Mormon theology ever written. There is nothing currently available that is even close to the rigor and sophistication of these volumes. B. H. Roberts and John A. Widtsoe may have had interesting insights in the early part of the twentieth century, but they had neither the temperament nor the training to give a rigorous defense of their views in dialogue with a wider stream of Christian theology. Sterling McMurrin and Truman Madsen had the capacity to engage Mormon theology at this level, but neither one did."

—Neal A. Maxwell Institute, Brigham Young University

Hugh Nibley: A Consecrated Life

Boyd Jay Petersen

Hardcover, ISBN: 978-1-58958-019-0

Winner of the Mormon History Association's Best Biography Award

As one of the LDS Church's most widely recognized scholars, Hugh Nibley is both an icon and an enigma. Through complete access to Nibley's correspondence, journals, notes, and papers, Petersen has painted a portrait that reveals the man behind the legend.

Starting with a foreword written by Zina Nibley Petersen and finishing with appendices that include some of the best of Nibley's personal correspondence, the biography reveals aspects of the tapestry of the life of one who has truly consecrated his life to the service of the Lord.

Praise for *A Consecrated Life*:

"Hugh Nibley is generally touted as one of Mormonism's greatest minds and perhaps its most prolific scholarly apologist. Just as hefty as some of Nibley's largest tomes, this authorized biography is delightfully accessible and full of the scholar's delicious wordplay and wit, not to mention some astonishing war stories and insights into Nibley's phenomenal acquisition of languages. Introduced by a personable foreword from the author's wife (who is Nibley's daughter), the book is written with enthusiasm, respect and insight. . . . On the whole, Petersen is a careful scholar who provides helpful historical context. . . . This project is far from hagiography. It fills an important gap in LDS history and will appeal to a wide Mormon audience."

—Publishers Weekly

"Well written and thoroughly researched, Petersen's biography is a must-have for anyone struggling to reconcile faith and reason."

—Greg Taggart, Association for Mormon Letters

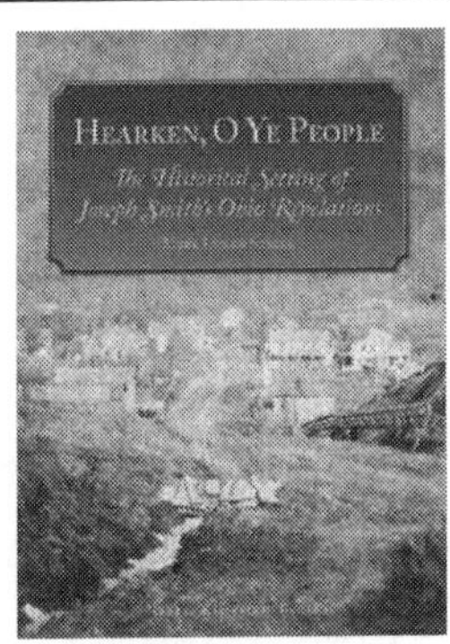

Hearken, O Ye People: The Historical Setting of Joseph Smith's Ohio Revelations

Mark Lyman Staker

Hardcover, ISBN: 978-1-58958-113-5

2010 Best Book Award - John Whitmer Historical Association

2011 Best Book Award - Mormon History Association

More of Mormonism's canonized revelations originated in or near Kirtland than any other place. Yet many of the events connected with those revelations and their 1830s historical context have faded over time. Mark Staker reconstructs the cultural experiences by which Kirtland's Latter-day Saints made sense of the revelations Joseph Smith pronounced. This volume rebuilds that exciting decade using clues from numerous archives, privately held records, museum collections, and even the soil where early members planted corn and homes. From this vast array of sources he shapes a detailed narrative of weather, religious backgrounds, dialect differences, race relations, theological discussions, food preparation, frontier violence, astronomical phenomena, and myriad daily customs of nineteenth-century life. The result is a "from the ground up" experience that today's Latter-day Saints can all but walk into and touch.

Praise for *Hearken O Ye People*:

"I am not aware of a more deeply researched and richly contextualized study of any period of Mormon church history than Mark Staker's study of Mormons in Ohio. We learn about everything from the details of Alexander Campbell's views on priesthood authority to the road conditions and weather on the four Lamanite missionaries' journey from New York to Ohio. All the Ohio revelations and even the First Vision are made to pulse with new meaning. This book sets a new standard of in-depth research in Latter-day Saint history."

-Richard Bushman, author of *Joseph Smith: Rough Stone Rolling*

"To be well-informed, any student of Latter-day Saint history and doctrine must now be acquainted with the remarkable research of Mark Staker on the important history of the church in the Kirtland, Ohio, area."

-Neal A. Maxwell Institute, Brigham Young University

"Let the Earth Bring Forth" Evolution and Scripture

Howard C. Stutz

Paperback, ISBN: 978-1-58958-126-5

A century ago in 1809, Charles Darwin was born. Fifty years later, he published a scientific treatise describing the process of speciation that launched what appeared to be a challenge to the traditional religious interpretation of how life was created on earth. The controversy has erupted anew in the last decade as Creationists and Young Earth adherents challenge school curricula and try to displace "the theory of evolution."

This book is filled with fascinating examples of speciation by the well-known process of mutation but also by the less well-known processes of sexual recombination and polyploidy. In addition to the fossil record, Howard Stutz examines the evidence from the embryo stages of human beings and other creatures to show how selection and differentiation moved development in certain favored directions while leaving behind evidence of earlier, discarded developments. Anatomy, biochemistry, and genetics are all examined in their turn.

With rigorously scientific clarity but in language accessible to a popular audience, the book proceeds to its conclusion, reached after a lifetime of study: the divine map of creation is one supported by both scientific evidence and the scriptures. This is a book to be read, not only for its fascinating scientific insights, but also for a new appreciation of well-known scriptures.

Made in the USA
Columbia, SC
07 December 2019

84507677R00176